Awaken

The

WARRIOR

A Practical Guide for a Troubled Time

By

Philip Paul Sacco

© 2002 by Philip Paul Sacco. All rights reserved.

No part of this book may be reproduced, stored in a retrieval system, or transmitted by any means, electronic, mechanical, photocopying, recording, or otherwise, without written permission from the author.

ISBN: 1-4033-3528-1 (e-book)
ISBN: 1-4033-3529-X (Paperback)
ISBN: 1-4033-3530-3 (Dustjacket)

Library of Congress Control Number: 2002092175

This book is printed on acid free paper.

Printed in the United States of America
Bloomington, IN

1stBooks – rev. 10/04/02

Dedication

To my Mother and Father. They have provided me with a perfect base camp to train in and from which to sail forth, always there to see me through and protect me when I have been in training and in need of repairs.

As all dangerous warriors are sought out by the enemy; I have suffered my share of ambushes and my parents have always been there to help put the pieces back together again.

If ever two names were to be used to describe the model of parenthood, they would be the names:

Agnes and Ulderico.

I have been blessed.

Acknowledgments

It is said 'a picture tells a thousand words,' and my thanks go out to Robert Valentine of Valentine Armourie for so graciously allowing me to use the many pictures of armor I have included. With four exceptions, all pictures in this book are from their website. Of the remaining four pictures, thanks to Legio XX for permission to use a picture of them in testudo formation. This picture can be found in chapter ten. I would also like to thank my companion-in-arms, Derrick Schroff, for helping me 'enlist young recruits.' Whenever I have needed a friend, Derrick has been there. He is the definition of a gentleman, and a fierce warrior as well. His picture is included in chapter two. Two pictures can be found of me: one in chapter seven showing me in my arming belts, and the final concluding shot at the end of the book. Thanks to my dear friend Louis DeBroux, for the proofreading, help finding scriptures, and rephrasing so many portions of the manuscript. When I was writing the chapters on character, Chrissy Mondell was there to give me examples of correct behavior, and see to it that I lived my own words. Chrissy has been called home by God, and I miss her greatly. I looked forward to sharing these printed pages with her. Special heartfelt thanks to Mick Spillane of Turn of Phrase, for his excellent job of final editing and proofing. Mick was uniquely experienced to work with me on the rough spots, and assured a flow to the material. My appreciation and thanks also go to my dear friend and "honorary Sacco," David Priessman. Dave has seen me through the best and worst times of my life. It is fitting that when I was in a pinch, he was there to save the day, and help me with the rear cover shot. Lastly, my thanks to God for making me the messenger for this material. The years of training He has given me helped bringing reality into these pages.

A Letter from the Author

I was the third child of four, born into the family of Ulderico and Agnes Sacco on January 11, 1955. I was raised Roman Catholic. In high school, I was exposed to the power of the baptism of the Holy Spirit, an experience that awakened in me a deep and committed love for the Lord, the study of the Scriptures, and eschatology. Much to the bewilderment of my fellow Catholics, not to mention my family, I pursued full immersion water baptism in the manner of John the Baptist. I became active with the Pentecostal or Charismatic movement in the Catholic Church, and clearly remember being told our group could no longer meet at the church. It was a number of years before our church came into the hands of a fire baptized priest, and our views of the scriptures and blessings of the Spirit were welcome again.

The imagery of the knight and the desire to see their form of chivalry and code of conduct expressed in society today has been part of my life since childhood. Long have I searched and long have I been disappointed. Times have changed…or have they?

Throughout my life, I have felt as though God was forging me into some sort of weapon for His own design or purpose, perhaps a sword. Today, rather than a sword, I feel that I could best describe myself as an arrow. While my life has had a few detours, and frankly at times has meandered, I have had a long flight to the mark, but feel I have finally arrived. The hand of the Master orchestrated numerous trivial incidents throughout the course of writing this book. It has not only made the completion of this book a pure joy; it has made the reality of presentations and seminars a blessing.

Now I believe my task is that of the bow, to deliver the message to others and see them fly on their way.

Having had over twenty-five years of training in the art of medieval marshal arms and finding a direct correlation between the values in the heart of the warrior and the values to be expressed as a Christian soldier, I find myself uniquely suited to presenting this material.

May God Bless all who read and contemplate the message of this book and may they find the strength and determination that will be required of them to complete the development of their Warrior within. Life's challenges will be easier to take on with the full nature of the Warrior to serve as an aid.

I invite you to write or call me and to offer any thoughts and comments on this book. Tell me what it has meant to you. I would also love to hear of the many adventures you have been sent on during your journey.

I have deleted the index of scriptures to save space. A full index of scriptures used in the book is available free of charge to anyone requesting one. Presentations and seminars of this material are also available.

Awaken the Warrior
Philip Paul Sacco
1097 Cherokee Heights, Stone Mountain, Georgia 30083
~~404-296-6332 ppsacco@attbi.com~~

800 483-6332
www.awakenthewarrior.com

Pray for me to be given an opportunity to open my mouth and fearlessly make known the mystery of the gospel of which I am an ambassador in chains; Pray that in proclaiming it I may speak as fearlessly as I ought to.

Ephesians 6:19-20

Table of Contents

Dedication iii
Acknowledgments v
A Letter from the Author vii

Introduction: Elements of the problem. Introduction to Archetypes xiii

Part One: METTLE—Man of Peace—The Warrior as a Man of Peace 1

Chapter One: The Battle—Spiritual warfare characteristics, knowing the enemy 3

Chapter Two: AWOL—The importance of Archetypes, our internal behavior models 16
    Section One—A World Gone Wrong—Evil rampant, the missing Warrior
    Section Two—Awaken the Warrior—Requirements
    Section Three—I Am a Warrior Of The Kingdom Of God—The missing character traits, societal factors, initiation rites

Chapter Three: Becoming Whole—Archetypes; the adolescent forms and adult forms. Internal images of the Warrior archetype, some historical comparisons 39

Chapter Four: The Forge—The makings of a Warrior's Character 55

Chapter Five: Awards, Standards and Appearances 87
    Section One: Awards—Merit for valor, penalty for wrong action
    Section Two: Crowns—The Seven Crowns as our heavenly rewards
    Section Three: Standards—Past representation of character or spirit; and Now—the expression of character in actions, moral codes, values, and ethics

Section Four: Appearances—Reality to the eyes of the body or the eyes of the Spirit

Part Two: METAL—Man of War—The Warrior as a Man-of-War, the tools of the trade, spiritual armor, armor proofing 101

Chapter Six: Shod Your Feet—The importance of good footing, characteristics of willingness and doing 114

Chapter Seven: The Belt of Truth—How truth serves us, use as a weapon 129

Chapter Eight: The Breastplate of Righteousness—Love and Faith, right action, matters of the heart 148

Chapter Nine: The Helmet of Salvation—Knowing and claiming salvation, the idle mind, protecting our thoughts 174

Chapter Ten: The Shield of Faith—Quenches the fiery darts, Faith binding us all together, the Testudo, covers us from attack in all directions 198

Chapter Eleven: The Sword of the Word of God—A terrible two-edged sword, cuts both ways, used for offense and defense 227

Chapter Twelve: The Twelfth Hour 250
    Section One: Salvation and Redemption—a call-to-arms
    Section Two: Fire and Empowerment—stories from the front lines

Epilogue: Autobiographical information about the author, the touch of the Masters hand 269

Bibliography and Suggested Reading 291

Introduction

Today's society is unique when compared to society past, due to one simple and particular fact. People are not the same due to changes in culture and the manner in which we develop as individuals of Character and Spirit. Proper development into full maturity is a two-step process. First, we must internalize behavior models that guide and develop our character to its fullest. Secondly, we must understand Spiritual Principles, then accept, and develop them. Societal changes brought problems on both these levels of development. These problems show themselves in the difficulties we struggle with in society, as well as the personal developmental flaws expressed in our individual character makeup.

This book deals with very real issues on the Physical and the Spiritual levels of perception. Part 1 discusses the physical level and certain common developed and undeveloped character traits. Part 2 deals with the Spiritual level and will elaborate on the "Armor of God," and how it relates to certain problems, or symptoms, and to their solutions, or cure. Demonstrating the integrated nature of character and our spiritual armor will associate parts 1 and 2. Scriptures support and exemplify spiritual truth specifically concerning the Armor of God. These spiritual elements correspond with real armor worn on the physical body. Armed with divine protection and assurance, the full power and might of the Godly armed Christian is developed and the spiritual enemy engaged as fearlessly and successfully as a physical enemy.

Abstract terms used in discussion of character development relate to physical or externally identifiable problems and issues of character and behavior. In contrast, strong visual images are used in depicting the Armor of God, the spiritual and nonphysical aspects of our protection. The dichotomy of Physical and the Spiritual aspects supporting each other is very important. The reader must recognize Godly Integrity requires the internal and external represent the same qualities. Reflect upon the expressions, "good through and through," and "rotten to the core." That which is good on the inside should be valued as good on the outside by an objective observer.

In other words, if your inner self is genuine and good, you should be seen as good by the outward manifestation of your character.

Part 1 expresses the character of the Warrior as a "Man-of-Peace" and is concerned with character development and behavior models representing the externalization of our internal character. We "see" the subject matter in the context of our own behavior and that of those around us. This is about as real as you can get. Part 2 deals strictly with the spiritual principles depicted by the Armor of God in a visual fashion, portraying the character of the Warrior as a "Man-of-War," and showing how the various characteristics of a well trained warrior are manifested in the Armor of God. As Christian Warriors, we have a duty to train in the use of this armor. These objects and their function carry an expressed spiritual message. When describing physical armor, the image drawn is of one prepared for combat. In effect, the most abstract concepts of character will be looked at as represented by real or external problems, while the most visually represented aspects of the book will deal with those intangible or internalized spiritual concepts.

To simplify, it is helpful to refer to various models of behavior ingrained in us all as "Archetypes." The classic four archetypes are known as the King (Queen), the Magician, the Warrior, and the Lover. These four basic behavior models give a clearer understanding of what full character development entails and the realization of what we should emulate in full maturity. The blending and maturing of these archetypes determine how we function as adults and how we express our character. Each archetypal model blends with and affects the others in a unique fashion within each of us. Ultimately it is the level to which we have developed each of these archetypes and how fully we have allowed them to mature and interact that determines our expression through word and deed.

While the full development and blending of our innate archetypes is essential to develop to our maximum individual capacity, it is uncommon in today's world to find a completely integrated person. We often meet and have dealings with people stuck in an adolescent or an undeveloped adult behavior model. Thinking of your many acquaintances, you can identify someone who seems to have their act together, but simply cannot get their personal life straightened out. They may have their professional life going full steam, but never seem to be able to make a decision or take a stand in their personal life. Studying them, it would appear likely their problems lay in the incomplete development of some aspect of their character. Even though it may be easy to see shortcomings in others, we are often blind to our own failings.

Though the internal archetypes of mankind appear timeless and universal, it is how they are recognized and individually developed which makes us different today as a society and a people. If we all were to develop completely and to our fullest potential, the world would be a much happier place. This would stand in stark contrast to the society and world surrounding us today. In dealing with societal problems, it helps to be better prepared and trained in certain spiritual principles. To be a person of "Character without Spirit" is as absurd a concept as to be a "Spiritual Person without Character."

The same difficulties we face in developing on the individual level must be faced on the societal level as well as both are related. Today's problems require the raising of higher standards than has been the rule in the past. Often, we are trained to deal with the appearances of a problem, or its symptoms, rather than its root cause or empowerment. The allopathic approach in treating illness is a good example of this. We as a society have followed this example, tending to treat the symptoms of the illness rather than "Cure the Disease."

An example of treating the symptoms may be seen in the way a child acting obtrusively or throwing a tantrum is typically dealt with by their parents. The child is scolded or sent to their room when in fact the poor behavior being expressed may be due to the child feeling ignored, or wanting to interact. If this is the case, including the child in your activities or spending a little time talking with them as an adult may correct their behavior by showing them a better form of coping. Our understanding of the underlying causes of poor behavior and dealing with the true cause is how a child learns to grow up or mature in a more acceptable way.

This is not to say discipline should be eliminated. On the contrary, discipline is essential to proper development. Improper or insufficient discipline may arguably be a primary fault leading to many of societal problems today. Many problems can be cured and eliminated if we but recognize the disease and treat it, rather than the symptoms. By illuminating the root of the problem, we recognize those things within us that have not developed as God and nature intend. Once this is done, progress towards true character development can occur. This, in turn, will have a reciprocal effect on society.

If we consider this dilemma an illness, it is of epidemic proportions. The archetype of the Warrior exists in men and women alike. Please do not think this book is for the development of character in only men. The concept of the Warrior being within us all is apparent in studying the scriptures and seeing that God intends us ALL to put on the armor he has prepared for us. Doing so assures a life rich with His assurances and blessings. We all carry the Warrior's basic character.

The Warrior image has suffered being ignored, rejected, denied, shunned, and spurned by our society and by us as individuals. This general misunderstanding and reaction to this aspect of character has typically led to the exclusion of women from association with the Warrior image. This stigma has prevented the Warrior in many of us from reaching full maturation, allowing us to be crippled by the attacks of the enemy. In a very real way, we have been rendered defenseless and the results have been disastrous. Those who have not developed this aspect never fully mature and struggle through life in a compromised state. Those so handicapped place a burden on the rest of society in attempting to deal with them. Society naturally suffers when its members cannot contribute to their fullest individually.

The cure can be found within the problems themselves. My proposal is not unlike the treatment for weak muscles; that being to exercise the muscles. The problem is in an aspect of ourselves being denied and cut off from our reach, understanding, use and full development into maturity. The cure is found within this key Warrior aspect of our beings. Recognizing the Warrior archetype can affect the cure for our immaturity disease by accepting all aspects of the

Warrior's archetype and developing the character and traits of the Warrior within us. Having matured our Warrior self image, we will enjoy the expression of our self understanding and development. Effectively, eliminating the cause cures the symptoms and the disease.

This maturing must take place on an individual level, for our society is but a composite of individuals. A society made up of nothing but children; no adults, just children-would be an immature, childlike society. Likewise, a society of freaks and twisted mentalities would be observed as being twisted and beyond the definition of a sane society recognizable to those possessing a whole spirit and a sane mentality.

Reflect on the days of your adolescence or young adulthood. Compare today's news and society with your memory of that time. Have the very principles and structure of society not changed since then? How would you compare the society of today to that of a generation ago? Societal turmoil, confusion, and moral decay are major concerns today. How many recognize the principles of our Founding Fathers in America today? Can a God-fearing society be made up of godless and wanton, unscrupulous individuals? Do the events reported in the daily news indicate something is terribly wrong? Think of the moral values of our public figures. Are there any good role models among them? All indications are there is a war going on in society today; a war unlike any we have seen in recent history.

We are all involved in a Spiritual War, though most do not want to recognize or acknowledge the fact. In this instance, ignorance is not bliss, but rather can kill us all.

This book is written to take you on a journey of self-awareness, to test you, and help train you for what must be done. I challenge you to take this journey within yourself and find that which needs identification and recognition. Develop the Warrior within yourself to help wage and win today's battles. Learn of the many tools with which the Warrior is equipped, and learn how to employ them. Train and become that Warrior and join the fray fearlessly! Your alternative is to become a destructive force in society rather than beneficial, or lie cowering on the ground as inconsequential as a rock when the Just Enemy comes for you.

One must first identify the Warrior archetype to train in the use of our spiritual armor. Once identified, you must understand how to develop that Warrior within yourself to maturity. Having done this, we can make use of and become adept with the many scriptural tools available to engage in effective spiritual warfare. This should become your "Order of the Day." When done, training in the use, the proper wear, and care for your Armor of God will become a treasured practice.

Be advised the initial chapters of Part 1 are drawn from current understanding of the human psyche and character development, information readily found in contemporary books of clinical psychology. Understanding why some problems occur will go a long way towards helping us deal with the problems and stem the social self-destruction we are witnessing. This material does not particularly rest in the scriptural realm. While this first section may strike many readers as being a little "dry," Part 2 will draw from this information. To have a complete understanding of the full nature and character of the Warrior, it is recommended that Part 1 be read first.

If you are simply dying to get into the heart of the scriptural basis of the "Armor of God," then by all means, feel free to start with chapter 4 which leads into the armor and the spiritual and scriptural discussions. This should excite the reader to become proficient in learning all there is to know about our wondrous protection and promises from God.

Scripture quotes are used throughout the material and are included in the text. This obviates your need to have a Bible handy. While some criticism may be leveled for such extensive inclusion of scriptures, I have chosen to include them for completeness. Those quotes including superscripts within the text are taken from the King James version, while all others are from the New Jerusalem Bible.

Jesus warns of sitting on the fence. To Him, you are either on his side, or AGAINST HIM. He wants us all to lay claim to His guarantees, and "FIGHT THE GOOD FIGHT!"

Fight the good fight of Faith and win the eternal life to which you were called and which you made your noble profession of faith before many witnesses.

1 Tm. 6:12

Part One

Mettle:

The Warrior as "The Man of Peace"

Part 1 deals with the internal, personal characteristics of the Warrior. This will serve as a guide to aid development of your internal Warrior or other character traits you are led to change or develop.

These character traits, while intangible, have very real effects when acted out. For example, compassion or discipline bear witness to themselves in expression of word or deed, and are easy enough to identify. An individual can truly be touched by an act of kindness or justice. These are examples of character traits of the internal Warrior that will be looked at in the chapter dealing specifically with character.

Many of the characteristics of the Warrior may be seen in the expression and action of our Lord Jesus, both as a "Man-of-Peace" and as a "Man-of-War." When Christ, our perfect role model, appeared to man for the first time, he was seen as a Man-of-Peace. His life was the epitome of honor and compassion: traits that should be our guiding force as we live our lives. His first appearance was to accomplish the redemption of man. Rather than appear as a King or military leader, as the Jews were expecting in a Messiah, He came, however, as a Man-of-Peace. It is fitting for us to refer to Him as "the Prince of Peace."

A good example of the expression of the Man-of-Peace is the occasion of Jesus' arrest in the Garden of Gethsemane. Jesus stayed the hand of a follower who had drawn a sword to protect Him. Jesus' response was simple and most revealing...*do you think that I cannot appeal to my Father, who would promptly send more than twelve legions of angels to my defense? But then, how would the scriptures be fulfilled that say this is the way it must be?* **Matt. 26:53-54**.

Philip Paul Sacco

How better may He have portrayed a Man-of-Peace? His actions revealed many of the qualities of the Warrior as a Man-of-Peace. Two that come to mind are discernment and control on His part. In order for us to develop all of the spiritual protection required by a Christian Warrior, we must understand how building up one fortifies the other. This protection is readily available, and extremely necessary, if one is going to engage in the spiritual war embroiling our world today.

Chapter 1

The Battle

I am a Spiritual Warrior. I have the ability to look upon a field of battle not yet engaged and discern the coming battle. I can sense the fight in the air around me as the battle lines draw near. I can easily look upon the ruins of a battlefield and tell of its many facets of destruction and the weapons employed thereon. The ebb and flow of Murderous Might is common to my eyes. Often on my mission I am alone in body, seemingly always outnumbered, surrounded and besieged by a hideous foe and yet...*I Stand*. My Lord has equipped me with His blessed Armor for my protection in my hour of need. His orders will I fulfill to the utmost of my ability. I have been blessed with the gift to heal, so that should I come across a comrade fallen or in need...with but a touch, a word, he may rise up and continue on his way, and always forward, forward to the fray. I have my orders. I will withstand the worst the enemy may throw my way, and yet **Stand**! I shall not give in! I shall not fail! The enemy fires arrows of death from shadows and yet I am protected from their peril.

I move with the preparedness to spread the gospel of peace and am furthered in my quest, my way made straight and clear before me. My actions come from the purest of direction and intent and my faith protects me from flaming words and deceit. I have secured all my defenses and made fast my wards with honesty and justice. While I am not to be trifled with or taken lightly by the enemy, I play in the streets and gardens with the children around me. No doubt or fear pervades my mind, as I am filled with direction and instruction from a higher order. My faith in an unfathomable redemption covers my approach upon my enemies. No keener weapon has ever been fashioned than the one I wield.

These are but some of my skills and attitudes as a true Warrior; attitudes and skills gained by seasons of hardness endured in combat, as well as the rigors of discipline and training, in preparation for the shock of war. As a true Warrior, I am prepared to give all, selflessly, to fulfill my orders.

The battlefields of days gone by looked quite different from the fields of war today. As I look at our society and the world today, I am aware of a battle being waged around us. I also recognize the remnant, shattered remains of many other battles fought in our very midst. The signs of this ongoing war are not seen by the severed limbs of the fallen and the fetid and bloated remains of the vanquished as in the wars of the past. I do not have to see the charred remains of cities besieged and sacked as in the days of old, nor the litter of discarded weapons strewn on the field by the faint of heart. I do not have to hear the cries of loss of those families left leaderless with a husband or father taken or slain by the enemy. Nor do I have to hear the soulful weeping of a wife or daughter subjected to rape or enslavement by the enemy as in the wars of the past.

I recognize a different type of war being waged today. I see a different type of refuse and shattered remains as a result of it. Do you see it? Can you recognize the destruction of homes from the doomsday weapon called divorce? Can you recognize the broken bodies of battle in the battered remains of abused children or wives? I see it in every single-parent family struggling to make ends meet with a spouse missing, not due to brutal invasion of an enemy occupation, but rather by abandonment! Husbands are leaving the responsibility of their families behind to pursue, not the lofty goals of truth, but their own personal pleasure. I see the effects of this war in the record number of child molestations each year, as well as spousal abuse and battering in all of its many diverse guises, i.e. spiritual, physical, sexual, and emotional. Like dysentery in the foul, unsanitary camps of campaigns fought too long in the open, moral corruption fills the hearts of men in positions of authority over others. I see the effects of poisoned water supplies in the rampant alcoholism and drug abuse by the adults and youth of our society. These are but the symptoms of a reality for the individuals who, for whatever reason, have turned to these measures as a means of escape, or to help them forget the trauma of their lives.

Where was compassion and love for these wounded people in their time of need? It has been supplanted by further persecution for their infirmity. Should they be the subjects of further discrimination and ridicule for displaying a symptom of a disease due to a society gone astray, at war with itself, or subjected to the wiles of an insidious and unseen, unchallenged foe? Do we tend to the root causes of the spiritual or character illnesses of these unfortunate masses? In short, we do not. This merely complicates and deepens the problems we all have to deal with. Had these individuals learned to develop the Warrior within them, many of these situations would not exist today.

Where are the Warriors of our Age? Where are the Warriors we expect to find defending the bastions of our society? Gone…NO—just not developed. They are all around us; consequently, not in the form we had hoped to find them. Rather they are hostage in the undeveloped character of many of those around us today.

Do you have the courage to embark on the most difficult journey we face as individuals today? This journey will take you within yourself to discover what truly lies there. Will you find a person of character? Will you develop those parts of your character you find absent? Will you face your fears and take a stand, to develop into the full mature being you are meant to be? Will you free one of the Warriors so desperately needed by society today?

Are you willing to admit that maybe, just maybe, you are not perfect, that none of us are? Can you come to that realization and do nothing? Are you willing to attempt to resurrect a part of your being that perhaps has been dormant for far too long? Humankind as a whole depends on you to develop this aspect of yourself at this most crucial time in humankind's history. The world is dependent upon us each to individually develop to our fullest capacity.

The material covered in this book concerns itself with real issues, real dilemmas we face in our daily lives and how we choose to deal with them. Will we make a positive choice to heed the call to action and meet our challenge's head on? Or will we avoid our responsibility to deal with the matter at hand? These are the two extremes we face, they ultimately define what we, in fact, do, and become. Character is a real issue. The Armor of God is a real issue. Without one, the other suffers, and we are vulnerable. "To what?" you may ask, and I shall answer, "The ravages of war." Today, we face a Spiritual War. If you are unaware of it, I challenge you to read the first few pages of this book and be accountable to yourself. You may realize that maybe, just maybe, you have blinders on your eyes.

Maybe you have elected them by past inaction. Perhaps they are the result of an oppressor. It could be that some part of you realized what you may have heard about spiritual warfare was true and this may have scared you to paralysis. You may have come to this realization some time ago. Perhaps you did not see your place in the fight or know how to take a stand. It could be that you have been just plain afraid to admit these facts to yourself. The Warrior within you will recognize the reality of this war. I submit to you that if you have not taken a stand by now, it may be that you have not developed your Warrior within. Maybe you tried at some time in the past and did not continue the training of your spirit. It is time you tried again. It is time to awaken. For those that recognize the reality of Spiritual War and are willing to find their post and take a stand—welcome to the fray and I hope this training manual assists you in polishing your armor and vanquishing the enemy.

Often the term "spiritual warfare" is mentioned with no further comment as to what the term entails, or how to engage in it victoriously. It is assumed the reader knows all about it and whom it concerns, typically leaving the reader to their own definition, limited understanding, and misperceptions. This myopic approach to such a crucial topic is unsuitable. In light of the vague or nondescript manner in which this topic is commonly presented, it is no surprise many people are not convinced of the reality of spiritual warfare. Many cannot discern it around them. Without proper definition, we have at best cloudy vision with which to view it. This is much like looking for a black cat on a moonless night with sunglasses on. That we as Warriors in the army of God may emerge victorious from this battle, the definition of what spiritual warfare embraces, who the combatants are, and what its effects are, must be clearly understood.

In the most simplistic terms, we define spiritual warfare as the battle between good and evil. While this sums it up, I find this definition wholly impersonal. A better way of defining spiritual warfare may be to think of it in these terms: spiritual warfare includes the activities of those forces aligned against the will of God and opposed to those who choose and try to do His will.

Spiritual warfare is unique in its scope and effects. It is far more insidious and dangerous than the typical physically waged war. While physical warfare may result in bloodshed and death, spiritual warfare goes far beyond this in its scope. The stake for its combatants is not mere mortality, but rather eternal life itself. Jesus' own words from the book of Matthew point this out clearly. *^{28}And fear not them which kill the body, but are not able to kill the soul: but rather fear him which is able to destroy both soul and body in hell.* **Matt. 10:28**.

To recognize the reality of spiritual warfare it is essential that we first recognize and understand that we are dealing with forces of a non-physical reality. The book of 2 Kings contains a revealing story that shows the reality and manifestation of other worldly powers involved in spiritual warfare. During a war with Israel, the efforts of the king of Aram were being frustrated by the prophet Elisha who was being continually alerted to the troop movements and threats of the Aramaeans. The heavenly host supporting Elisha, as well as the spiritual blight upon the aggressors, is clearly presented…*The king of Aram grew very much disturbed over this. He summoned his officers, and said, 'Tell me which of you is betraying us to the king of Israel.' 'No one, my lord king,' one of his officers replied. 'It is Elisha, the prophet in Israel. The words you utter in your bedchamber, he reveals to the king of Israel.' 'Go and find out where he is,' the king said, 'so that I can send people to capture him.' Word was brought to him, 'He is now in Dothan.' So he sent horses and chariots there, and a large force; and these, arriving during the night, surrounded the town.*

Next day, Elisha got up early and went out; and there surrounding the town was an armed force with horses and chariots. 'Oh, my lord,' his servant said, 'what are we to do?' Do not be afraid,' he replied, 'for there are more on our side than on theirs.' And Elisha prayed. 'Yahweh,' he said, 'open his eyes and make him see.' Yahweh opened the servant's eyes, and he saw the mountain covered in fiery horses and chariots surrounding Elisha.

As the Aramaeans came down towards him, Elisha prayed to Yahweh, 'I beg you to strike these people sun-blind.' And, at Elisha's word, He struck them sun-blind. **2 Kings 6:11-18**.

As we are dealing with matters of a different nature, understanding certain prerequisites enables us to recognize spiritual warfare for what it is. First, it is imperative that we as individuals understand that we are primarily "spirit" in nature, represented with a physical form. When we hold this to be true, we must then answer the question: "From where did our spirit originate?" This leads us to recognize and acknowledge our divine creator, God, and the truths revealed to us by His holy Word. The scriptures testify to our spiritual nature: *[8]But there is a spirit in man: and the inspiration of the Almighty giveth them understanding.* **Job 32:8**. *[5]Before I formed thee in the belly I knew thee; and before thou camest forth out of the womb I sanctified thee...* **Jer. 1:5**.

Next, we must identify the agendas and strategies of this war and recognize they may be played out in the physical realm, while the objectives reside in the spiritual. *The weapons with which we do battle are not those of human nature, but they have the power, in God's cause, to demolish fortresses. It is ideas that we demolish, every presumptuous notion that is set up against the knowledge of God, and we bring every thought into captivity and obedience to Christ; once you have given your complete obedience, we are prepared to punish any disobedience.* **2 Cor. 10:3-6**.

As we cannot expect to avoid spiritual warfare, we must learn to fight and be victorious. We must recognize failure is a matter of opinion. Only if we accept defeat in our mind *are* we *then* defeated. As long as we struggle, we claim victory. Failure and defeat only come with our admission. The nature of spiritual war is quite different from what we are exposed to in our every day news. Spiritual war cannot be won with the same type of logic and logistics of a conventional war. Rather, it is waged with faith, love, and patience. We must assume that our spiritual enemies are everywhere, and we must be ready at a moments notice to face them down. Paul, in writing to the Ephesians, not only points out our equipment for this battle, he further identifies the enemy we face. *[10]Finally, my brethren, be strong in the Lord, and in the power of his might. [11]Put on the whole armour of God that ye may be able to stand against the wiles of the devil. [12]For we wrestle not against flesh and blood, but against Principalities, against Powers, against the rulers of the darkness of this world, against spiritual wickedness in high places.* **Eph. 6:10-12**.

Continuing in Eph. 6, we find explicit direction as to how to equip ourselves to wage spiritual war. The above scripture tells us we are to equip ourselves with spiritual armor. We are encouraged to learn exactly what that armor is, and how to use it. *¹³Wherefore take unto you the whole armour of God, that ye may be able to withstand in the evil day, and having done all,* **to stand.** *¹⁴Stand therefore, having your loins girt about with truth, and having on the breastplate of righteousness; ¹⁵And your feet shod with the preparation of the gospel of peace; ¹⁶Above all, taking the shield of faith, wherewith ye shall be able to quench all the fiery darts of the wicked. ¹⁷And take the helmet of salvation, and the sword of the Spirit, which is the word of God…* **Eph. 6:13-18**.

The war is real. The enemy is dangerous. The stakes are high. Our societal problems are going to worsen, and worsen far quicker around you unless you learn to take a stand and become empowered to do battle as you were equipped and blessed to do.

Being able to identify the enemy is crucial to effectively defeat them. God has proclaimed in various names, who the enemy is. Satan is perhaps the most well known. It is the influence of Satan and his minions that we are pitted against. While it is unlikely most of us will confront Satan or one of his fallen angels directly, it is possible. What is most likely to face us is a confrontation with an individual who has been influenced by the forces of Satan. *³⁸The field is the world; the good seed are the children of the kingdom; but the tares are the children of the wicked one…* **Matt. 13:38**. The scriptures contain many incidents in which an evildoer is said to be possessed or under the control of an evil spirit. The story of Jesus' encounter with the unclean spirits known as Legion in Mark 5 or Luke 8 is representative. Jesus instructs his disciples they (we) are to cast out these unclean spirits as well as perform other miraculous acts.

Bear in mind that one of the first goals of Satan and his minions is to remove our attention from doing that which God would have us do. This accomplished, Satan would love nothing more than to pervert our understanding to the point of our denial of God in any context. Ultimately, Satan wants us to recognize *him* as god. He wants us to accept his gifts of death, damnation, and destruction, rather than God's gifts of grace, love, and eternal life. Satan showed his hand quite clearly in his temptation of Christ. **Then leading him to a height, the devil showed him in a moment of time all the kingdoms of the world and said to him, 'I will give you all this power and their splendor, for it has been handed over to me, for me to give it to** *anyone I choose. Do homage, then, to me, and it shall all be yours.'* **Lk. 4:5-7**.

Satan's greatest desire is to destroy our faith. To accomplish his goal, Satan has deception and lies at his disposal to bring us into a condition of doubt, fear, worry, or frustration. Satan also has the ability to use physical dangers to bring this frame of mind about. While the inception of a spiritual attack may be from the non-physical realm, the actual attack is not confined to the non-physical. We, or those we love, may be physically threatened in such a fashion that fear, doubt, worry, and frustration are created in our mind. The story of Job is very clear on all of these points. *[7]**So went Satan forth from the presence of the LORD, and smote Job with sore boils from the sole of his foot unto his crown.*** **Job 2:7.**[*] When we allow ourselves to be distracted in this manner, our attention is not on God. Rather than singing praise and giving thanks to His holy name, we focus on worldly concerns. The fields of defeat and failure are then created in our minds. When Satan succeeds in removing our attention from God, he has effectively "cut our lines of communication." This is an objective of any wise and schooled warrior, even in a conventional war.

As his vanguard, Satan will often use deception and lies. He can use any weakness in our character to assail us. While Satan may never have been a Boy Scout, he is nevertheless a master of tying us up in knots. His knots are unique and function exceptionally well at binding us. He and his servants may literally immobilize us: *[4]**And that because of false brethren unawares brought in, who came in privily to spy out our liberty which we have in Christ Jesus, that they might bring us into bondage...*** **Gal. 2:4**. His bonds are capable of restricting our will to act. The immobilization of the enemy is a primary goal in any war. Once the individual soldiers are neutralized, or immobilized, *there is no army*. This is a very effective means of dealing with an army which otherwise cannot be defeated. An army of soldiers *acting as if* and *believing* they are defeated, ***is defeated***! When his deception and lies have beset our minds, we admit defeat

---

[*] Satan beset Job with trials to make him curse God; however, it did not work.

and often think, "I cannot," "I am not," and "I will not." We must "Untie the Not's" by giving thanks and singing praise to God's holy name. It is amazing how this simple act will loosen Satan's knots. When an enemy is immobilized and has its lines of communication cut, it is doomed. This is the simple, ultimate goal of Satan—to steal, kill and destroy. *¹⁰The thief (Satan) cometh not, but for to steal, and to kill, and to destroy...* **John 10:10**. In general, the enemy's primary focus is to take our attention away from God and turn it towards worldly concerns. We may then be disposed of in leisure.

By consistently turning our worries, fears, doubts, and anxieties over to God, we display our faith and trust in His promises. Ezekiel gives us an admonition from God on this point: *³¹Shake off all the crimes you have committed, and make yourselves a new heart and a new spirit! Why die, House of Israel? ³²I take no pleasure in the death of anyone-declares the Lord Yahweh-so repent and live!* **Ezk. 18:31-32**. Being a loving and responsible Lord, He will always safeguard us, and show us the way to victory.

Having a better understanding of the generalities of spiritual warfare, we should become aware of where and how this war is waged, and have a clear picture of the enemy himself in his many guises. As with any war, there must be battlefronts. One front in which we have little involvement is the theater in which spiritual warfare is waged by God and His angels, and the forces of Satan; however, there are two realms of spiritual warfare that may directly involve us. They are the following:

1. **Direct or Internal**—This battlefront effects our lives directly and those of our loved ones, and
2. **Indirect or External**—This battlefront includes those influences that effect our society.

While these prospects may seem daunting, we must know that we have already been given the victory in this war, and the enemy knows it. The enemy will do everything in their power to test your resolve to hold onto that victory and claim it.

Our internal battlefields are often heralded by our daily concerns, worries, anxiety, fear, and doubt. These may be piqued by such things as the actions of co-workers, criminal acts, or the immature acting out of family members. Bad habits, addictions, personal illness, and concerns for financial security or job security are also typical daily battles for many people. For these reasons the scriptures instruct us not to give in to any of these. They are the tools and devices of the enemy to preoccupy us and divert our attention. This tactic is common in combat. It is essential to divert your enemy's attention. Diversion accomplished, it is much easier for the *real* threat to go unnoticed until it is to late. Has any amount of worry or fretting ever amounted to anything fruitful in you life? How often do you worry about things that never happen? If you are anything like me, our track record on productive worry amounts to a perfect "0." The internal battlefield is the area in which Satan loves to immobilize us with his "knots." We combat the "I cannot," "I will not," and "I am not" with "I can," "I will," and "I am!"

The external battlefield can include situations around us in the environment, and society in general. Often the enemy can place us in situations in which we question our beliefs and values. Alcohol and drug abuse, family violence, and crime have touched all our lives. You may be forced to take a position on abortion, capitol punishment, and corruption of public officials, or other societal issues. Our country's foreign policies are another arena to consider. After all, that which represents us internationally represents us individually in the eyes of the world. Compromise, or lack of proper discernment in dealing with any of these issues, can lead to an erosion of our values, and ultimately society teaches these values through our media and schools.

The effects of enemy action on both of these battlefronts can be seen in broken homes, irresponsible adults, and abusive or destructive conduct. Spiritual warfare is also manifested in infirmities, spiritual bondage, spiritual oppression, and in the worst cases spiritual or demonic possession.

None of us are assured a life of leisure and contentment: Quite to the contrary. We are told that God chastises only those He loves, and that our life will be filled with trials and tribulations: [33]***These things I have spoken unto you, that in me ye might have peace. In the world ye shall have tribulation: but be of good cheer; I have overcome the world. John 16:33. Not only that; let us exult, too, in our hardships, understanding that hardship develop perseverance, and*** *perseverance develops a tested character, something that gives us hope, and a hope which will not let us down...* **Rom. 5:3-5**. We show our true mettle in how we choose to cope with trying situations. Even when under severe attack by the enemy, we may take heart by contemplating one of many scriptures of power, reassurance, and strength. Remember this simple admonition: *[13]Wherefore take unto you the whole armour of God, that ye may be able to withstand in the evil day, and having done all, to stand.* **Eph. 6:13**. You see, when properly equipped, we can take anything the enemy throws at us.

While victory is not always quick, clean or neat, it is assured us by God through His Son. Here is an example to show you what I mean: *[57]But thanks be to God, which giveth us the victory through our Lord Jesus Christ.* **1 Cor. 15:57**. *[15]Thus saith the LORD unto you, 'Be not afraid nor dismayed by reason of this great multitude; for the battle is not yours, but God's.'* **2 Chron. 20:15**. So long as we maintain our lines of communication and persevere in the face of opposition, we are guaranteed to meet victory.

Perception and discernment are important keys to properly identifying true spiritual attacks. Some people consider certain vices such as smoking tobacco, or listening to certain music as spiritual warfare. It is important to use wisdom and discernment when considering whether one is dealing with a spiritual attack. Whenever a situation arises in which the enemy may have a hand, it is extremely important to turn your situation over to God with prayer and ask for His guidance, wisdom, and knowledge. This is one way we keep our lines of communication open, and is essential as appearances can be deceiving. We typically classify something ugly or not to our liking as evil; while those things we see represented as beautiful, we attribute to good. Unlike the caricature of the devil so often represented with a pitchfork and a long forked tail, Satan's appearance is actually quite different. *[14]...Satan himself is transformed into an angel of light.* **2 Cor. 11:14**. We should be prepared for the image of the enemy to present him as one of beauty, guile, and seduction. Furthermore, Satan has some identified personality traits, such as pride: *[4]the Enemy, who raises himself above every so-called god or object of worship to enthrone himself in God's sanctuary and flaunts the claim that he is God.* **2 Thess. 2:4**. Another trait is his subtlety *[3]...as* *the serpent beguiled Eve through his subtlety, so your minds should be corrupted from the simplicity that is in Christ.* **2 Cor. 11:3**. Among other things, he is also known to be the father of lies...*He was a murderer from the start; he was never grounded in the truth; there is no truth in him at all. When he lies he is speaking true to his nature, because he is a liar, and the father of lies.* **John 8:44**.

With all of this clearly understood, the question must be asked, "Who does God use to wage His war on Earth?" The answer is "His Warriors." Accepting a commission to fight in the army of the Lord endows one with a new personal commitment and attitude. The attitude is one of victory and not defeatism. God Himself tells us where He will be when we encounter the enemy in His name. *²I will go before thee, and make the crooked places straight: I will break in pieces the gates of brass, and cut in sunder the bars of iron.* **Isa. 45:2.** Rather than choosing to play it safe and not rock the boat, we choose to engage the enemy on the front lines, and with this accept and cherish the excitement of trials and challenges. This brings home to us that the enemy we engage is real. All warriors need provisions and supplies, and as God's Warriors, we are to turn every day to the Word of God for our supplies and provisions. These come in the form of inspiration, wisdom, guidance, strength, discernment, and continued focus.

If we are to be God's *Warriors*, then we need to hold dear His instruction and develop those characteristics essential to being a steadfast, effective, and victorious warrior.

God has given His word. God has given His warnings. God has given you a place in it all. God is calling you to come to awareness. Will you answer the summons? Will you do your part? Or will you have to be accountable before God's throne for being caught asleep—taken unarmed and quaking by the enemy?

This book is about hearing that call, and having recognized that, TO DO SOMETHING ABOUT IT! This is a training manual for character development, spiritual awareness, and combat. It is long overdue; but then again, some of us have been asleep and not heeding the call. It is time to awaken the warrior within yourself.

I have awakened. I have answered that call within myself. I beseech you to do the same!

For your sake!
For My Sake!
For the sake of us all!
For God's Sake!

Chapter 2

AWOL

As simple and straightforward as the preceding information is, the reality of spiritual warfare is lost on many Christians today. They have neither trained, nor entered the fray. The overwhelming majority of readers have heard, if not sung, the hymn "Onward Christian Soldiers." Certainly Christian Soldiers exist, so where are they you may ask. A vast number of them are AWOL (absent without leave). As a result, many disruptive problems and forces are at liberty to work in our society. We encourage those sitting on the fence to make a decision, prepare themselves, and join in this most glorious fight. To that end, we study the character of the warrior and how his attributes support the spiritual armor of God.

The human psyche is an interesting composite of instincts, and to a large measure, what may be referred to as "genetically determined behavior." The very "hardwiring" within us helps to guide us in acting in a "right" or "good" manner. Our choices and the decisions, which define our character, are guided towards full maturity by these internal directives, these built-in behavior characteristics, or models. These behavioral patterns, instilled in mankind through eons of development, are ingrained in our unconscious as models to be called for in various life situations. These internal behavioral models are referred to as "archetypes."

The noted psychologist Carl Jung described the "double quaternio" in the four primary archetypes he coined as the King (Queen)/Magician, Lover/Warrior. To become a fully developed mature individual, it is essential all of our basic internal directives, or archetypes, are properly accessed and brought to maturity individually as well as in concert with each other. Only if this is done, can a person become a fully functional, integrated, and mature adult, capable of acting in a constructive and beneficial manner for us as individuals and for society as a whole. We are all in this together. As Paul states…*we are all parts of one another.* **Eph. 4:25.**

Grasping what occurs when an archetype is not balanced may elude many readers. Think of what are referred to as masculine or feminine traits and how they are expressed and function within society and us. All of us embody masculine and feminine traits. Individuals not in secure enough touch with both their masculine and feminine side are very lopsided or unbalanced when faced with situations calling for a balanced reaction. A man having not developed the typically expected masculine traits may be viewed as a "wimp" or "effeminate." Similarly, a woman expressing strictly masculine traits may be labeled a Tomboy or described as "butch." The opposite extreme is also seen in society. Men without the slightest representation of feminine traits are dubbed "macho," while women without the slightest expression of their internal masculine traits are seen as, for lack of a better term as "prissy." Our attention is typically focused on the male expression, creating a particular bias in the way we refer to and evaluate masculine behavior. This topic is generally deliberated under the topic of "The Male Dilemma," or "The Male Identity Crisis" in any number of books. A wealth of information pertinent to the male crisis is readily available at your local library.

Much like masculine and feminine traits, archetypes conform to specific and readily identified behavior models. In simplest terms, an individual expressing a lopsided or biased development of their sexuality will convey a specific and easily defined pattern of behavior. Therefore, it is with our archetypes that when underdeveloped they are out of sync with each other. These distinctive character traits or imbalances can be noted in an individual.

A World Gone Wrong

Society, from the local level to a world societal view, depends on each of us developing to the best of our abilities. If this is absent, a world full of distress, disorder, and societal disease is inevitable. In general, a sweeping ignorance of proper behavior is seen today. The level of dysfunction may arguably and easily be an overall societal dysfunction or hindrance preventing individuals from developing freely and fully. The more widespread the individual problems, the greater the effect will show in society.

In viewing society both on the micro and macro level, it appears there is something wrong, something amiss. Some would simply say "Evil" is rampant in the world. This sentiment, in fact, may not be far from the truth. The archetypal character of the Warrior is an essential ingredient we all carry needed to face off Evil. If we do not realize this and use it, Evil will run rampant. Is this the character of the world today?

What if those very elements of character carried by the archetype we as a society shun and disregard are required for us to exist in freedom and love? What if we discover the one archetype required to keep Evil in check were not allowed to develop? What if this one model of behavior is such a cornerstone of development to prevent Evil having a free hand, Evil itself permeates society to KILL its most dangerous opponent? A simple observation can answer that question. **Without the Warrior archetype, we would never be able to fully recognize and enjoy the true freedoms we are intended to have.** Strange as it may sound, we would never know a society of peace and harmony, one filled with love and encouragement. We would live with fear of calamity, strife, and war. Life would become a regular experience of violence erupting in traditionally safe areas such as our schools, shopping malls, and homes. Can you deny this is, in fact, what we are seeing more and more of?

Something has been missing…and that is the Warrior within us all. We ignore and shun the Warrior in our society. As a result, the characteristics of the Warrior have been reassigned and our personal development has been lacking. Without allowing *all* of our character to develop to maturity, we can never fully appreciate the full joy of knowing who we really are. The Warrior within us all has been either targeted for destruction or due to societal dysfunctions, has been stunted and denied maturation. This gives a new insight into the expression *Character Assassination.* This has allowed evil elements to run amuck in society and exacerbated societal problems. The symptoms are explained by the prominence of the expression of the Warrior's undeveloped or regressive behavior characteristics. When the disease is cured, the symptoms go away. The cure lies in recognizing and allowing the Warrior's archetype to develop in us individually for the benefit of us all. It is crucial we awaken and develop the Warrior within us to face and challenge the world's problems and combat Evil. It will be a battle on two fronts-the Physical and the Spiritual.

Each behavior model we carry is important for very distinctive reasons. We must recognize, develop, and liberate each archetype, or we can never truly enjoy being who we are meant to be. Suppose a youngster blessed with the special gifts of a composer or artist were never to mature that aspect of their being and unlock the special gift that may be waiting within. If that composer or artist is not developed, we would all be deprived of the fruits of a Mozart or Picasso.

Just imagine a fine castle: walls fresh and stout, gate wide and open, the drawbridge down. All the King's finest artisans are busy in their shops, and all the children play carefree in the market place where scholars, clerics, and dignitaries mingle in open exchange. Only one necessary ingredient is missing—the watchtower is empty. No guards stand at the gate ready to secure the King's domain and all within it. No sentry walks the wall with a vigilant eye on the people and countryside below for signs of trouble. What is the likelihood of peace, security, and harmony existing with no safeguards? This analogy may be considered: the castle represents society, and all the people therein represent each of us as portrayed by the various role models or archetypes. This could be expanded to consider a world, or macrocosmic view. With no Warriors on guard to watch over us in this sense—society on the grand scale is a sitting duck.

To bring the analogy closer to home, the castle can represent each one of us individually. The people within represent the composite behavior models we emulate. With no Warrior to protect the rest, any bully in the street could terrorize the rest of our character. What develops is a lopsided or weak character. Once this condition becomes widespread, the effects become apparent in society as well as in the individuals.

As the Warrior is essential for the protection of the rest, if he is delinquent in his duties or not at his post, not only will the innocent suffer, but he will be held responsible. This example warns this part of our nature is imperative for wholeness and wellbeing. Consider these words from the book of Ezekiel: ***The word of Yahweh was*** addressed to me as follows, ²*'Son of man, speak to the people of your country. Say to them, 'When I send the sword against the people of that country, take one of their number and post him as a watchman; ³if he sees the sword coming against the country, he must sound his horn to warn the people. ⁴If someone hears the sound of the horn but pays no attention and the sword overtakes him and destroys him, he will have been responsible for his own death. ⁵He has heard the sound of the horn and paid no attention; his death will be his own responsibility. But the life of someone who pays attention will be secure.'*

⁶'If, however, the watchman has seen the sword coming but has not blown his horn, and so the people are not alerted and the sword overtakes them and destroys a single one of them, that person will indeed die for his guilt, but I shall hold the watchman responsible for his death.' Ezk. 33:1-6.

Therein lies the obligation laid upon the author to write this book, for in continuing from the next verse: ⁷ *'Son of man I have appointed you as watchman for the House of Israel. When you hear a word from my mouth, warn them from me. ⁸If I say to someone wicked, "Evil-doer, you are to die," and you do not speak to warn the wicked person to renounce such ways, the wicked person will die for this guilt, but I shall hold you responsible for the death. ⁹If, however, you do warn someone wicked to renounce such ways and repent, and that person does not repent, then the culprit will die for this guilt, but you yourself will have saved your life.'* Ezk. 33:7-9.

All the behavioral archetypes are required to balance us as individuals. All the characteristics enhance and support one another. Consider the Warrior with no "Lover" characteristics to balance him/her. How would the Warrior express compassion or mercy? Consider the Warrior with no kingly attributes: how would he dispense justice for his lord, or act evenhandedly? Likewise, a Warrior with no "Mage" or Magician attributes would be without the benefit of new weapon development, or the ability to heal himself or others, both valuable traits for a Warrior to have.

Can an archetype become obsolete? No, these hidden and ignored parts of our character will constantly struggle for expression and recognition in some way. As a backlash of the captive traits, the suppressed or repressed behavior will be expressed through a regressive character trait. The question then becomes: What behavior may indicate the subversion of the Warrior characteristics? An undeveloped or ignored Warrior may be seen in a boss who may verbally abuse employees, or even sexually harass women in the workplace. Gangs thrive as places for the continued twisted development of psyches incapable of interfacing constructively with society. Husbands abuse their children or spouses physically, mentally, or sexually, or they may show delinquency in financial duties and in the care and support of his family. Wives may be unmindful of their husband's wishes, or may become abusive verbally or physically. They may deny husbands the simple pleasures to be lovingly shared between a husband and wife. Children would be denied the benefit of mentoring by fully mature individuals, thus filling our society with out-of-control kids bent on self-gratification and disrespect. Belittling of character and bickering over seemingly insignificant occurrences may divert valuable time otherwise spent with family members and friends. Public servants, or employees dealing with the public, put an edge on our days by treating the public and customers callously and rudely. Courtesy on the roadways becomes the exception rather than the rule as road-rage becomes increasingly typical of driving behavior.

People find self-expression via sex, drugs, and alcohol because characteristics are being walled up within the individual and stifled. Self-abuse and lack of self-esteem become endemic as no valid forms of self expressions may be found adequate for the immature psyche which will otherwise become dominant.

For these reasons it is imperative we—

Awaken the Warrior

This section is intended to make you aware of those elements of your character needing development. There is a Warrior in each of us, and it is time we recognize that part of our makeup. Come back to these quotations often and dwell on them, as they will instill in you a calling of the Spirit.

Rom. 13:11-14 *Besides, you know the time has come; the moment is here for you to stop sleeping and wake up, because by now our salvation in nearer than when we first began to believe. The night is nearly over, daylight is on the way; so let us throw off everything that belongs to the darkness and equip us for the light. Let us live decently, as in the light of day; with no orgies or drunkenness, no promiscuity or licentiousness, and no wrangling or jealousy. Let our armor be the Lord Jesus Christ, and stop worrying about how your disordered natural inclinations may be fulfilled.*

...You know the time has come... This recognition comes from the Holy Spirit within you. Knowing the time for action is not enough; you must take action as well. This can only be done after one awakens to the day. Time is short. When you arm yourself in the might of our Lord Jesus, the desire to fulfill orders from above quickly and decisively replaces your own selfish desires. All that matters is completing His will.

Judg. 16: 20 *The Philistines are on you. He awoke from his sleep, thinking, 'I shall break free as I have done time after time and shake myself clear.'*

The Philistines were the mortal enemy of the children of Israel. Reference to the Philistines for us today serves as a rallying cry and warning of the most desperate urgency. When the Philistines are announced, there is no time to consider what must be packed away, or stored. The enemy is at hand. It is time to join the fray. Awaken from your sleep and jump to arms! No matter they have returned undaunted from past defeat. You simply resolve yourself to fight them until they are again turned away in defeat. While this is a quotation directed at Samson on arrival of the Philistines, his sentiments are quite clear. His reaction shows the immediate reaction of a trained and well-disciplined Warrior—no questions, just the doing.

1 Cor. 15:34 *Wake up from your stupor as you should and leave sin alone; some of you have no understanding of God; I tell you this to instill some shame in you.*

One must recognize the error of his ways to waken from this type of stupor. It calls for turning away from impropriety. Without the understanding of God, you may never awaken; it is His truth within that sounds the alarm. Knowing God brings with it the responsibility to act as He directs. To have the understanding and knowledge of God and not act as He directs is the most self-serving expression of free will. Recognizing one has acted in this fashion is to admit a truly shameful act of poor choice or disobedience. Coming to the understanding of what has driven their actions, shame for the action is appropriate. Do not deny the call of the Spirit.

Eph. 5:16 *Make the best of the present time, for it is a wicked age. This is why you must not be thoughtless but must recognize what is the will of the Lord.*

Making the best of this wicked time does not mean to take advantage of the accepted wickedness of our times for your own pleasure or gain. It means you should use the time to act as God has directed you. If wickedness abounds, there must be lots of opportunity to act against wickedness…***but where sin abounds, grace abounds much more…*** Rom. 5:20. In these times of depravity, it's when God's redeeming qualities should most abound. As I know of few instances of God acting in the first person in the real world, He counts on us to allow Him to act through us.

It is time to awaken the Warrior within you and declare:

I Am a Warrior of The Kingdom of God!

The following scripture quotes address many of the actions, or rather inactions, we encounter daily and what proper actions should best be practiced. Doing so will reinforce proper behavior and help to correct the problems of misbehavior or those acts of an underdeveloped character. Character itself will be the topic of chapter four, and these quotes should be borne in mind later, when you consider the many aspects of character you will be asked to address in yourself:

Eph. 4:17-32 *So this I say to you and attest to you in the Lord, do not go on living the empty headed life that the gentiles live. Intellectually they are in the dark, and they are estranged from the life of God, because of the ignorance which is the consequence of closed minds. Their sense of right and wrong once dulled, they have abandoned all self-control and pursue to excess every kind of uncleanness. Now that is hardly the way you have learnt Christ, unless you failed to hear him properly when you were taught what the truth is in Jesus. You were to put aside your old self, which belongs to your old way of life and is corrupted by following illusory desires. Your mind was to be renewed in spirit so that you could put on the New Man that has been crated on God's principles, in the uprightness and holiness of the truth.*

So from now on, there must be no more lies. Speak the truth to one another, since we are all parts of one another. Even if you are angry, do not sin: never let the sun set on your anger or else you will give the devil a foothold. Anyone who was a thief must stop stealing; instead, he should exert himself at some honest job with his own hands so that he may have something to share with those in need. No foul word should ever cross your lips; let your words be for the improvement of others, as occasion offers, and do good to your listeners; do not grieve the Holy Spirit of God who has marked you with his seal, ready for the day when we shall be set free. Any bitterness or bad temper or anger or shouting or abuse must be far removed from you-as must every kind of malice. Be generous to one another, sympathetic, forgiving each other as readily as God forgave you in Christ.

Eph. 5:16-33 *Make the best of the present time, for it is a wicked age. This is why you must not be thoughtless but must recognize what is the will of the Lord. Do not get drunk with wine; this is simply dissipation; be filled with the Spirit. Sing psalms and hymns and inspired songs among yourselves, singing and chanting to the Lord in your hearts, always and everywhere giving thanks to God who is our Father in the name of our Lord Jesus Christ.*

Be subject to one another out of reverence for Christ. Wives should be subject to their husbands as to the Lord, since, as Christ is head of the Church and saves the whole body, so is a husband the head of his wife; and as the Church is subject to Christ, so should wives be to their husbands, in everything. Husbands should love their wives, just as Christ loved the Church and sacrificed himself for her to make her holy by washing her in cleansing water with a form of words, so that when he took the Church to himself she would be glorious, with no speck or wrinkle or anything like that, but holy and faultless. In the same way, husbands must love their wives as they love their own bodies; for a man to love his wife is for him to love himself. A man never hates his own body, but he feeds it and looks after it; and that is the way Christ treats the Church, because we are parts of his wife, and the two become one flesh. This mystery has great significance, but I am applying it to Christ and the Church. To sum up: you also, each one of you, must love his wife as he loves himself; and let every wife respect her husband.

The true expression of a Warrior is one in control; control learned through discipline. A True Warrior is never hasty, never belittling, but rather always supportive and protective. These are the masculine expressions of a true Man, not the macho, patronizing form of behavior so readily pointed out by feminists and erroneously ascribed to as "masculine behavior." A True Warrior is never denigrating or destructive in his actions. Rather, a Warrior is a nurturing, constructive force. As a character, a Warrior is someone children willingly and readily trust, and clamor to. After all, we all know a

Warrior is prone to telling tales of far-off adventure, deeds done to defeat evil, and the righting of wrongs (not to mention the neat things they have to show off). These are the true qualities of masculinity, rather than the belittling, denigrating, destructive mannerisms so often portrayed in our world and mistaken for masculine behavior.

As if this situation were not bad enough, there are processes in society that further contribute to the short-circuiting of access and development of our mature archetypes. This inhibition prevents development and expression of the mature forms of behavior for these archetypes, barring their natural activation.

Two societal factors in particular have contributed to the entrapment of each of our internal Warriors. The result is this archetype's becoming hostage rather than a freely expressed contributing factor in our lives. As with all hostages, it is only natural for the Warrior to find some form of escape or expression wherever possible. As this behavior role model is underdeveloped, it finds its expression through either an adolescent behavior pattern, or unbalanced, undeveloped adult behavior patterns. Most often, we see the masochistic or sadistic behavior patterns expressed rather than the balanced approach of the Warrior through truly masculine traits. In effect, true masculine behavior is thus mislabeled, and we find our society confusing it with boyishness and inappropriate macho behavior.

The combined effect of many of these pseudo-masculine traits has been the production of a demeaning and patronizing society. Our patriarchal and patronizing society is one of the primary factors contributing to the suppression of the Warrior archetype. A vicious cycle has been formed. Traditionally, we as a society have been based on, directed by, and focused on the masculine gender, i.e. "Masculinity." The word itself, masculinity, has become a dirty word to many due to widely held and expressed misunderstanding and misrepresentation. It is wrong to believe this patriarchal or patronizing expression is due to true masculinity or simple male dominance. True masculinity has no need for deprecating or demeaning behavior, ultimately destructive and divisive. True masculine behavior is instead supportive and constructive. When this is understood, the mask begins to come off; the problem begins to show its true face and can be seen for what it is. Our patriarchal society is instead suffering from dominance of the immature behavior patterns found in adolescent behavior, or rather Boyhood or boyishness.

By its very approach to this dilemma, society shows how deprived of Warrior characteristics it is. As our society fails to recognize the true nature of masculinity, we have lashed out at the masculine nature rather than cope with the real problem, that being inappropriate patriarchal and patronizing behavior. This, in itself, is more of an automatic reaction rather than a well thought out and controlled action, incisively dealing with the true problem. A more controlled and deliberate approach would be consistent with the true and accurate expression of the masculine attributes of the Warrior.

Machismo and overbearing behavior in all its many forms have led to the advent of the equality, or the feminist movements. Many people, not just women, have fought to bring about more recognition of female influence and rights in society. Their efforts have been excellent in focusing attention on defining masculinity, not by it's true nurturing and protective nature, but rather the brutish, aggressive mannerisms of machismo. As a result, men often find any expression of their more dominant or masculine traits is confronted with the pressure of sexual discrimination, sexual harassment, or some aspect of a violation of "EQUALITY." This movement, in its actions and approach to what is believed to be our societal problem with masculinity, is no better at representing true feminism than it is correct in attacking all things masculine in nature. Men and masculinity are not the root of this problem. It is our misunderstanding of the true issue compounding the problem. The feminist movement, while attempting to represent "true womanhood," presents itself as a poor representation of feminism. The entire movement is generated by adolescent behavior patterns much the same as the very thing which it hopes to correct. This has resulted in our society not only having a distorted understanding of what is truly masculine, but we have now muddled our understanding of womanhood as well. This has only served to further confuse the issues at hand and forced true masculinity further from sight. The few "True Males" in society are faced with a complex dilemma.

While the efforts of the equality movement are not without merit or cause, it should be remembered, equality is not sameness. Men and women are different. A simple look at the anatomy of the two sexes will support this position. This is not to say men and women do not have feelings and thoughts, and in characteristic ways show the same inner drives. They do, however, think differently, and this has been the subject of many a best seller. The simple fact is, the scriptures give both men and women specific and different duties to be mindful of. This is how natural order is created. Reread the last verse of the above scripture **Eph. 5:33**. This topic alone can fill a book.

If the proponents of feminism truly understood the power of Womanhood, they would understand their acquiescence to Manhood is where their power lies. Ultimately they ***DO*** hold the power they want. However, as boyishness is confused with manhood in their eyes, they find themselves barking up the wrong tree. The key to understanding is simply this: Manhood's power resides in the head; Womanhood's power is of the heart. Manhood's directive is to be considerate of Womanhood, and allow their lessons of the heart to speak to their head before action is taken. This is a great topic to do a specific Bible study on, and it is hoped you will poke around in the scriptures a little on this subject.

The roles of men in society, as well as of the family, were clearly defined a generation ago. Today's men find those traditional roles vied for by women in both the workplace and the home. Many men have had to learn to cope as best they could with the shifting sand under their feet, and just hang on while society turns a determined eye on destroying itself. Tragically, any action they were to make would be seen as further male dominance attempting to maintain control, and would further isolate and erode the situation. They are truly "damned if they do, and damned if they don't." The result is the simple resolve of these men to hold on to what they can and make the best of it.

The overreaction resulting from the feminist movement has created a certain mindset among women that men and their male dominant ways are the cause of today's problems. The crux of the problem is that true masculinity has been in the back-seat all this time. The adolescent energy or undeveloped forms of the masculine model have been driving the car all along, rather than the energy and spirit of the mature man. Consequently, patriarchy has been under siege.

A simple example of the contrast between a true masculine response and a boyish or patriarchal response may help to clarify the difference. Suppose a World-Champion Martial-Arts Expert were making an appearance and casually asked for a challenger to prove his expertise in a public setting. Any adult with a modicum of intelligence would realize this is not a setting for a show down with a world title expert, unless you would like to be made an example of. However, this is just the setting that would prompt some young buck to step forward to prove his stuff.

Another example of a situation as ridiculous as this would be to affront an armed assailant who is looking for an excuse to "pop-a-cap" on someone in the midst of a robbery. Unless you are seriously ready to meet your maker, prudence would dictate you make yourself scarce. However, there is always some rash youngster full of false bravado ready to make a point, and usually makes a headline instead. Rashness and impudence are notable trademarks of a boyish response. In marked difference to this, calculation and control are true masculine traits.

Another situation, which addresses the patriarchal aspect of our society, can easily be found in any office environment. Suppose a delivery is being made to an office in which both a man and woman have a desk. Whom do you suppose would be addressed first by a stranger walking into the office and looking for the supervisor? Studies have shown the first approached will be the man.

The second major contributing factor to suppress the Warrior has been the loss of the most basic and fundamental initiation rituals in our culture. Without these simple ritualistic initiations, the adult archetype of the Warrior never receives his wake up call and misses his ride to the real world. This Initiation Rite serves to signal the new model it is time to take over. As the fully mature archetype role model is never thus recognized or activated, we fall prey to trying to live an adult life with old, inappropriate, and outmoded forms of behavior in place, the adolescent role models we have had on line since our childhood. To this day, those societies still existing with a tribal structure have rigid initiation rituals specifically tailored for the rite of passage of a young man into full manhood.[*] We may claim to

---

[*] An excellent movie that portrays how this operates is *The Emerald Forest.*

be more civilized, yet this simple and crucial rite of initiation is missing from our culture.

In the minds of most hot-blooded American high school students, there are perhaps two experiences thought of as a rite of passage. These include their first fumbling attempt at making love in the back seat of the family car, or learning to smoke. Hormones certainly serve as a natural drive for the one, while peer pressure is the typical inducement for either of these behaviors.

The closest pseudo-initiation rituals to be found in our culture today with any semblance of, or association with, tribal cultural rites may be: enlistment into the military, graduation from high school, joining a gang, or getting married/having a baby. All of these experiences indoctrinate the initiate into a shadow reality of true adulthood/manhood and mock some facets of the true Warrior's nature. Certainly, these situations may be hallmark moments in one's life, but have very little to do with that required to specifically activate the Warrior's archetype within us. Many gangs today require an initiate to kill an innocent person or in the basest of ways take advantage of an innocent through a violent act. With such a requirement as this, only the basest of behaviors are instilled and exalted. That created is a "Shadow Knight" at best and a continued exaggeration of the immature archetypes found in the adolescent.

Two religious rituals found in our culture today come closest to a true initiation. One is the Catholic confirmation, and the other is the Jewish bar mitzvah. Another ritual is the reciprocal of the bar mitzvah, the bat mitzvah, performed for young Jewish girls who have "come of age." These ceremonies are intended to instill in the mind of the initiate the notion they are now recognized as an adult. As it specifically pertains to young ladies coming of age in secular society, another example comes to mind that was prominent in society just a generation ago. Young ladies in aristocratic families were recognized as coming of age as a debutantes and formally brought into society as a young woman through a debutante ball. The purpose of this ceremony was to recognize the young woman's entrance into adulthood, attendant with all the duties and responsibilities of being an adult. This coming of age and formal "coming out" into society was typically distinguished by the proper introductions being made to those within society she may best find her advancement though.

Prospective mates were also carefully included in the introductions. This is certainly a far cry from the hallmarks identifying a true initiation.

To introduce a true initiation rite, consider the European dubbing of Knighthood. This ritual, designed to instill in the mind of the young squire he had "arrived," and formally recognize his advancement in society, was recognized by all of society, secular as well as nonsecular. His moment of advancement into full manhood was at hand. Nothing approaches this ritual in our culture today. Without even this simplest form of initiation rite present in society today, most people are locked into expressing the adolescent form of the Warrior or the "Hero." While the Hero may portray a fully balanced archetype of behavior, it is an adolescent form, and can never rise to the power and expression of the adult Warrior model. There are few, if any, live Heroes, while a Warrior is most content to see the enemy die for their cause. The question to be answered is this: "How can we activate this archetype when the ingredients required to awaken it are difficult to find, or non-existent in our society?" Understanding the hallmarks typifying the dubbing ceremony of Knighthood shed light on how our Warrior archetype can be awakened today.

The hallmarks of the dubbing ceremony, or any true initiation, rite is as follows:

1. **The Holy Place:** There must be a recognized Holy Place, a sanctum, or specially prepared venue in which the initiation may take place. While this may be a remote place for the benefit of isolation and the likelihood of being undisturbed, isolation is not required. What the location denotes is the site of a significant occurrence. A prescribed location will typically assure isolation. Usually it is a place prepared for the rite or the rite is held typically at this specific location for other intrinsic reasons. The location is held as sacred or sanctified and may be specifically reserved for the process.
2. **The Mentor:** The initiation is performed or overseen by someone seen as being of a higher level of wisdom or status in regards to the initiation, someone capable of executing the rite and revered as being able to confer a new status. A wise old

man or Holy Man is traditionally required, or one holding a position which is deferred to.
3. **A Symbolic Death:** This is typically the death of the old outdated characteristics being replaced with the New Self created by the initiation.

These three characteristics are readily visible within both the confirmation and bar mitzvah. While the religious ceremonies may be quite significant for those involved, few individuals in society recognize or apply any significance to them. The debutante ball may be a social occasion, but unless there is a truly mature young adult being recognized, the affair simply denotes a specific age having been reached, little else. A true initiation ritual is both recognized by society as being a significant occurrence and will carry a heart felt, if not religious, significance for the initiate.

Let us take a look at a typical historic dubbing ceremony, and see how the elements of initiation were represented. This rite of passage was typically held in a church or holy place. This quite often included the field of battle, as blood makes the land hallowed ground. The location of a great victory or defeat conveys upon the land a sort of reverence. Gettysburg, Pennsylvania, is a good example of this. The ceremony was overseen and conducted by the candidate knight's sovereign king or lord. In a more formal setting, the ceremony could have been officiated by a bishop or local priest. The ceremony was conducted only after the candidate had purified himself in some fashion to make himself ready mentally and spiritually. Typically, this was accomplished by the initiate spending a certain amount of time in prayer and observance in a chapel. Combining an officer of society with a matter of personal purification, matters of the heart are recognized and conjoined with society and its needs. The vigil was often before the Eucharist and the knight's tools-of-the-trade, which would have included his arms and armor. The initiate considered his old station and way of life behind him now. He looked forward to his new station and the attendant responsibilities and duties he would soon be accepting. This passing away of his old station in life represented the symbolic death of his boyhood as it gave way to his new life of Manhood.

Having been knighted, and therefore, reborn anew and granted a certain new recognition, the new knight was acknowledged as properly trained. His sword may now be used to dispense justice as he found it necessary to correct wrongs. He had no need to check with a higher authority, as the authority has been dispensed to him for these situations. He was duly empowered to act.

For us to recognize the Warrior within and undergo an initiation to bring about this liberation is essential for our individual development and the betterment of society. A simple way of accomplishing this is by first coming to the realization there exists within one's self the need for this change. Taking an inventory within oneself may reveal this need, but as the required forums for this to occur are no longer provided by society, a real problem is encountered in following through with the process. Remember, a characteristic of the true mature Warrior is the ability to take action. If an individual recognizes the Warrior within is not developed, or lacking in expression, this is the first characteristic I would ask you to call forth and claim. For without action...NOTHING CAN BE ACCOMPLISHED!

The first hallmark of the process to healing and reconciliation within one's self is recognizing an error or deficiency in one's make-up and electing to change it. Once the election is affirmed, it must be acted on. This is, in effect, being called out, or "Answering the call." While society may not provide the outward ritual, the inward process will be sufficient in this instance, and can prove to be useful in awakening the internal Warrior.

"How does this meet the conditions of initiation?" you may ask. Consider what has been said about our body in the scriptures: The body has always been referred to as the Temple of God, so what more sanctified place can you go to for a change of your inner being?

John 2:21 *But he was speaking of the Temple that was his body...*

1 Cor. 6:19 *Do you not realize that your body is the temple of the Holy Spirit, Who is in you and Whom you received from God?*

That which recognizes our lack of a spiritual truth, or a flaw in our make-up, is something more than conscience it is the Holy Spirit. The Holy Spirit knows all spiritual truth and stands above our carnal nature, thus is of a "higher level of wisdom or status." The Holy Spirit calls us out and identifies what needs to change within us, calling this to our own spiritual awareness. It is the Holy Spirit, then, which we have recognized as our Mentor capable of performing the rite. He acts on us in this fashion by calling upon our spirit to bring about the necessary change. The Roman centurion recognized this Higher Authority and had enough faith to act on it in the book of Matthew: *^{5}And when Jesus was entered into Capernaum, there came unto him a centurion, beseeching him, ^{6}And saying, Lord, my servant lieth at home sick of the palsy, grievously tormented. ^{7}And Jesus saith unto him, 'I will come and heal him.' ^{8}The centurion answered and said, 'Lord, I am not worthy that thou shouldest come under my roof: but speak the word only, and my servant shall be healed. ^{9}For I am a man under authority, having soldiers under me: and I say to this man, Go, and he goeth; and to another, Come, and he cometh; and to my servant, Do this, and he doeth it.' ^{10}When Jesus heard it, he marvelled, and said to them that followed, 'Verily I say unto you, I have not found so great faith, no, not in Israel…'* **Matt. 8:5-10**.

Your "Greater Self," or Spirit, induces the junior self into a process of maturing or growing up, by the recognition or identification of a higher level of development or maturity. This is, in fact, what maturing is. Just getting older will not do it. Just being taught what is mature is not enough either. The need for the change must be called for and performed within ONESELF. This is one of the greatest challenges one can place before one's self, as the effort and experience of self-examination is one of great trial and personal pain. The end result is the symbolic death of the old self and the birth, or awakening, of the new self. This *must* occur, and without it there has been no true initiation.

Rom. 12:1 *I urge you, then, brothers, remembering the mercies of God, to offer your bodies as a living sacrifice, dedicated and acceptable to God…*

1 Ptr. 3:18 *¹⁸For Christ also hath once suffered for sins, the just for the unjust, that he might bring us to God, being put to death in the flesh, but quickened by the Spirit...*

Ps. 51:10 *¹⁰Create in me a clean heart, O God; and renew a right spirit within me.*

Many Christians may describe what I am referring to as being accomplished during the moment of conversion. That would not be a bad comparison at all, actually. However, conversion to follow our Lord is specifically a conversion experience of the heart or spirit. With continued nurturing and training, a conversion experience may operate within an individual as the type of initiation mentioned above. All of the elements are there. Unfortunately, the continued training and development typically do not occur. What is required is a change in spiritual recognition and identity. A good person remains a good person, so there is no real change in their behavior.

The real change is in the spirit and recognizing there is a Divine Creator, God. This must happen to allow a person to move from the collection of the well-intentioned good people, to the ranks of the spiritually alive Warriors for Christ. I am referring to the awakening of a part of your character to empower you to claim the promises our Lord has assured His Warriors of the Faith. When the Spirit within an individual moves them to change, a part of their old self will die and a new creature emerge. Acknowledging what the Holy Spirit has called upon your heart to change is one thing; *making the change* is often the most difficult action.

Water baptism would be, in a sense, a better analogy to the type of initiation we are discussing. The baptized individual recognizes they emerge from the water a changed person, Born-Again, afresh, renewed. The old self is passed away and a New Self emerges. Typically missing from our modern pseudo-initiations is the life long awareness the day would come, and constant preparation to meet the day of fulfillment.

To challenge ourselves to recognize the Warrior within and undergo a true initiation and to awaken him is the dilemma we all face individually today. Society is no longer of any assistance in meeting this particular need. In understanding what elements are missing, we may understand the necessary ingredients to awaken the Warrior Archetype within ourselves.

Once an individual has accessed the Warrior within and made a compact within himself to go forth and declare himself for the Kingdom of God, he should be made aware of the weapons and defenses with which he is to claim as his own.

Rom. 10:9-10 *...that is you declare with your mouth that Jesus is Lord, and if you believe with your heart that God raised him from the dead, then you will be saved. It is by believing with the heart that you are justified, and by making the declaration with your lips that you are saved.*

Eph. 6:12-13 *...For it is not against human enemies that we have to struggle, but against the Principalities and the ruling forces who are masters of the Darkness in this world, the spirits of evil in the heavens. That is why you must take up all God's armor, or you will not be able to put up any resistance on the evil day, or stand your ground even though you exert yourselves to the full.*

As enough of us access and develop our internal Warrior archetype, the effects will be seen in society.

God's army is recruiting. You are being called upon to enlist.

Take it from me...but then "Who Am I?" How do I know and see these things:

I am a Warrior of the Army of God!

Chapter 3

Becoming Whole

The Human psyche has been described as a composite of various archetypes. As we mature, these archetypes develop in very specific ways. Each archetype has a definite form of expression that is identifiable by these characteristics. From an adult perspective, these behavior patterns are recognizable and distinguished through immature adolescent behavior into full maturity. The typical behavior expressed by a child is easy to identify as adolescent and immature in nature, children will act as such. Yet, even for children, while there are certain behavioral patterns accepted for the adolescent, there are other expressions such as the malicious treatment of playmates that will be dealt with as unacceptable even for the adolescent. It is hoped these expressions will work themselves out and the youngster will learn to act in a mature fashion as they grow up. An adolescent is viewed as mature when we can recognize they act in a manner beyond their age. Some youngsters are fortunate in developing earlier than their years would indicate and showing a very mature character for their age.

Take a moment to reflect on some of the children and adults you know. Think in terms of their behavior. Are there any people you know who seem to be wrestling with simple decisions or situations most adults would deal with very easily? Do you know any adults who never seem to get their lives straightened out or on a level footing? What about the young adults you know. Can you single out any young adults who display a great level of maturity for their age?

When you call these individuals to mind, you are consciously comparing them to behavior models you have come to know as "adolescent behavior" and "adult behavior." You are assigning them mature or immature classification according to the behavior you have witnessed them express, and judge these actions against what you have come to know as mature behavior. Our inborn behavior models, our archetypes, are the models upon which we hang the decisions we make in our lives and where we hang our experiences. What remains part of this behavioral framework becomes the person we are identified as, or becomes our character. All of our failings, weaknesses, strengths, and victories are shown in our various forms of expression. Some expressions are supported by adult behavior models, and some by various degrees of undeveloped or outdated adolescent behavior models.

When faced with the prospect of developing a yet unrecognized archetype, the problem areas each of us face in our progress can often be better pointed out by those who know us than by any degree of personal self examination. How many of the people you called to mind in the simple exercise above would agree with your assessment of their character? Listening to the critical comments others may have about our character is one of the best ways to address self-examination for problem areas we may need to focus on. It requires a special kind of frankness to recognize these messages when we receive them, and a special kind of determination to face up to the challenge and effect growth and change.

Try this exercise: Of the following character types, pick the one that closest represents you. How would you best describe yourself? Are you a Teacher or a Student, a Lover or a Player? Perhaps you are yet something else…are you a Coward or Bully, or a Sadist…possibly a Masochist? Are you a Victim or a Martyr? Can you speak and act on your own behalf as a Leader, or do you merely follow the lead of others as a Follower? Are you a Warrior or a Mercenary?

Each of the above descriptive models is readily identified as portraying a certain trend of behavior. If you can identify with these forms of personality expressions, you are not alone. We are all familiar with them. All of us show in some way the various forms of the inadequately developed, self-canceling psyche at one time or another. None of us is perfect, and even if we have developed a mature archetype of any one particular model, we will not always have the benefit of acting fully within that model's trait at any given moment. It is not something we as individuals dwell on before we open our mouths or act. Repeated correct actions, when called for, will tend to produce a more consistent character. Even so, being human, we will never get it correct all the time. Thus, the weaker expressions of the immature character models are far more prominent in our society today than the mature character trait expressions of the fully matured archetypes.

Adolescent and Adult Archetypes

Just as our behavior may be described as adolescent or adult, our innate behavior models, our archetypes, come in both adolescent and adult forms. Each form, be it the adolescent or adult form, will develop through an immature expression and hopefully into a mature expression. Therefore, en route to full maturity, we must first develop through the immature expression of the adolescent form into a fully developed, mature, adolescent form. The next process may sound a little peculiar, but it is how we develop into maturity. We carry forward our maturation process by transcending beyond the mature adolescent form into the formative immature expression of the adult behavior form. In effect, we have two fully developed forms of each of our archetypes: the adolescent and the adult. Each of these forms develops through an immature expression, into a mature form.

There have been many different archetypes defined as making up human behavior. Some treatments of the subject will use as many as a dozen archetypes to define human behavior. In their simplest forms, they may be best defined in four simple models: The Magician, The King/Queen, The Lover, and The Warrior. It is the basic understanding of what archetypes are and the mechanics of one in particular, the Warrior, with which we will be concerning ourselves.

The process of developing character begins in adolescence and continues into adulthood. What we show as our character today is primarily due to the choices we have made in the past. Hopefully, development will continue to its fullest. The result is a person of character in the finest sense. These internal guidelines of character are easily considered as our innate hardwiring that compels such behavior as our "fight or flight" behavior. Whether we choose fight over flight, or flight over fight, will have an effect on our character. These innate forms direct our development into maturity and are described with the basic four forms. Each of these adult archetypes has a precursor, or adolescent form, which is developed in the adolescent child. These adolescent forms of the adult models are known as: "The Precocious Child," "The Divine Child," "The Oedipal

Child," and "The Hero."* These adolescent forms will hopefully mature into their fullest stage of development before the end of adolescence. As we enter our young adult age, we hope to develop into full maturity by building upon the behavior models we have developed in our adolescence. Then we may accept the maturation process and develop the full adult forms of each archetype of character.

With regard to all aspects of character, the goal for the adolescent is to mature into the full character of the mature behavior models. We must come to terms with the immature forms of our characters and develop them to the best of our abilities as we grow up. When we have gone beyond adolescence and approach adulthood, we are called upon to develop and continually express the mature face of the adult archetypes. Remember, developing all the archetypes of behavior in us is important if we are to develop into full maturity and be on the best footing to deal with the complications and situations of life as a fully matured individual. To just develop one archetype would leave us unbalanced and not fully developed.

So, you, the reader may have a clearer understanding of how these behavior models, or archetypes, function and express themselves, and how they form the basis for our adult expression, a brief overview of the maturation process of the basic four archetypes follows. First described is the adolescent forms and how they are best described and developed. This will then be followed by a brief explanation of how this adolescent form develops into the fully mature adult form. Considerable insight into our actions, and those of others, will be gleaned from this information.

The Precocious Child In The Magician

"The Magician" in his adolescent form is identified as "the Precocious Child." The Precocious Child may be typified by their eagerness to learn, wanting to know the "why and what" to

---

* This information is easily found in *King, Warrior, Magician, Lover: Rediscovering the Archetypes of the Mature Masculine,* by Robert Moore, and Douglas Gillette.

everything, possessing talents in one or more areas, and is the wellspring of our adventurous impulses and curiosity.

When this adolescent form is itself undeveloped, it produces what may be described as the character traits of either the "Trickster" or the "Dummy." The Trickster may be characterized as loud mouthed, and a con-artist. He will sell us on the appearances of something he has created and get us to buy into his con. Then he derives a sick satisfaction in our misfortune once we are taken in. He may be quick to verbally abuse someone, and in many ways creates many more enemies than friends.

Contrary to this, the Dummy shows no real personality at all. Typically, a slow learner, the Dummy is a dull wit, lacking personal vitality, and creativeness. He may show a total lack of physical aptitude as well. For all his appearances, however, the Dummy is usually not as naive as he may seem. Most of his portrayal is a put on. This stems from the fact of his not having any personal fortitude.

To develop the balanced aspects of the Precocious Child is to allow ourselves the ability to tap into an interest for learning in general, and to generate a playful spirit as we mature. This will then allow us to continue beyond the Precocious Child into the next step in the maturation process, the development, and manifestation of the fully developed adult behavior traits of the Magician.

The Magician

The adult form of "The Magician," also known as the "Wizard," is best described as commanding wisdom and possessing the understanding of technology. He works wonders not easily understood by those of a lesser knowledge. If not fully developed in the adult form, the Magician is often represented by the "Manipulator" or the "Innocent One."

When expressed as the Manipulator, the characteristics most prominent are his underlying cruel nature and his unwillingness to fully educate those studying with him. This denies others their full understanding and creates dependency. This is opposed to the actions of the Magician, which are focused on liberation, which true understanding brings.

Acting as the Innocent One, the characteristics often expressed are an unwillingness to accept full responsibility and a desire to block others from achieving his level of stature. Acting out as the Innocent One shields an individual from being asked to take positions of responsibility and authority.

When fully developed, the Magician offers liberation from the unknown, and is a true mentor to those seeking knowledge.

The Divine Child Becomes The King/Queen

"The King/Queen" in the adolescent form is described as the "Divine Child." As defined by Carl Jung, some of the attributes of the Divine Child are his love and enthusiasm for life, his sense of well-being and carrying the heart of joy and peace.

When not developed to its full adolescent form, the Divine Child has been described as the "High Chair Tyrant" or the "Weakling Prince/Princess." With respect to the behavior of the High Chair Tyrant, typical traits include: his belief he is the center of all attention, everyone and everything exists to please his needs, and never being satisfied with anything. The High Chair Tyrant will display lack of responsibility, aloofness/arrogance, and a high degree of immaturity or childishness in the strictest negative connotation.

The Weakling Prince/Princess is typified as reclusive from life, possessing a dull personality, a constant complainer who gets his way by whining. He will belittle those around him, and will portray the helpless victim, waving his hands in the air and crying out for help-constantly.

It is important to fully develop the Divine Child so all the creative and life-giving influences he commands will develop and represent themselves in maturity as the King/Queen.

The King Or Queen

In the fully mature nature, "the King/Queen" serves as the center of the world. He serves as the support for all of the other archetypes. He relates to them all and helps direct them. He willingly makes himself accessible, and places himself at the disposal of his subjects.

He functions to create order and prosperity for all. In an undeveloped state, the King/Queen is often described as the "Tyrant," or the "Weakling."

The Tyrant may be characterized as destructive and ruling to serve his own wants rather than the good of the whole. Being self-serving and self preoccupied, he will disregard those he feels are below his station in life; meaning everyone.

The Weakling, while he may know well what needs to be done, will fail to muster up the strength needed to do what needs to be done. While noting injustices around him, he will typically wonder why nobody else takes notice, or does anything about them. All the while, the Weakling will point his finger and cry out, all the while conspicuously sitting immobile himself.

The presence of the fully developed King/Queen can be recognized in the able efforts of one in control. Concern is expressed for all. Recognizing they have achieved the pinnacle of authority, election to serve those whom they rule over is chosen to set the example.

The Oedipal Child Becomes The Lover

In his adolescent form "the Lover" is described as "the Oedipal Child." The Oedipal Child may be typically portrayed as having a high level of connectedness with things at a deep level. He will display passion and affection for all things. The Oedipal Child is the root of our spiritual sense of identity. The characteristic most notable in the Oedipal Child is best described as the symptoms of the Oedipus/Electra complex. While this malady may affect either sex, the subject is typically described as having a desire to search out and engage in a relationship with a woman who portrays the internal characterization of his mother. The opposite would be true for a female suffering from the condition known as the Electra complex.

While in the undeveloped adolescent form, the Oedipal Child has been described as "Mama's Boy" or "the Dreamer." Mama's Boy is characterized by the strong attachment to their mental construct of what is believed to be the ideal mother. He may continually strive to obtain a relationship with a real woman, all the while seeing her as the unobtainable non-existent mother model he has created in his mind.

Typical of this undeveloped model, relationships driven by the Mama's Boy attitude always fail because they are developed around obtaining the unobtainable. As a rule, the Mama's Boy mentality will generally also express a fascination with pornography and excessive sexual self-gratification. When referring to this malady in a female, the expression "Daddy's Girl" may be more appropriate. The young girls fascination would be for her father, rather than her mother.

While a Mama's Boy attempts to have relationships, the Dreamer removes himself from all relationships, into his own dream reality. The Dreamer relates typically to inanimate objects to the exclusion of any interpersonal relations. Content to exist within the boundaries of his imagination, the Dreamer will wile away the hours lost in thought rather than playing with friends and developing real relationships.

If fully developed in a balanced fashion, the Oedipal Child will continue to develop into the Lover and bring with him the sense and ability to develop fully integrated, intimate and passionate relationships.

The Lover

"The Lover" as a fully developed behavior pattern may display a sensual relationship with everything he/she touches. No shame is associated with the body, and delight is gained in relishing all sensations. The Spanish word "simpático" well describes the nature of the Lover.

When not properly balanced, the Lover may manifest the behavior of "the Addict," or "the Impotent."

The Addict lacks the ability to separate from the hedonistic delight derived from simple sensuousness, everything must coalesce in orgasmic release. Contrary to this, the Impotent lacks the ability to derive the pleasure desired in the least.

The Lover has the ability to accept pleasure for what it is at any level. Well aware of the dangers of investing personal affection, the Lover gives unselfishly.

The Hero At The Heart of The Warrior

Finally, we come to the archetype at the focus of our concern. As with the previous archetypes, we will first discuss the adolescent form of the Warrior, the "Hero." Just as the previous terms, this term evokes many mental pictures, and may cause some confusion in its use in this context as traditionally the hero is seen as the penultimate conqueror, the vanquisher of evil. How then could it be an adolescent development stage? When used as a descriptive term within the developmental sciences, we associate a different definition to the term. Recognizing the Hero by this new definition, we will then have an understanding of how the Hero develops into the Warrior, and more readily identify his behavior in those around us.

What we encounter in society today is the behavior of the adolescent Hero model, or possibly some immature aspect of the Hero. In standard usage, we typically say a "hero" is that individual who has risen to a higher level of achievement above the common warrior—not so in the development of our archetype.

In the simplest of definitions, a "Hero" is a term we tend to use to describe an individual who has risen to the occasion when an uncommon act was required. This act would typically be an uncommon thing by its very nature, and not something to be expected again. For this reason, the term Hero is used to describe the adolescent form of the Warrior archetype, for while we hope our youngsters will rise to the occasion when they need to, more often than not, they don't. This is typically due to the fact they have not yet learned what will be expected of them in full mature adulthood. Until they have grasped this type of behavior is to be expected from them and their Warrior nature, to act in a fashion that would require them to be singled out is uncommon ground for them to tread on. For this reason, many times they will shirk their duty to act, and fall short of our hopes for them. Consequently, for many adults today, it is still uncommon or uncomfortable ground to tread on. This is why the term Hero is used to address the character of a person who may rise to the occasion when conditions are just right. The action taken will generally entail something not normal or ordinary for the individual to perform at their age, or point of development.

The individual who *regularly* rises to the occasion and does the uncommon holds the true heart to the Warrior archetype. To act in such a fashion regularly is the result of having learned proper behavior patterns, and accepting the responsibility that goes with them. Character patterns are learned through repeated action.

A Warrior is expected to be there at the right time. A Warrior is expected to always come through in a pinch. It is the Warrior who is relied on in the fight. The Hero cannot be counted on to show his stuff. When a castle was under siege and the attacking army began scaling the wall by grapple and ladder, it was not countless Heroes who scaled up the walls to take the rampart. It *was* countless Warriors who were relied upon. As a whole, their efforts were heroic. Out of the many that did perform this common feat of taking the battle to the enemy, a few may be singled out as having acted classically heroically and shown themselves to be heroes in the traditional sense. This recognition after-the-fact by the Warrior is not to be confused with the jargon used to describe the typical aspects of character the adolescent Hero model represents. Just remember, even though the Warriors may have singled out the courageous acts of one of their own as being truly heroic, it would not be something that would be expected of that individual to perform again. This is the distinguishing difference: the Hero is one who may rise to the occasion in one instance, while the Warrior is expected to do the uncommon as a matter of duty and devotion regularly. Every one of those Warriors who scaled that wall was in fact a hero in their own right.

Aside from the psychological use of the term, perhaps a title that better fits the traditional representation of the hero may be the "champion." Among any number of Warriors, there may be one individual who represents the paramount in all the Warrior endeavors to do. This individual would be singled out of the entire force as the Champion. This individual would be without compare. He would be the best of the best, the warriors Warrior. A good example of one individual the reader may associate with in this manner would be the champion knight of King Arthur's court. Do you remember his name? He was none other than Sir Lancelot. Sir Lancelot was unquestionably the best Knight-in-Arms; he was the unquestioned champion, undefeatable in combat.

The Hero harnesses all the energy of the immature masculine energy. His rashness and bravado must be tempered into true masculine traits, or full maturity will never occur and show in the adult. In his immature form, the Hero has been described as the "Grandstanding Bully" or the "Coward."

The Grandstanding Bully believes the whole world revolves around him and anyone challenging this is likely to get a punch in the nose at worst and verbally abused at least. Being a lone-wolf, he will find it difficult to work with others in a concerted effort. A chance taker, he will often bring harm to those around him. He has no real understanding of his limits and does not accept he has any. Where females and all things feminine are concerned, he is out to conquer them. This in some way makes him feel masculine.

The Coward, on the other hand, is that undeveloped immature side of the adolescent Hero who does not recognize his own worth, or will not live up to it. The Coward shows himself as the individual turns his head from wrong and looks for someone else to intercede…all the while thinking, "Why doesn't somebody do something…?!" while he himself stands idly by and watches, usually from the shadows, fully capable himself. He will not stand up for himself and would rather be abused or walk away from a confrontation than defend his character or position in the slightest way.

Traditionally the Hero dies for his cause. In this sense, the cause for which our Hero *must die* is to become fully mature as a Warrior. It is through the sacrifice of the Hero the Warrior is born. While we typically view the death of anything in a negative way, in this particular incident, the death of the Hero is essential for the birth of the Warrior. Formatively, this sets the stage for the future actions of the Warrior as in many ways the Warrior my destroy many things, but whatever he kills or destroys always serves as the fertile ground for something greater to spring from: urban renewal, the "Phoenix from the fire," is the result.

The Warrior

"The Warrior" is the cornerstone to resolving many of our problems. Fully developed, the Warrior is a motivator. He is aggressive and alert. Discriminating in his destructiveness, his actions create the room in which society builds. He is not wantonly destructive.

In his immature stages, the Warrior may be described as the Sadist, or the Masochist. Neither of these two immature adult stages have the ability to construct by their actions. In the simplest definition, the Sadist relishes inflicting pain upon others, while the Masochist relishes having pain inflicted upon them. One is simply harmful to others and the other is harmful to himself. These two character models may be seen easily as the abusive boss, the tyrant husband, or the head-in-the-sand-deniers who are downtrodden by society. Of these forms, they may be readily found in either S&M clubs or the underbelly world of dominatrix and bondage.

We are all a constantly changing blend of these character types at various times. To be truly balanced, an individual should show representative portions of the Mature Archetypes, but we *ALL* have perfectly imperfect pasts that show themselves in our occasional release of the immature character forms. The amount to which our immature patterns show versus the full appearance of the mature forms, will indicate the amount of maturity development needed. Simply put, the more regularly we display immature actions, the more maturing is required.

That said we should understand the added complexities that are placed before the budding child when a well-defined male or female role model are absent in a child's development. Even when they are present, chances are these adult models will not have been fully matured themselves. This is a polite way of saying the vast majority of parents raising children today are not ready or are ill prepared for representing the various fully matured archetypes parenthood is expected to serve in the form of role models. This has nothing to do with age, simply with full character development. This may sound a bit harsh, but rest assured that this has been typical throughout the history of man. Who can honestly say they are ever ready for parenting. We all do the best we can with what we have.

When asked to describe a particular type of individual or role model, we draw on our encounters with individuals whom we believe would exemplify the role model in question. Unless we have had direct dealings with the particular role model, we will derive a mental image that, we believe, will be imbued with the requisite characteristics. For example, If I asked you to close your eyes and picture a King, you would probably imagine a fellow wearing regally ornamented robes and bearing a gold crown on his head. You would probably imagine him sitting on a throne looking very serious. This image comes to us courtesy of history books and movies of days long gone. Considerably many nations in the world today still have Kings ruling over them, and many of them spend their days dressed in suits, although very nice suits. Few would make a habit of wearing a crown on any but the most solemn or important of occasions.

Before we discuss in detail the various characteristic traits of a Warrior, let us try something. Let's take an inventory of how you perceive a Warrior, what you understand the nature of a Warrior to be. A powerful individual, such as a Warrior, will bring to mind many preconceived notions as to the nature and character of such a person. These mental images, or preconceived notions, are direct results of our encounters with people of our past. They are also rather revealing when one considers them against the backdrop of the characteristics to be discussed.

Think for a moment of the purist, fullest description of a Warrior that you can conjure in your mind. Keep that image clear and take a careful mental inventory of all the details about your Warrior. Describe this individual to yourself. Put as much detail into your image as you can imagine.

Animate this image and watch how it moves and acts. See the various things this Warrior may do, and how your Warrior may react and respond in various situations. Try to hear what type of sounds may be associated with this image. What types of settings do you picture this Warrior in?

At this time, sit back, relax while you let your imagination whirl. Once you have a very solid picture in your minds eye of the Warrior, ponder these simple questions in regards to your image:

1. Is a Warrior an AUTHORITY FIGURE? Do you see the image of a person you would listen to in times of crisis? Does your mental image of a Warrior bring to your mind a person you would follow if so directed, or take orders from?

2. Is this a person you would trust? Is this someone you would entrust your possessions with? Is this someone you would entrust with the welfare and safety of your family? Would you feel comfortable knowing the Warrior was at home with your kids, alone?

3. Do you see this Warrior as a threat? If you were in close contact, would this presence evoke fear in you? On the contrary, would you feel safe in your Warrior's presence? With this Warrior's immediate presence, would you feel uncomfortable, or protected? Would the fact of having this Warrior present, in itself intone to you that you were in imminent danger? Do you fear the Warrior's presence, or is it something else?

4. Does this person embody a destructive force? Would acts of wanton violence be in character for this Warrior, or does the Warrior embody controlled or focused violence?

5. Bearing in mind I have purposely not applied a gender to the Warrior, have you? Is your Warrior a Male, Female, the same sex as yourself, or of the opposite sex? Can you describe any particular reason for the gender you have applied to the image?

Although we typically think of a warrior in terms of masculine images, it is important to remember the character of a warrior is present in women too. To think otherwise would lend one to fall to the argument men do not have any feminine traits or character attributes. It is just as foolish to consider women to not posses any masculine traits. Neither is true. A good example of this is the mothering instinct or nurturing of the young. This instinct is imbedded in both men and woman. As a race, in order to develop completely, it is advantageous to have the influence of both a mother and father. Having both male and female role models, the natural development of the youngster into a character of value and merit are substantially improved. A good example of a woman seen as a Warrior is Joan of Arc. She led the French people to a National freedom from the invading English King and his army, and helped them regain lost lands. A woman Warrior in contemporary science fiction is Princess Leah from the movie *Star Wars*. A popular contemporary fantasy television series based upon the exploits of a Warrior as expressed in a woman would be none other than the heroine *Xena*. If Xena seems a little lopsided as an individual, this may be simply be for the reason she expresses a predominance of the Warriors archetype to the exclusion of many of the attributes of the other archetypes (this is not to say the writing for the show may be a little lacking...).†

A literal historic figure of a comparable position can be found in the book of **Esther**. We are told the story of a Jewess who becomes Queen of 127 provinces from India to Ethiopia. How she becomes Queen is not as important as how she obtained her claim to fame. Esther succeeds in saving the entire nation of the Jews by her honor, courage, devotion, and self-sacrifice. All of these characteristics are represented as traits of the Warrior. Female warrior figures such as Esther, Deborah, and Joan of Arc, have been more than an occasional anomaly. Many have been immortalized in various forms of art, theater, film, print, and sculpture. Anyone familiar with opera is no doubt accustomed to the depiction of the female Valkyrie. In addition to the Valkyrie we may consider the Amazons. In the Amazons, we have an entire culture run by woman. The Valkyrie and the Amazons serve as excellent reminders of the character of the warrior that is present in all women. This must not be forgotten. Even ancient civilizations revered the woman warrior as goddesses and appropriate figures to be immortalized in effigies and statues. Warrior goddess figures such as Athena and Diana are good examples of this.

---

† The scriptures tell the tale of two women in particular, who portrayed much in the way of the Warrior's character. In the Book of **Judges**, chapters 4 and 5, we read of Deborah, who was a prophetess of Israel and traveled with the army, wielding a sword and standing as judge over Israel. In **Judges 4** we encounter Jael, who entices Sisera, a hunted enemy of Israel, and after nailing his head to the floor, smites it off and presents it to Barak and Deborah.

The warrior images you have conjured up may have been as versatile as a fireman, policeman, American Indian brave or a soldier from some period of American history. As well suited your mental image may be to fill the warrior role, I question whether many of us have a full and true understanding of the Warrior's full character and role in society. This is due, in part, to the fact this role model isn't given free rein in society today. We generally rely on storybook images or movies of some era long gone when referring to the description of a Warrior. Few of us have daily encounters with a Warrior of this description. This is not as it should be, however. It should be as natural as encountering a schoolteacher or a doctor, as each of us carries the role model of the Warrior within us.

The point is many of us do not have a fully matured image of a Warrior. Instead of envisioning a "True Warrior," many will instead envision a "pseudo-Warrior," or a Mercenary. The primary difference would be any other man-of-war image would fall short of the full character of a true Warrior. I would venture to guess your mental image of a warrior would be full of wanton destruction, acting in an individual and carelessly destructive fashion. The typical impression may have him acting alone for his own personal gain and fighting when it suited him rather than for a higher ideal. A pseudo-Warrior may actually fight for the gain of his leader, but the force for which he fights and the energy he harnesses is of evil, darkness, or chaos rather than goodness, light, and balance.

Borrowing another popular character from the movie *Star Wars,* a good example of a pseudo-Warrior, or "Shadow Knight," can be described in Darth Vader. Vader as the Shadow Warrior as opposed to a true Warrior contrasts many of the major differences between the two while embodying many of the same characteristics. Awesome in his power, and ultimately destructive, he does take command from a higher authority as a true Warrior does, but Vader serves "Darkness." He fights on his own terms and his wake of destruction leaves brokenness and disorder. If he were to charge into a room full of innocents in pursuit of his enemy, he would kill indiscriminately and mindlessly, never losing any sleep over what he has done. We can almost hear him say in defense of his actions, "Oh Well…They should not have gotten in the way…!" This is a very good example to consider when put in the context of spiritual war.

A true Warrior may be a destructive force in his own right, but the destruction results in development and beneficial change, the growth of society versus the total destruction and wasteland left in the wake of the Shadow Warrior. Vader would be content to destroy whole worlds to make a point, and does, while the true Warrior would rather develop and nurture whole worlds to make his point.

Another good example of a pseudo-Warrior would be the legendary son of King Arthur, Mordred. Anyone who knows the story of Camelot and the Knights of the Round Table should be familiar with the closing chapter of the legend in which Arthur's bastard son, Mordred, lays claim to the throne and by sowing the seeds of dissent, destroys the very notion of "Good Triumphant" over "Might is Right." Everything Mordred does leads to the destruction of something. What is left is ruin, not tilled fields but, fallow, not fertile fields.

Both of these examples pale when contrasted to the two perfect knights brought to us in the tales of the Round Table, Percival and Galahad. Depending on the version read, either of these knights was the sole perfect exemplification of Chivalry and Knighthood. Both suffered the loss of everything they possessed, were imprisoned, and suffered unendurable hardships in their quest for the Holy Grail. Although they slew their fair share of the enemy, and had hand-a-plenty in the ruin of castles and towns, they left behind the fruit of justice, and their actions never served their personal gains.

Rather than finding ourselves dealing with the mature role model of the Warrior, we have instead been typically confronted with some immature form of the Warrior archetype, or even an adolescent behavior model. A well-matured child's character may show all the trappings of the Hero, falling short of the Warrior by becoming an "Example Figure" or "Hero," but not truly empowered to act as a Warrior and truly *be* that example. Generally ready to point fault and belittle, tearing down, or gloat, instead of building up as a Warrior would.

The image of the warrior that the scriptures describe is of the Roman Legionary. Another good example of a Warrior is the European crusader. History tells us how they followed the encouragement of the various Popes of Rome. They gave up all of their possessions to fight against the forces of Islam to free the Holy

Lands. Wearing their white tabards bearing the characteristic red cross, we tend to think of the crusaders as living by some higher moral code, living on a plane somewhat closer to the throne of God, fighting for a just cause. Constantly wearing their battle dress, they were ready for combat in an instant.

From that period, we can reference the Hospitalers, a special Order of the Crusaders, wearing black tabards bearing a white cross. The Hospitalers are the forbearers of the Red Cross of today, and practiced what little was known of medicine in their day. Staunching wounds and setting bones was just becoming understood, but the cause of infection was still a mystery to them. Their special calling was to administer aid and support to their wounded comrades, as well as serve in the rank and file. The modern day Corpsman, or Medic, would be a close comparison. To date, much of what is known about surgery and medical care comes directly from the front line and support service of the Medical Corps, direct ancestors from the Hospitalers. The horrors and effects of war have provided mankind with a rich field of study with no shortage of patients or variety of trauma to learn from.

Bear in mind the image of the Roman Legionary, or crusader, to develop a full mental and spiritual impression of the Warrior's character and a mental physical image. This image is best served by the following presentation. The scriptures will be used as a source to further define this image.

Chapter 4

The Forge

Col. 3:12-17 *As the chosen of God, then, the holy people whom he loves, you are to be clothed in heartfelt compassion, in generosity and humility, gentleness and patience. Bear with one another; Forgive each other if one of you has a complaint against another. The Lord has forgiven you; Now you must do the same. Over all these clothes, put on love, the perfect bond. And may the peace of Christ reign in your hearts, because it is for this that you were called together in one body. Always be thankful.*

Let the Word of Christ, in all its richness, find a home with you. Teach each other, and advise each other, in all wisdom. With gratitude in your hearts sing psalms and hymns and inspired songs to God; and whatever you say or do, let it be in the name of the Lord Jesus, in thanksgiving to God the Father through him.

Mark 16:16-18...*proclaim the gospel to all creation. Whoever believes and is baptized will be saved; whoever does not believe will be condemned. These are the signs that will be associated with believers: in my name they will cast out devils; they will have the gift of tongues; they will pick up snakes in their hands and be unharmed should they drink deadly poison; they will lay their hands on the sick, who will recover.*

Now that we have had a closer look at the archetype of the Warrior, we must look at his mettle, his character, and thereby gain a fuller insight into what exactly drives this part of our being. If these aspects of character are left undeveloped, it will be easy to imagine the consequences once we understand how essential these characteristics are. Each character aspect described is integrated and represented through our spiritual armor. When this is understood, it will be easy to see our weak spots, our exposed underbelly if you will, due to the lack of protection some missing aspect of character would have afforded us.

In the earliest stages of childhood, our character develops; character is learned, but *CANNOT* be taught. It is subject to maturation when the individual considers it, but not before. It is essential to remember: character develops out of the experience of having made a choice of action. Without role models, the lessons of character have no true score card for the individual to measure their performance against. It is not "What happens" to a person that dictates how that person develops, but rather what the person does "*AFTER it happens*" that defines character. Inaction in circumstances demanding action constitutes a choice, a decision, and an action, regardless of the inaction expressed by the individual. For this reason, we must remember that character cannot be taught, but we choose the type of behavioral choices we wish to express.

Bad things do not happen to "Bad people" anymore than good things happen to "Good people." Bad things happen to "Good people" just as good things can happen to "Bad people." It is only after the person has responded to an incident that you can truly evaluate their character. After all it is what one *does* that is used as a measuring stick, a definition of their character. We must understand it is not merely the willingness to do something by which we are measured, but by the doing of what is willed. A Warrior displays "willingness and the doing." Inaction will thus define ones character. When called upon to take a stand and one does not, they may be defined as a coward or someone who is "all mouth," willing to lend lip service, but never adding any backbone to an issue.

There is an expression that speaks to the matter of dealing with bad situations, with good character: "When life hands you nothing but lemons, make Lemonade!" Acting in such a fashion allows us to take adversity with a smile, and make good things happen, regardless of the adversity of the moment. Many aspects of a Warrior's character may be expressed with such an attitude and by taking such action. Besides, it is fun to turn adversity around and see good things happen in spite of the current turn of events.

Where does the role model of the Warrior come from, you may ask? It is programmed into our genes, in our very "behavioral hardwiring."

We have discussed archetypes briefly and we all have the same hardwiring for these archetypes, be we male or female. Men and women all carry the same drive to develop character in all its many aspects. This includes those traits we define as characteristically male or female. We are all influenced by many factors and countless decisions that, in the end, will determine what the results may be for each of us.

The Warrior is cut from a most "Noble Spirit." It is with this Spirit we are all imbued and created. The Spirit wants us all to develop into full maturity and take on all situations fully prepared. Before we can understand that which we are created to be, we must be able to identify those characteristics that make up the Warriors' archetype. Once these characteristics are recognized and identified, we will then be able to fully understand how those parts of our makeup operate. If we have identified an aspect of character we feel may need some improvement, we will be in a position to make constructive change.

It is imperative each of us recognizes all of these characteristics as being ours and lay claim to them. Having done so, and only by having done so, can we then own them and express them. After we have claimed ownership to these characteristics, we may then be able to fully express them and develop into full maturity. In the mean time, we may have some holes in our character, some virtual holes in our spiritual defenses.

Remember: Character is learned by actions and decisions made. We determine how much and in what fashion our character is molded and shaped by the decisions we make and the actions we take.

Just as there are various metals in an alloy, the components of our character blend and work with each other. As we strengthen one aspect, we often find we have bolstered another. For this reason, all components of an archetype must be understood and handled in a unique manner. Building our character with the blueprints for each archetype is the only surefire way of building our character in a fully cohesive and integrated fashion. The components of an archetype may be difficult to deal with separately as they are all so closely interrelated and alloyed. They are melded with the spiritual principles governing the archetypes as well as the separate character traits of the individual archetypes.

It is not with just a well-integrated character a warrior is armed. He is also equipped with real armor that protects him and serves to support his stance on the field of conflict. His training in the terms of character is only part of it. His training in the use and reliance in his armor is a crucial part in understanding the mindset of the Warrior. Truly, one has to consider his mettle as well as his metal. The subject at hand is his mettle; so let's take a look at the mindset and character of the Warrior. What traits constitute a Warrior's character?

A Warrior's Character encompasses **Devotion** and **Honor** to a greater power or allegiance and **Justice**, so right, freedom, and truth or "right action" may be expressed freely and abundantly. A Warrior is **Compassionate**, **Merciful**, displays **Rightness**, **Nobility**, **Courage/Fearlessness**, and **Trustworthiness**. A Warrior fights selflessly so as not to get in his own way. He is well **Disciplined**, **Humble**, **Willing and Able to Act**, **Strong** as well as **Dogged/Persistent**. All of these traits help a Warrior identify the battle to be waged and the enemy to be fought with **Discernment** and **Wisdom**. Nevertheless, all of this is not enough; recognizing a battle must be engaged is not enough: A warrior must also ACT.

I think the following scripture says a good deal about the nature of a Warrior's character and how we should all act. Take some time to read it and let it sink into your mind before you proceed into the section on character:

James 1:19-27 Remember this, my dear brothers: everyone should be quick to listen but slow to speak and slow to human anger; God's saving justice is never served by human anger; so do away with all impurities and remnants of evil. Humbly welcome the Word, which has been planted in you and can save your souls.

But you must do what the Word tells you and not just listen to it and deceive yourselves. Anyone who listens to the Word and takes no action is like someone who looks at his own features in a mirror and, once he has seen what he looks like, goes off and immediately forgets it. But anyone who looks steadily at the perfect law of freedom and keeps to it—not listening and forgetting, but putting it into practice—will be blessed in every undertaking.

Nobody who fails to keep a tight rein on the tongue can claim to be religious; this is mere self-deception; that person's religion is worthless. Pure, unsoiled religion, in the eyes of God our Father, is this: coming to the help of orphans and widows in their hardships, and keeping oneself uncontaminated by the world.

While it is easy to become bogged down in the details and intricacies of what comprises character, it should always be remembered a Warrior: 1) Appreciates Life, and 2) Has Fun. Wearing a smile and allowing the easy approach of strangers and friends, best represent this. This amiable and approachable demeanor stems directly from the fact a Warrior *has a heart*, and is aware of the tremendous responsibility he bears. It is the people around him the Warrior will fight to protect and preserve, and the underlying love for what God has created remains always close to the surface of his demeanor.

Mettle

Now that you have had a little primer, let us look at the traits of a Warrior a little more closely and claim them each and everyone as ours.

Devotion/Honor—Honor is gained by noble and correct action. The aspects of the Lover temper the actions of the Warrior.[*] Without the emotions and caring of the Lover, the actions of a Warrior may be seen as bullish or uncaring. A Warrior shows and gives honor to a greater power or allegiance: a Warrior does not act for his own self-interests. He subjects himself to the will of a Great Leader or Sovereign. Fighting for his Lord's cause, he serves a greater cause than his own self-interests. God is a "True Warrior's" King. Recognizing this at all times, a Warrior remembers he is under the direct supervision of this Great Sovereign and acts with Honor in

---

[*] In Medieval times, when tournaments were regularly held, it was typically a requirement of participants to display a token of a "Lady Fair." This was to show that the individual fought for the honor of, and in devotion to, someone other than his own personal gain.

respect to his Lord's cause. This can be seen as a form of Devotion, if not simply Honor.

Only when a Warrior acts honorably for the greater cause can he be trusted to do the right thing. Acting in this fashion keeps the Warrior's motives clear and undisputed. He is not acting out of self-motivation or with personal gain in mind. He is being directed by a code of honor derived from a higher authority. The Warrior is ever mindful of this fact and acts accordingly. With his actions directed by a "Higher Good," the next two aspects of character follow close behind: justice and compassion. An honorable Warrior would not take advantage of a situation by destroying that which may be saved. Until the very last blow is delivered, a True Warrior would still hope his adversary might capitulate, or, recognizing true goodness, give in. An eye is always turned to this eventuality. Our Lord's compassionate nature is our model for this type of behavior. To quote from *The High History of the Holy Graal,* Percival (the holiest and purest of all of King Arthur's Knights) slays a belligerent Knight and accepts his two companions as prisoners, telling his mother, "…one ought to make war on the warrior, and be at peace with the peaceable."

Actions directed by devotion, honor and a selfless nature generally infer righteousness or right action. While this may be true, acting rightly will be discussed in greater depth when we look at the breastplate that the Warrior is armed with. It represents "right" or correct action. When the benefits of wearing a breastplate of protection such as this become clear, it becomes easier to act appropriately with time and practice. Remember, behavior of a mature character comes with action over time.

Lev. 27:28 [28]***Notwithstanding no devoted thing, that a man shall devote unto the LORD of all that he hath, both of man and beast, and of the field of his possession, shall be sold or redeemed: every devoted thing is most holy unto the LORD.***

Ps. 119:38 [38]***Stablish thy word unto thy servant, who is devoted to thy fear.***

Our Lord Jesus served as the perfect example of devotion to a greater cause and authority. *My Father, He said, if it is possible, let this cup pass me by. Nevertheless, let it be as You, not I, would have it.* **Matt. 26:39.**

Justice—Not fighting for his own gain, the Warrior is always vigilant to safeguard and act upon the truth and justice of his Lord God. The Justice he supports and protects is not derived from his own goals and concept of fairness. He follows the guidelines set for him by One greater than himself. This enables freedom and truth to live freely and abundantly. With an eye towards preserving Justice, an infraction of the peace can count on being dealt with by an agent of the Lord. Justice in this context is the Law of God. *Wisdom comes from the lips of the upright, and his tongue speaks what is right; the Law of his God is in his heart, his foot will never slip.* **Ps. 37:30-31.** By following the Laws of God and speaking for His Justice, our way is secure.

Justice for Justice sake would at times be cruel. It takes a Wise King to dispense Justice fairly, which means there must be some latitude available to convert ill actions for good. This ultimately is True Justice, which can only be meted out by the King. We are told where Justice is dispensed; Compassion is measured (Zech. 7). The best dispensing of Justice would result in reparations and constructive benefit for the wronged party and a conversion of intent on the part of the wrong acting party. Remember: our Higher Authority defines what is just and right, and this governs our actions. We all have access to His wisdom. As justice emanates from our Higher Authority, and the sword of the King or His duly appointed authority historically meted it out, it serves us well to remember Justice is carried in the Word of God. This is represented in a Warrior's armor as the Sword of the Spirit. Being a Warrior's only offensive weapon, bear in mind it is the Word of God we are instructed to bear as our sword.

Additionally, justice can only be rightly dispensed in the light of Truth. Truth makes up the girdle of protection for a Warrior. When girt in Truth and acting with justice, think how impeccable one's actions become in the eye of our King.

Gen. 18:19 *[19] For I know him, that he will command his children and his household after him, and they shall keep the way of the LORD, to do justice and judgment.*

Ps. 82:3-4 *[3] Defend the poor and fatherless: do justice to the afflicted and needy. [4] Deliver the poor and needy: rid them out of the hand of the wicked.*

Compassionate—Compassion may be shown for the victim who has been wronged, or for the misguided individual who has committed a wrong. One way or the other, this obligates a Warrior to act on someone's behalf. When finding those wounded by the many battles waging in the world today, a Warrior will take the time to help those in need and bend his back to help those needing a strong back to aid them. Compassion being shown for the enemy can be found in virtually every recount of a battle throughout history. A Roman slave may save the life of a cruel or abusive Master. The end result may be in the freeing of the slave. There is a good example of this in the movie spectacle *Ben Hur*. At one point in the story, Ben Hur (who has been unjustly sentenced to slavery for an act he did not commit) is chained to an oar on a Roman Galley and subsequently saves the life of a Roman Senator when their ship is sunk (this was made possible when the Senator himself had seen the character of Ben Hur for what it was, and had his chains released just at the beginning of the battle in which their ship subsequently sank). In return, Ben Hur is given his freedom and adopted as a son into the influential Roman's family. These just rewards were in recognition of the actions of a true Warrior by a true Warrior. There was nothing compelling the Senator to bestow freedom, or even more surprisingly, accept Ben Hur as his son. These actions themselves were a show of compassion and justice from one Warrior to another after having recognized the true character of Ben Hur. Other good examples may be found in many accounts of battles during the American War Between the States. It was not uncommon for one wounded soldier to offer aid and water to a fallen enemy after a battle had raged.

As we have been taught the great must become low and the servants will reign above all, a Warrior never assumes a greater station for himself over any under-privileged, hurt, or needy individuals he encounters. His mission is to right wrongs, fight for justice, and be mindful of the needs and compassion required by those having suffered the onslaught of the enemy. What would happen to those victimized by alcoholism or abuse if even the avengers of God will not pay them heed, treat them with compassion, and help bind their wounds? Compassion is inextricably tied to a Merciful and Humble Spirit. *[8]Finally, be ye all of one mind, having compassion one of another, love as brethren, be pitiful, be courteous: [9]Not rendering evil for evil, or railing for railing: but contrariwise blessing; knowing that ye are thereunto called, that ye should inherit a blessing.* 1 Ptr. 3:8-9.

As portrayed by the Warrior's armor, the sacrifice of our Lord is a symbol of his compassion, which he has shown us all. The salvation we were graced with by His action serves the Warrior as a Helmet. This serves to protect our mind, our value judgments, and our decisions.

Ps. 86:15 *[15]But thou, O Lord, art a God full of compassion, and gracious, longsuffering, and plenteous in mercy and truth.*

Merciful—A Warrior well disciplined and trained can recognize the disadvantaged and display his Lord's Justice with Mercy towards those having a change of heart or recognizing the wrong action they had done. He can recognize when the fight has been won and is not mindlessly going to continue destruction. The innocent, bereaved, and those recognizing they have been on the wrong side and show earnest desire to make right, are given the opportunity to bring their petition before the Higher Authority. These are a Warrior's orders from above. Seldom will the hand of reconciliation be withheld, as a Warrior has been shown this lesson by His Lord. Mercy is not shown for the hardened heart, obstinate, or belligerent. To treat even the enemy without regard to compassion and Mercy would ultimately be the act of a Sadist, or a Shadow Knight.

Mercy is a strange thing in today's light as compared to the medieval era. In Europe between the twelfth and sixteenth centuries, there was in common use a piece of armament known as a Misericorde, or Mercy Dagger. The actual translation of the weapon's name literally means "mercy for the body." The mercy dagger was a long, edgeless, slim blade constructed with a strong point. Not for use as a primary weapon, rather the mercy dagger was intended for use on those having fallen in combat. The final act of raising the blade before dispatching the enemy was often enough to force a change of heart in the enemy, and rather than accept ultimate death, capitulation may have been obtained. The alternate use of the blade was to end the suffering of mortally wounded family, or a loved one whose only other alternative was a slow and painful death. Amends would be made, and blessings offered before the final *coup de grace* was delivered. Obviously, this duty historically fell to the Hospitalers.

The dagger represents Mercy; therefore, remember the Warrior is armed with the Sword of God, which is His Word. True mercy is an expression of a noble spirit and it is from God this virtue is given to us.

Ps. 89:14 *[14]Justice and judgment are the habitation of thy throne: mercy and truth shall go before thy face.*

<u>Displays Rightness</u>—The Warrior must be seen by all as a constant reminder of the will of a Greater Authority. The breastplate he wears represents this. It is bearing in mind the will of his higher authority and measuring his action against this, which constitutes "right action." It is the display of Rightness that enables the Warrior to be seen as a Bastion of Might, a leader, and a role model; someone not just to be followed, but also to emulate. It is this part of his character which helps single him out as someone to be trusted and welcomed with a warm heart, and openly. His actions are clear, his motives directed for the good and benefit of all. This marks the Warrior as a person to be trusted to do the right thing at the right time in the right way. The path he clears, and the way he leads, makes it easier for those following him to do so with unswerving support and faith. His actions bring those around him closer and forge a bond of faith and love. This bond is based on his actions of clear conscience and right acting. This trait additionally makes the Warrior dependable and above reproach.

The Breastplate of the Warrior is represented by righteousness or right action. It is by the Warrior's right actions that bonds of faith and love are forged. Paul, in **1 Thessalonians**, uses the typical chain-mail body protection to represent the joining together of faith and love to form a protective garment. It is faith and love which welds us one to another, and through this is forged a close fitting protective garment for the whole body's protection.

Prov. 10:2 *²Treasures of wickedness profit nothing: but righteousness delivereth from death.*

Prov. 21:21-22 *²¹He that followeth after righteousness and mercy findeth life, righteousness, and honor. ²²A wise man scaleth the city of the mighty, and casteth down the strength of the confidence thereof.*

<u>Nobility</u>—Knowing he is cut from greater stock than mankind itself, and belonging to a greater Kingdom, a Warrior can easily lay claim to the fact he is a true Brother and rightful heir to a greater realm and way of being. This is not an attitude one accepts; it is a fact a Warrior lays claim to as part of his being. Accepting the fact and not effecting airs, the true Nobility of the Warrior is seen in his Gentle Spirit and Compassionate nature. Only true nobility can be merciful, for the true dispensing of mercy is ultimately reserved for those in a position of authority. God has shown us the model for noble action, and He expects us to follow His example.

The noble acts of a Warrior cannot help but elevate those who witness them. Consider the wounded leader knocked from his horse who goes on to lead his companions on foot, putting himself to no less risk than those he commands. Acting in such a way can only endear and galvanize the hearts of those witnessing his actions. Noble acts enrich us all, and show the true caliber of our human nature. Noble actions enable us to show that, contrary to the general dictates of human nature, we can act in a manner that exceeds normal bounds or understanding. These are acts that cause us all to stand a little taller, endure a little more than we normally could, and stand when we may have fallen or accepted defeat.

We are all from the same stock, be we White, Black, Red or Yellow. Recognizing a noble act on the part of another speaks to our spirit. In this way can we identify these actions by saying, "Hooray for our side" or, "I wish I had done that." The key here is if we all adopt a sense of our nobility, we will be more disposed **to Act.**

When Nobility is called for, a lesser being may instead display disregard or partiality to those suffering. This type of action is typical of the Coward or Bully and when seen in the proper light will be seen as callous, uncaring, or inactive, rather than as one acting out of a noble character. Neither disregard, bias, nor partialities are traits of a Warrior. Oftentimes, when acting simply as your Nobility directs, one may be labeled as courageous, another trait of the Warrior.

The armor protecting the legs and feet of the Warrior may best reflect the aspect of nobility. As this armor represents the willingness and the actual doing of certain acts directed by our Sovereign Lord, we may be compelled to frequently display acts of courage that others would see spiritually as emanating from a reserve of Nobility. This type of action, when called for, may be supported by our security of salvation (represented by the helmet) for we would not be distracted by errant thoughts that may otherwise dissuade us from acting at all.

Rom. 8:14-16 *[14] For as many as are led by the Spirit of God, they are the sons of God. [15] For ye have not received the spirit of bondage again to fear; but ye have received the Spirit of adoption, whereby we cry, Abba, Father. [16] The Spirit itself beareth witness with our spirit, that we are the children of God…*

<u>**Courageous/Fearless**</u>—A good definition of courage may simply be: *being afraid to do something, and doing it anyway.* When we allow our fear to justify our inaction, we effectively shoot our self in the foot, using our excuses as the ammunition. Face any excuses you may use for what they are, excuses, and then simply **DO**. Win or lose, you learn from the experience, and this builds character. Remember, it is what you do after something happens, that determines your character. When confronted by a challenge or a "bigger than life" problem, we are to turn to God and involve Him in the solution. Nothing is bigger than Him. God is the Commander-in-Chief. He empowers us with super human abilities and blesses us with miracles when need be. We are never in the fight alone so long as we remain prayerful, and ever mindful we are not fighting our

fight, but God's. God most certainly can beat all the odds. He simply needs us to take a stand, and become the conduit for His blessings.

By removing our self-interest and concern from a situation, we become dispassionate observers, and allow God's blessings to flow. By being overly concerned or self-invested emotionally, we can block the flow of God's blessings. Being quiet and listening for His orders is a very important part of a Warrior's training. When we effect a change within our being, we create a change in our surroundings. We become the instrument of change. If we sit idly by, we are onlookers, and onlookers do not change the circumstances around them.

As a Warrior knows he fights for a greater cause than any he could conceive of, and he is selfless, he is therefore ready to act in a Fearless manner, having vanquished fear with love and devotion. This sort of action is additionally supported by his understanding the power of Faith; the belief he is secured by the protection of his spiritually bestowed armor and shield. Believing there is no weapon the enemy may employ to harm him, he does not fear those dangers appearing imminent. He recognizes the true dangers are the strategies and tactics he may not see at all. Everything before him takes on the proper perspective. He can act automatically when action is called for. His training has given him this ability, for it frees him to stay aware of the unseen perils that are the true dangers. A good way to define Fear is this way: **F**alse **E**xpectations **A**ppearing **R**eal. Now consider the word **Fearless**—a true Warrior can be fear-less because we are taught to Love more. Love conquers all. Just imagine if every stab were instead a kiss, every shot instead a loving word of encouragement or act of reconciliation. Under conditions such as that, what war would ever begin? To love one's enemy is, after all, one of the primary charges we are given. Fear is a weapon of the enemy. It is quite capable of rendering the most powerful Warrior ineffective if he is not adequately prepared and armed. When filled with love, however, there can be no room for fear, and even the slightest, least assuming Warrior can become a fearless force to be reckoned with. *In love there is no room for fear, but perfect love drives out fear, because fear implies punishment and whoever is afraid has not come to perfection in love.* **1 John 4:18.**

The one piece of armor that may best assist this aspect of character is the Shield of Faith. Faith is what protects us from the needling attacks of the enemy, the fiery darts. Faith offers protection from attacks in all quarters, seen or unseen. Faith may be used as a weapon, delivering enough impact to dash the enemy to the ground and crush bones. When a Warrior surrounds himself with Faith, he moves within an impenetrable bastion of protection. When this spiritual principle is mastered, what Warrior would fail to move forward against the enemy? Courage may also be defined in this way: *Courage is fear that has said its prayers.*

To be truly fearless, a Warrior would best don all his accouterments, for then he would not rely entirely on any one of them. God intends us to wear all of the armor for a reason. The enemy is devious.

Deut. 31:6 *⁶Be strong and of a good courage, fear not, nor be afraid of them: for the LORD thy God, he it is that doth go with thee; he will not fail thee, nor forsake thee.*

Josh. 1:9 *⁹Have not I commanded thee? Be strong and of a good courage; be not afraid, neither be thou dismayed: for the LORD thy God is with thee whithersoever thou goest.*

Ps. 31:24 *²⁴Be of good courage, and he shall strengthen your heart, all ye that hope in the LORD.*

<u>Trustworthiness</u>—As his principles are of an order derived from a higher code, a Warrior can be trusted to do the Right thing and not harm or take advantage of the innocent, weak, or disadvantaged. There is a certain comfort in knowing the Warrior can be welcomed into one's home without regard for one's safety or possessions. He can be counted on in a pinch, for that is what he lives for. Even though a Warrior is trained to the utmost in the full destructiveness of total war and empowered to wreak awful destruction, a true "walking terror," he can be trusted to put his feet up amongst the finest things of life and not even leave a blemish on the finish. When he leaves, do not be surprised to find your silver polished, as it is in his nature not to allow tarnish to blemish his armor. He knows all to well what today may be a small blemish, tomorrow can be a spot of rust that no amount of polishing can remove from the finish. If left untended long enough, this blemish can compromise all the armor, leaving it a heap of rust. Think of a lie in this manner and I believe you will understand the concept; a lie, no matter how well intended or innocuous, will always seem to find a way to erode some aspect of our character or our relationships. It may take some time, but a simple lie has the capacity to ruin relationships and break trusts that may never be the same again. The reason a lie affects relationships stems from the simple fact we felt we had to lie to someone else. A relationship of some fashion has to be involved. Generally, this means a trust has been broken, a word not kept, or a confidence betrayed. This not only affects the relationship, but also will have an effect upon our character in some way. When we lie to ourselves, we directly damage our character in that we forestall some aspect of development, or retard development that has been made. A blemish is created; ruin will follow.

In all ways, the Warrior can be expected to bring the best out of any situation, for he is entrusted with caring for and protecting all in his Masters Realm. He does not think of himself, as he is trained and disciplined to think of and consider others before himself. This is what makes him a truly reliable "Brother-in-Arms" in combat. Additionally it is a character trait that makes him terrible in the face of the enemy, as it is known he has taken orders from above and acts in accord with this trust. A Warrior's unswerving trustworthiness makes him dependable in all ways. He is not faint of heart, as he believes in a greater cause, has faith, and thus has no doubts, or fear. This allows him to see past and through many of the common attacks of the enemy. As he has deprived himself of personal possessions, he cannot be tempted with trappings of materialism. This allows him to remain focused on his duty, concentrating on doing what he has been entrusted to do. He has been directed to protect and preserve the innocent and the defenseless. He will go where no one else is willing to go, and nobody will question his carrying out his orders, no matter how hopeless his situation may appear to become. It is the element of his selfless sacrifice and commitment that develops his Trustworthiness.

Another aspect of Trustworthiness stems from the Warriors unswerving devotion to Truth; therefore, it is represented by the belt, or girdle, the Warrior girds himself with. Typically, the belt was made of leather. Leather is impervious to rusting and in many ways much easier to care for. Truth, when thought of as surrounding oneself, can offer a very restive mind to the Warrior, as Truth is undeniable, untarnishable, rust-free, and eternal.

Ex. 18:21 *Moreover thou shalt provide out of all the people able men, such as fear God, men of truth, hating covetousness; and place such over them, to be rulers of thousands, and rulers of hundreds, rulers of fifties, and rulers of tens…*

Josh. 24:14 [14]*Now therefore fear the LORD, and serve him in sincerity and in truth…*

<u>**Selfless**</u>—A Warrior's selfless willingness to put himself in harm's way and risk all he has for a cause greater than himself is a characteristic which makes him a dangerous foe. Not allowing his own concerns to interfere with what he is told to do, he can be a single-minded adversary knowing, seeing, recognizing, and accepting nothing but victory before him. When a Warrior dons his armor, his mind is set that he is, in effect, already "dead." This means he has counted himself as having paid his admission to fight to the fullest, and has no fear of losing something he considers already sacrificed. This is an act of volition. Nobody has demanded it from him. He has surrendered it all so he may fight without a care for personal loss. This is a strange concept for many to understand being easily misconstrued as a defeatist attitude. For clarity, consider this: When everything is on the line, and you maintain the understanding *"They can't Kill Me,"* you can devote yourself to the fullest exertion against the enemy! This sort of conscious reality was impressed upon the Japanese Samurai whenever he donned his armor to fight for the Shogun. Having already considered he had paid the ultimate sacrifice, there was no need to concern himself with losing his life. It was already forfeited. This is not to be construed as a defeatist attitude, but rather one of resolve to pay the ultimate price if need be. He no longer has to consider what to do, but rather just do it!

To put it another way, a Warrior who commits an act out of regard for his personal self would be putting himself above the very thing he has devoted himself to—that being the higher cause he has been bound to by honor and devotion. Remember, all these character traits are integrated. Being so closely related to each other, in trying to resolve an issue for one aspect of character, it will at times be necessary to reflect on how the other traits would reflect their presence in the resolution. If an incongruity occurs, then a bad decision or improper action may have been considered. All actions of the Warrior must conform to his entire character. An attempt to look at a situation involving one characteristic alone would be very difficult. You must consider how the other related characteristics would govern the chosen course of action.

Understanding the proper training and use of the Warrior's Spiritual Armor, many of these fine points will become clear. You see, the Warrior doesn't go to battle with only character, he has been completely prepared to face his challenges with armor to support his stance and position and to allow him to hold his ground and fearlessly engage the enemy. Just as his combat is both real and physical, we must remember it is unseen and spiritual also.

The Helmet of Salvation represents this aspect of selflessness, and serves to fortify ones resolve. With his mind at ease and confident of salvation, no stray thoughts can enter into the mind of the Warrior and distract him from what need be done. Not having any concerns in the moment for himself, the Warrior is free to devote his attention and energy solely against the enemy.

Gal. 5:24 *All who belong to Christ Jesus have crucified self with all its passions and its desires.*

Rev. 12:12...*because even in the face of death they did not cling to life.*

Disciplined—As part of his training, a true Warrior understands there is a time to fight, and he will be guided by discernment and led by the greater cause, and a time to retreat and fight another day. If discernment is lacking, a Warrior may fall prey to "flying off the handle," picking a fight he best not be involved in, and making hasty decisions. This action would display the trait of the Bully, an incomplete form of the adolescent warrior or Hero archetype. The Warrior's Discipline directs him to act according to the situation.

A Warrior is drilled and disciplined to understand the strength and weaknesses of his protective armor, and trained in the fine art of choosing the place to take his stand and fight. Not all ground is favorable to attack an enemy from, or defend on. Sun Tzu's *The Art of War*, speaks about the "killing fields." The killing fields refer to a situation where one has but one outcome to expect: DEFEAT. To be caught in the killing field is to be annihilated. The Warrior would choose to fight only when the Enemy is positioned in "the killing fields," as Sun Tzu refers to it. Doing so, the battle is virtually already won and actually having to fight the enemy may be averted entirely, for they may recognize the poor state of their position and choose to retreat rather than suffer a terrible loss. If indeed engaged, they may be fought with much less expenditure of valuable resources and manpower than would otherwise have been needed to bring about their defeat.

Inadequate discipline would generate a Coward, one unwilling or unable to act. Without the benefit of thorough training in both the mastery of his arms as well as the mastery of his own actions, an ineffective soldier is the result. If unable to act when called for, or indecisive in how to act when he recognizes he needs to, the end result is typically a tragic loss of some sort. In mortal combat, **seconds determine eternity**! Without full mastery of his actions and weapons, a soldier is rendered inconsequential. Without the personal confidence to carry on, or without a clue as to how to proceed, the would-be-warrior is left waiting to be told what to do. The missing ingredient, which he has forgotten or not learned, is that he has been empowered to act. With proper training and discipline, the Warrior knows unquestioningly he has been empowered to act, to mete out Justice, and will do so unconsciously in an instant of action. All decisions are acted on in an instant; done without hesitation, doubt never crossing his mind. Without the benefit of this kind of foundational training, doubt and indecision will fill the mind of the would-be-warrior, the moment will be lost, and the results often are catastrophic.

The best disciplined troops act in one accord, as if they were a machine. Each large force being made whole by many smaller parts, each acting individually, will be ever mindful of the rest of the unit and the entire situation, and the end result is a cohesive integrated behemoth, each part acting as it needs to in its individual situation for the good of the whole. The individual parts of any unit made up of true Warriors would act with the entire body of Warriors in mind. Instead of acting as individuals intent on personal gain and glory, as would a Mercenary, the army of Warriors acts out of a consistent set of entrained behaviors. The army itself acts as if it were a single organism. Discipline is closely related to Faith. Suffice it to say here, a well trained army of devoted, well disciplined, and trained Warriors will act with a sort of single-minded energy. Just as the scales of a snake never leave a gap and flawlessly move over each other to the benefit of the snake, the Shields of an Army of Warriors remain so well configured no soft underbelly is exposed.

We have all heard the expression, "The idle mind is the playground of the devil..." I submit to you, when properly trained and focused, the mind of a Warrior is never idle, but rather constantly focused on the enemy and how to engage and destroy him. With the mind filled with simple resolve and direction, questions about one's salvation, well-being, and course of action never enter the mind to create a distraction. This covers an easy mark for the enemy to attack, the mind, behind an impenetrable Shield of Faith and Helmet of Salvation, a metal the enemy cannot pierce, and both crucial pieces of armor for the Warrior. This is the very essence of the protection rendered for the mind in the Helmet of Salvation.

Prov. 10:17 *Whoever abides by discipline, walks towards life, whoever ignores correction goes astray.*

Job 36:5-7, 10-11 *^{5}Behold, God is mighty, and despiseth not any: he is mighty in strength and wisdom. ^{6}He preserveth not the life of the wicked: but giveth right to the poor. ^{7}He withdraweth not his eyes from the righteous: ^{10}He openeth also their ear to discipline, and commandeth that they return from iniquity. ^{11}If they obey and serve him, they shall spend their days in prosperity, and their years in pleasures.*

Humble—Having recognized there is a Greater Being than himself, the Warrior is careful not to allow himself to get "bigheaded." This is endemic of the Bully, and is a characteristic that I hope the Warrior has long ago vanquished. Only a Bully filled with himself and his abilities would needlessly and recklessly pick a fight, often without adequate "military intelligence." While a Bully acting in this way and picking on easy or unprepared targets can often get away with it and suffer little harm, the failure to adequately humble oneself in the face of the Enemy will almost certainly end in unneeded risk. Underestimating the enemy has led to the defeat of many great Generals in history. If the Enemy were to have properly sized you up as a Bully, they could count on you to throw your weight around and easily lay a trap for you. In contrast, by acting in a humble fashion and calculating, the enemy would prepare a trap for what he sees as easy prey, only to have fallen prey to you instead. This is the hallmark of a true strategist, one who presents the aspects of his fighting force he wants the enemy to see and judge, rather than what the facts may otherwise represent. To dupe the enemy in this way is much preferred to being duped yourself.

In the martial art of Judo, one learns to use his enemy's weight and movements against them. This allows you to seemingly throw your enemy around effortlessly. What is really happening is you are simply adding a little energy to help your enemy do what he is already doing. He winds up on the ground wondering, "What Just Happened...?" and you can turn your attention to the next unsuspecting clod to cross your path.

In remaining humble, a Warrior is ever mindful he serves a greater authority whose ways and orders he can never understand in man's limited way. Having already acknowledged he will put his life on the line for causes he may not fully understand, the Warrior is committed to simply fight when told to, thus he displays discipline and courage. A Warrior acting out of a true humble nature often comes across as acting on Faith. This is simply because he isn't directing his fate himself for himself, but rather doing what he is told without a second thought or hesitation. Wouldn't it be comfortable to have such an understanding of where you fit in that you would never hesitate or act in a questioning way? Wouldn't that really lend an immense amount of comfort to your life? To have a life of no doubts, no fears, just the doing; getting it over with and getting home to play with the kids.

Another important aspect of humility is to recognize none of us are perfect; we all make mistakes. As justice recognizes this aspect of our being, it is important we submit to the fact we are all prone to err, and admit it when we do. To do otherwise is to become defensive about a situation. This only raises confrontation. An important element along this line is accepting the errors of others and offering forgiveness. This is more likely to bring about a reconciliation than rubbing someone's nose in what they have done wrong. If it is obvious to you, it most certainly is obvious to them.

To be in a position of leadership, a Warrior needs to be mindful of service and humble in spirit. Jesus gave his disciples an excellent lesson in leadership and the meaning of humility: *[14] If I then, your Lord and Master, have washed your feet; ye also ought to wash one another's feet. [15] For I have given you an example, that ye should do as I have done to you. [16] Verily, verily, I say unto you, The servant is not greater than his lord; neither he that is sent greater than he that sent him. [17] If ye know these things, happy are ye if ye do them.* John 13:14-17.

Prov. 15:33 *[33] The fear of the LORD is the instruction of wisdom; and before honour is humility.*

1 Ptr. 5:5-11 *[5] In the same way, younger people, be subject to the elders. Humility towards one another must be the garment you all wear constantly, because God opposed the proud but accords his favor to the humble. [6] Bow down, then, before the power of God now, so that he may raise you up in due time; [7] unload all you burden onto Him, since he is concerned about you. [8] Keep sober and alert, because your enemy the devil is on the prowl like a roaring lion, looking for someone to devour. [9] Stand up to him, strong in faith and in the knowledge that it is the same kind of suffering that the community of your brothers throughout the world is undergoing. You will have to suffer only for a little while: [10] the God of all grace who called you to eternal glory in Christ will restore you, he will confirm, strengthen and support you. [11] His power lasts forever and ever. Amen.*

Willing and Able to Act—All of the characteristics of the Warrior are meaningless unless he is empowered to act and he wills himself to do so whenever the time comes. He is ever vigilant and aware of the enemy's presence, and yet never cowers from action when directed to action by his Higher Authority. To do anything less would be negligent and cowardly. Having been properly trained with discernment and exercising wisdom, a Warrior is not an oafish automaton easily goaded into a fight. It would be unwise of a Warrior to ignore his training and greater sense and therefore fall prey to ambush and deceit.

Willingness and the ability to act relate directly to the armor that is worn on the feet; the willingness to spread the gospel of peace. If a Warrior's footing is not sound, he can easily be pushed out of the way, or knocked to the ground. To truly be a stumbling block to the Enemy's minions, a Warrior must at all times have the utmost sound footing and the ability to press forward against the Enemy. Should a Warrior become bogged down in mud, or have no footing or handholds to scale the enemy's wall, he will be unable to act or be where he needs to be. He may want to fulfill his orders in a most desperate way but not be in a position to do anything about it because of his inability to act. A Warrior who is cornered and put into a position of inaction is defeated. A trained Warrior would not allow himself to fall into this position. A competent Warrior is at all times ready to move on a moment's notice and do what needs to be done.

Now let us consider the another possibility. The ground may be level and dry. No obstacle may lie in your path, and you are given the order to go forward. What would happen if you thought you stood alone and you were outnumbered? It wouldn't matter that you had excellent footing, and no real danger of tripping over anything other than your own two feet. If you are unwilling to go forward, you will not. Willingness and the ability to do are both required for you to act as a Warrior. You may know exactly what to do because of your excellent discipline and training, but if you have no willingness or secure footing, nothing will be done due to inability.

James 1:22-25 *But you must do what the Word tells you and not just listen to it and deceive yourselves. Anyone who listens to the Word and takes no action is like someone who looks at his own* *features in a mirror and, once he has seen what he looks like, goes off and immediately forgets it. But anyone who looks steadily at the perfect law of freedom and keeps to it-not listening and forgetting, but putting it into practice-will be blessed in every undertaking.*

2 Chron. 20:32 *^{32}And he walked in the way of Asa his father, and departed not from it, doing that which was right in the sight of the LORD.*

Gal. 6:7-10 *^{7}Don't delude yourself: God is not to be fooled; whatever someone sows, that is what he will reap. ^{8}If his sowing is in the field of self-indulgence, then his harvest from it will be corruption; if his sowing is in the Spirit, then his harvest from the Spirit will be eternal life. ^{9}And let us never slacken in doing good; for if we do not give up, we shall have our harvest in due time. ^{10}So then, as long as we have the opportunity let all our actions be for the good of everybody, and especially of those who belong to the household of the faith.*

The above attributes of the Warrior are the "boot camp" imperatives. As these traits are mastered through action and repeated drills, secondary traits will begin to manifest. These secondary traits are ancillary to the primary characteristics, as they develop after certain behavior is entrained. They function to further enhance your reliability and service. Once action is taken, character begins to develop. This is how we learn character. Just as the opening of a flower's petals invites the visit of a honeybee, as one aspect of the Warrior is allowed to develop, the other characteristics of the Warrior are free to flourish.

Having the benefit of the above characteristics, a Warrior will soon show the remaining hallmark characteristics. With training and exercise, a Warrior will gain Strength, relentless Doggedness, Perseverance, and will fight any odds when told, or rather led to, with Discernment and Wisdom.

<u>Strong</u>—By proper training and seeking arduous tasks constantly, a Warrior is brought to the peak of his ability, and he knows this. He also knows he will never be burdened with more than he can endure.

This inward recognition and heartfelt claim allows him to perform what may only be called Herculean feats at times. Truth serves as a spiritual principle to bolster and aid strength.

Ps. 37:23-24 *Yahweh guides a strong man's steps and keeps them firm; and takes pleasure in him. When he trips he is not thrown sprawling, since Yahweh supports him by the hand.*

Deut. 31:5-6 *[5]And the LORD shall give them up before your face, that ye may do unto them according unto all the commandments which I have commanded you. [6]Be strong and of a good courage, fear not, nor be afraid of them: for the LORD thy God, he it is that doth go with thee; he will not fail thee, nor forsake thee.*

Josh. 10:24-25 *...and said unto the captains of the men of war which went with him, Come near, put your feet upon the necks of these kings. And they came near, and put their feet upon the necks of them. [25]And Joshua said unto them, Fear not, nor be dismayed, be strong and of good courage: for thus shall the LORD do to all your enemies against whom ye fight.*

1 Cor. 16:13-14 *[13]Be vigilant, stay firm in the faith, be brave and strong. [14]Let everything you do be done in love.*

Strength is called upon when a Warrior is to choose an action that may be seen as weakness. Suppose a Warrior is challenged to a confrontation that can only result in mindless destruction. Exercising wisdom and discernment, rather than brute force, requires greater strength. Acting in this manner may be seen as the act of a coward or a weakling, but ultimately the Warrior's actions will be born out as a choice backed by a strength only understood and in control of the Warrior...Strength of Character. There are many dictates and demands placed on a Warrior that makes him/her highly principled. The choices are not always clear, nor are they always easy to be made. It is in the exercise of discipline and control that true strength may be mastered. This is much more difficult to master than developing brawn.

It must be remembered it is the power and might of our Lord which may be marshaled when in His service. This is obviously greater than any amount of physical strength that may be developed by an individual. *Finally, grow strong in the Lord, with the strength of His power.* **Eph. 6:10.**

1 Chr. 29:11-14 *[11]Thine, O LORD, is the greatness, and the power, and the glory, and the victory, and the majesty: for all that is in the heaven and in the earth is thine; thine is the kingdom, O LORD, and thou art exalted as head above all. [12]Both riches and honour come of thee, and thou reignest over all; and in thine hand is power and might; and in thine hand it is to make great, and to give strength unto all. [13]Now therefore, our God, we thank thee, and praise thy glorious name. [14]But who am I, and what is my people, that we should be able to offer so willingly after this sort? for all things come of thee, and of thine own have we given thee.*

2 Chr. 20:6 *...Yahweh, God of our ancestors, are you not God in heaven, and do you not rule all the kingdoms of the nations? Your power and might are such that no one can resist you.*

Isa. 40:29-31 *[29]He giveth power to the faint; and to them that have no might he increaseth strength. [30]Even the youths shall faint and be weary, and the young men shall utterly fall: [31]But they that wait upon the LORD shall renew their strength; they shall mount up with wings as eagles; they shall run, and not be weary; and they shall walk, and not faint.*

Dogged/Persistent—Having been engaged with the enemy and still having them in his sight, a Warrior can be a relentless and dogged enemy. He seems tireless, with the full wellspring of the Almighty at his disposal. He will not let go of the enemy until called off by his master, rather like a Pit-Bull. Tenacity is his left arm.

A Warrior is ever willing to continue in his pursuit of the enemy regardless of the obstacles in his way. Although he may seem to be a mindless automaton when in pursuit of the enemy, he may in some instances, be willing to sit and wait at a road bend for the enemy to double back and fall unwittingly into his hands. A Warrior understands patience can be a powerful ally in a fight with a wily enemy, whereas mindless adherence to some possibly outwitted or outmoded form of battle will lead to unnecessary hardship. A Warrior knows to always and relentlessly pursue the fleeing enemy is to fall prey to a possible ambush or trap. "Sometimes it's best to let the fight come to you" is an adage he is well familiar with. With this and the enemy in mind, the Warrior is always in pursuit, although it may not seem so.

I found the following poem in an unusual place. It was taped to the wall of a holding cell in a jail in Georgia. A former inmate had written it on a piece of paper. The guards had yet to discover and remove it. It is simple, yet powerful and puts the point across easily.

Don't Quit
author unknown

When things go wrong, as they sometimes will,
When the road your trudging seems all uphill,
When the funds are low, and the debts are high,
And you want to smile, but you have to cry,
When fear is pressing you down a bit,
Rest if you must—
BUT DON'T YOU QUIT!

Heb. 12:6-7...*Perseverance is part of your training; God is treating you as his sons. Has there ever been any son whose father did not train him?*

<u>Discernment and Wisdom</u>—Being charged with a responsibility from a higher authority, a Warrior's training teaches the power of observation and the wisdom to know when to act as well as how to act. The shifting sands of the battlefield can be treacherous for the unwitting and foolish warrior. A Bully can be easily goaded into a fight, but not a Warrior. A true Warrior is well trained in recognizing a good fight from a bad one, and when to act as well as when not to act. It is important to consider inaction at the wrong moment can be just as disastrous as action when none is called for. Think of the many examples in history when a much superior force was goaded into pursuit of what appeared to be helpless, broken enemy in full flight, only to end up themselves the object of a clever ruse and ambush. Without discernment and wisdom, a warrior would be an ineffective sideliner, or fool rushing into the snare of the enemy. It is through proper training and control a Warrior may use discernment and wisdom to choose a course of action which best utilizes his resources. Jesus himself taught there are times when one of us alone will not be sufficient, and that we should seek comrades to aid us with prayer and fasting.

Prov. 2:6-7 *[6]For the LORD giveth wisdom: out of his mouth cometh knowledge and understanding. [7]He layeth up sound wisdom for the righteous: he is a buckler to them that walk uprightly.*

Ecc. 9:15-18 *[15]Now there was found in it a poor wise man, and he by his wisdom delivered the city; yet no man remembered that same poor man. [16]Then said I, Wisdom is better than strength: nevertheless the poor man's wisdom is despised, and his words are not heard. [17]The words of wise men are heard in quiet more than the cry of him that ruleth among fools. [18]Wisdom is better than weapons of war: but one sinner destroyeth much good.*

Suppose a Warrior was to charge into a room in pursuit of the enemy and find it full of noncombatants, innocents. He would charge on through the room if he sees no immediate need among them or danger to them, leaving them unharmed and safe knowing he is on duty and in pursuit of Evil.

Discernment comes from long, arduous training in most instances and is of immense benefit to the Warrior. His Spirit is in tune with his Lord's Will. He has become proficient in the use of all his weapons and has learned to fight only when he has to; personal discernment and spiritual truth lead him. This is an exercise of Wisdom so as to fight the correct battles and fight them correctly: to win. Remember the story of *Don Quixote*, the old confused knight, whose vision of the world differed from reality. One day Don Quixote meets what he perceives to be several giants in serious need of a lesson in humility when they do not get out of his way. What they are, in reality, are windmills. Now just imagine this fearless old warrior fighting windmills. The result was as you would expect. The harsh reality of the situation compelled itself upon the misguided, however well intentioned, knight. Rather than bringing a giant to heel, his relentless attacks against unrelenting windmills ended in the only way possible: with the poor misguided knight defeated by his own misjudgment.

The wake of destruction wrought by the Warrior may be terrible indeed, but this destruction is of that which needs destroying. It is not wanton destruction, but instead, because of what has been destroyed, makes it is possible for a greater rebuilding and a greater loving, caring, civilization that will enjoy and outwardly show more of God's Goodness.

Wisdom supports Discernment in a very subtle way. One tends to follow the other. We are also taught wisdom brings true understanding and we are to regard wisdom as a mother of sorts. Proverbs Chapters 3 and 4 speak quite specifically about this. The following two short readings from Proverbs are loaded with notes relevant to the character of the Warrior:

Proverbs: Chapter 3

[1]*My son, forget not my law* (the Warrior is under a Higher Authority); *but let thine heart keep my commandments* (Faithful and devoted): [2]*For length of days, and long life, and peace, shall they add to thee.* [3]*Let not mercy and truth forsake thee: bind them about thy neck; write them upon the table of thine heart* (Merciful and truthful): [4]*So shalt thou find favour and good understanding in the sight of God and man.* [5]*Trust in the LORD with all thine heart; and lean not unto thine own understanding* (expresses faith, and is secure in salvation). [6]*In all thy ways acknowledge him, and he shall direct thy paths.*
[7]*Be not wise in thine own eyes* (humble): *fear the LORD, and depart from evil* (acting right). [8]*It shall be health to thy navel, and marrow to thy bones.* [9]*Honour the LORD with thy substance, and with the firstfruits of all thine increase:* [10]*So shall thy barns be filled with plenty, and thy presses shall burst out with new wine.* [11]*My son, despise not the chastening of the LORD; neither be weary of*

his correction (well trained and disciplined): *¹²For whom the LORD loveth he correcteth; even as a father the son in whom he delighteth.*

¹³Happy is the man that findeth wisdom, and the man that getteth understanding. ¹⁴For the merchandise of it is better than the merchandise of silver, and the gain thereof than fine gold. ¹⁵She is more precious than rubies: and all the things thou canst desire are not to be compared unto her. ¹⁶Length of days is in her right hand; and in her left hand riches and honour. ¹⁷Her ways are ways of pleasantness, and all her paths are peace. ¹⁸She is a tree of life to them that lay hold upon her: and happy is every one that retaineth her. ¹⁹The LORD by wisdom hath founded the earth; by understanding hath he established the heavens. ²⁰By his knowledge the depths are broken up, and the clouds drop down the dew (wisdom and discernment).

²¹My son, let not them depart from thine eyes: keep sound wisdom and discretion: ²²So shall they be life unto thy soul, and grace to thy neck. ²³Then shalt thou walk in thy way safely, and thy foot shall not stumble (surefootedness). *²⁴When thou liest down, thou shalt not be afraid: yea, thou shalt lie down, and thy sleep shall be sweet* (secure in salvation and faith). *²⁵Be not afraid of sudden fear, neither of the desolation of the wicked, when it cometh* (fearless). *²⁶For the LORD shall be thy confidence, and shall keep thy foot from being taken.*

²⁷Withhold not good from them to whom it is due, when it is in the power of thine hand to do it (just). *²⁸Say not unto thy neighbour, Go, and come again, and to morrow I will give; when thou hast it by thee. ²⁹Devise not evil against thy neighbour, seeing he dwelleth securely by thee. ³⁰Strive not with a man without cause, if he have done thee no harm* (just and discerning). *³¹Envy thou not the oppressor, and choose none of his ways. ³²For the froward is abomination to the LORD: but his secret is with the righteous. ³³The curse of the LORD is in the house of the wicked: but he blesseth the habitation of the just. ³⁴Surely he scorneth the scorners: but he giveth grace unto the lowly. ³⁵The wise shall inherit glory: but shame shall be the promotion of fools."*

Proverbs: Chapter 4

¹Hear, ye children, the instruction of a father, and attend to know understanding. ²For I give you good doctrine, forsake ye not my law (faithful and devoted). *³For I was my father's son, tender and only beloved in the sight of my mother. ⁴He taught me also, and said unto me, Let thine heart retain my words: keep my commandments, and live. ⁵Get wisdom, get understanding: forget it not; neither decline from the words of my mouth. ⁶Forsake her not, and she shall preserve thee: love her, and she shall keep thee. ⁷Wisdom is the principle thing; therefore get wisdom: and with all thy getting get understanding. ⁸Exalt her, and she shall promote thee: she shall bring thee to honour, when thou dost embrace her* (devotion). *⁹She shall give to thine head an ornament of grace: a crown of glory* (see Chapter 5) *shall she deliver to thee. ¹⁰Hear, O my son, and receive my sayings; and the years of thy life shall be many* (wisdom). *¹¹I have taught thee in the way of wisdom; I have led thee in right paths. ¹²When thou goest, thy steps shall not be straitened; and when thou runnest, thou shalt not stumble* (surefooted and persevering). *¹³Take fast hold of instruction; let her not go: keep her; for she is thy life...²⁰My son, attend to my words; incline thine ear unto my sayings. ²¹Let them* (wisdom and understanding) *not depart from thine eyes; keep them in the midst of thine heart. ²²For they are life unto those that find them, and health to all their flesh. ²³Keep thy heart with all diligence; for out of it are the issues of life. ²⁴Put away from thee a froward mouth, and perverse lips put far from thee. ²⁵Let thine eyes look right on, and let thine eyelids look straight before thee. ²⁶Ponder the path of thy feet, and let all thy ways be established. ²⁷Turn not to the right hand nor to the left: remove thy foot from evil.*

Now that the character of the Warrior is better understood, let's take a look again at **James 1** and see how many different aspect of the Warrior's character we can find in these nine verses:

James 1:19-27 *Remember this, my dear brothers: everyone should be quick to listen but slow to speak and slow to human anger; God's saving justice is never served by human anger; so do* *away with all impurities and remnants of evil. Humbly welcome the Word, which has been planted in you and can save your souls.*

But you must do what the word tells you and not just listen to it and deceive yourselves. Anyone who listens to the Word and takes no action is like someone who looks at his own features in a mirror and, once he has seen what he looks like, goes off and immediately forgets it. But anyone who looks steadily at the perfect law of freedom and keeps to it—not listening and forgetting, but putting it into practice—will be blessed in every undertaking.

Nobody who fails to keep a tight rein on the tongue can claim to be religious; this is mere self-deception; that person's religion is worthless. Pure, unsoiled religion, in the eyes of God our Father, is this: coming to the help of orphans and widows in their hardships, and keeping oneself uncontaminated by the world.

If you can find more than nine different aspects of the Warrior's character in the above verses, that is good—Keep at it, and as you grasp more of the traits of the Warrior, finding a dozen shouldn't be difficult.

As an additional exercise, try the following quote out and see how many of the qualities of the Warrior you can find within it:

2 Cor. 6:3-10 *We avoid putting obstacles in anyone's way, so that no blame may attach to our work of service; but in everything we prove ourselves authentic servants of God; by resolute perseverance in times of hardships, difficulties and distress; when we are flogged or sent to prison or mobbed; laboring, sleepless, starving; in purity, in knowledge, in patience, in kindness; in the Holy Spirit, in a love of affection; in the work of truth and in the power of God; by using the weapons of uprightness for attack and for defense: in times of honor or disgrace, blame or praise, taken for impostors and yet we are genuine; unknown and yet we are acknowledged; dying, and yet here we are, alive; scourged but not executed; in pain yet always full of joy; poor and yet making many people rich; having nothing, yet owning everything.*

Understanding what has been missing from our behavior and, subsequently, what has been denied society, we will now have a chance to release the Warrior from the dungeon he has been imprisoned in and allow him to take his rightful place at our table. Understanding the Warrior within us may at first glance seem a little out of place in our world today, but now that it is clear how important the Warrior's behavior traits are there is a great likelihood improvements will soon follow around these newfound guardians of God's faith and assurances. If we open ourselves to the development of the Warrior each of us carries within, concrete change is destined to occur in society. The bad guys always seem to win because the good guys haven't been "playing the game."

Don't you agree it is time this changed? He can only express the empowerment wielded by the Warrior, as he is the only trained combatant entrusted with all the keys to the manor. When he is unleashed upon the problems of society, we shall see God's will manifested.

Chapter 5

Awards, Standards and Appearances

In addition to the character traits discussed in the previous chapter, there are three facets involved in the life of every Warrior that add some perspective to the way the world was viewed by the Warriors of long ago. These three facets helped to further identify and clarify the character and purpose of a Warrior. This was accomplished by showing the Warrior the rewards he was assured of for correct action and devoted service by his Lord's promise, and were represented by the symbols with which he identified himself. They served in some respects as guideposts to aid the Warrior in the approach he took to the way he lived.

Although they have changed somewhat from what they used to be and how they were represented, they are just as present and serve the Warriors of today in much the same way. These three aspects are Awards, Standards, and Appearances.

AWARDS

The Romans began, for the civilized world, a system of recognition for the heroic deeds of the common soldier in the line. "Into the Breach" was an expression used by them to urge the closest elements of their forces onward into a collapsed section of wall during the siege of a fortified position. The man first into the breach was later decorated if he survived. The efforts and deeds of the men of a specific Legion were similarly recognized by the Legion's Standard being decorated, typically with ribbons, for exemplary service or duty in battlefields far from home. Metallic discs of specific designs were also employed for specific service. A Legion's Standard represented the fighting spirit of the Legion, was ever-present, closely guarded, and revered by the men serving under it. This type of unit honor was applicable to the lower components of the Legion as well, its cohorts. This tradition has been carried over to the military of today and can be recognized in unit commendations as well as individual medals such as the Congressional Medal of Honor, the Purple Heart, and the Bronze and Silver Stars given for peculiar and individual acts of heroism. Campaign ribbons are also awarded to servicemen seeing duty in certain regions of combat. These are worn on dress uniforms, being displayed above the heart, denoting the various fields of service participated in by the individual.

There are Awards awaiting us all as good and faithful Christian Warriors. There are many references to "rewards" with which we will be blessed by God. Seldom are they expounded upon to any great extent. However, there are several awards described in the Bible. These awards are referred to as "Crowns" and will be given to each of us by our Heavenly Father in recognition of our obedience and actions in His name.

The following scripture quotations will familiarize the reader with the promise of rewards for good and faithful service. It is surprising to note how few Christians are familiar with these promises our King has made us, especially in light of the many references to rewards for correct action. There is even a direct reward for wickedness or evil actions. Here are a few of the promises:

Ps. 58:11 *The upright does have a reward; there is a God to dispense justice on earth.*

Matt. 6:4 *...and your Father who sees all that is done in secret will reward you.*

Matt. 10:41 *Anyone who welcomes a prophet because he is a prophet will have a prophet's reward; and anyone who welcomes an upright person because he is upright will have the reward of an upright person.*

Matt. 16:27 *For the Son of man is going to come in the glory of his Father with his angels, and then he will reward each one according to his behavior.*

Eph. 6:8 *Never forget that everyone, whether a slave or a free man, will be rewarded by the Lord for whatever work he has done well.*

Rev. 22:11-14 *[11]He that is unjust, let him be unjust still: and he which is filthy, let him be filthy still: and he that is righteous, let him be righteous still: and he that is holy, let him be holy still. [12]And, behold, I come quickly; and my reward is with me, to give every man according as his work shall be. [13]I am Alpha and Omega, the beginning and the end, the first and the last. [14]Blessed are they that do his commandments, that they may have right to the tree of life, and may enter in through the gates into the city.*

Now, lets see what the reward for acting wicked is:

Rom. 6:20-23 *When you were the servants of sin, you felt no obligation to uprightness, and what did you gain from living like that? But, now you are set free from sin and bound to the service of God, your gain will be sanctification and the end will be eternal life. For the wage paid by sin is death; the gift freely given by God is eternal life in Christ Jesus our Lord.*

Matt. 13:49-50 *This is how it will be at the end of time: the angels will appear and separate the wicked from the upright, to throw them into the blazing furnace, where there will be weeping and grinding of teeth.*

The Seven Crowns

There are seven crowns mentioned in the Bible that are promised as rewards. God himself will award these crowns to those Warriors who are deserving. Judgment day will be quite a celebration party for some of us! Please bear in mind that each version of the Bible may be slightly different in its translation. These scripture quotes are from *The New Jerusalem Bible*.

CROWN OF JOY: *For those whom Yahweh has ransomed will return, they will come to Zion shouting for you, their heads Crowned with Joy unending.* **Isa. 35:10.**

CROWN OF GLORY AND HONOR: *...you have Crowned him with Glory and Honor.* **Ps. 8:5.**

CROWN OF KNOWLEDGE: *The prudent are Crowned with Knowledge.* **Prov. 14:18.**

CROWN OF RIGHTEOUSNESS: *I have fought the good fight to the end; I have run the race to the finish; I have kept the faith; all there is to come for me now is the Crown of Righteousness which* *the Lord, the righteous judge, will give to me on that Day; and not only to me but to all those who have longed for his appearing.* **2 Tm. 4:8.**

CROWN OF LIFE: *Blessed is anyone who perseveres when trials come. Such a person is of proven worth and will win the Prize of life, the Crown that the Lord has promised to those who love him.* **James 1:12.**

Rev. 2:10 *Even if you have to die, keep faithful, and I will give you the Crown of Life for your prize.*

CROWN OF GLORY: *When the chief shepherd appears, you will be given the unfading Crown of Glory.* **1 Ptr. 5:4.**

Prov. 4:9 *⁹She* (referring to Wisdom) *shall give to thine head an ornament of grace: a crown of glory shall she deliver to thee.*

CROWN OF VICTORY: *I am coming soon, hold firmly to what you already have, and let no one take your Victor's Crown away from you.* **Rev. 3:11.**

Rev. 6:2 *...he was given a Victor's Crown and he went away, to go from victory to victory.*

Philip Paul Sacco

STANDARDS

The Romans used the symbol of the Eagle as a Standard for their Leader/Emperor. It symbolized something above them with greater vision and power than a man or a thing. The individual Legions carried Standards that typically depicted some animal of great power or tenacity, an emblem of a known quality or trait. This Standard represented a particular internal power the members of that particular Legion identified with personally in some way. The soldiers were unified by it. They would individually identify themselves by the virtues depicted and represented by their Legion's Standard. It led to a certain esprit-de-corps for the Legion, having given each man an emblem that represented the Legion as a whole. The symbol of their Standard would be the heart of that unit's fighting spirit, lending a cohesive energy to the men following it. The unit's Standard was a thing revered and protected with great jealousy and devotion. *[22]Thus saith the Lord GOD, Behold, I will lift up mine hand to the Gentiles, and set up my standard to the people: and they shall bring thy sons in their arms, and thy daughters shall be carried upon their shoulders.* **Isa. 49:22.**

There are instances in history when the outcome of a battle was affected by the fate of a Legion's Standard. One example of this would be a Legion on the brink of losing the battle at hand, having its

Standard fall into enemy hands or fall to the ground potentially precipitating the collapse of the unit. If the cohesive force and unity of the unit had not been broken, the symbolic or virtual loss of their Standard could galvanize the remnants of the otherwise broken unit to rally. It could then, through force of will and esprit-de-corps, carry the day in their efforts to regain their lost emblem of unity, their Standard. This redoubling of effort was usually of enough force to not only carry the original objective, but additional objectives as well.

Alternatively, an enemy well appraised of Roman cohesiveness could use subterfuge and demoralize the Roman force by capturing, or besmirching a unit's Standard. With adequate preparation and properly executed, a Roman Legion could be demoralized and defeated before blows were struck in a fully developed battle. The loss of their Standard by a unit would spell almost certain defeat, for the fighting will of the unit would be gone, quite literally in the hands of the enemy. While this is an uncommon experience for the Romans historically, it is not unknown to have occurred as a matter of well-conceived forethought and strategy on the part of an enemy.

Not many military forces in the history of mankind before or since the Romans have been as disciplined and unified. This fact, combined with their excellent engineering skills, craftsmanship, skill, and training in the art of war made the Romans the dynamic fighting machine they have historically been recognized to be.

The Standard was used as a point of Rally in time of disarray, and a point of concentration for directing their energy in an attack.[*] The Romans led their Legions forth with their Standards, and protected them with "Honor Guard's" much as we do today with our National flag in the various branches of our Military. The Honor Guard's specific duty was to protect and preserve the Standard, and show the devotion of the men under it to support, lift up, and follow it.

---

[*] While in modern warfare, the Standard is no longer used as a focus for the attacking energy of a unit. It did fulfill this role as late as WWI, and still forms the center for rallying units in camp situations. The use of the flag as a point of rally may best be thought of in use during the Civil War in the 1860s.

Philip Paul Sacco

In our society today, standards are best seen in a different way. The Standards that we look toward today for direction and encouragement are the Moral Standards of our leaders and role models, i.e. our political leaders, teachers, and parents. We look for their lead in our society rather than a flag or emblem held before us. How does this compare to the connection the Romans felt to their Standards? A quick evaluation of the morals and values typically represented by our political leaders today should give cause to reflect on our hesitance to follow the majority of the leaders paraded before us. In this sense, our moral standards should serve us today to rally us in opposition or support of issues in our lives. In a very real way, it is time to "Raise our Standards" and fight the good fight.

Take a moment and reflect on how standards and leadership have eroded in the last forty years in our society. What standard do you follow? What emblem best serves to identify your spirit?

Is there any wonder that, as a society, we display what seems to be a constant loss of direction? This is primarily because of our lack of a *TRUE STANDARD* to follow. Are our children being taught values, morals, and character in our schools today? I do not understand how they could be unless they were allowed some direction and guidance by their religious expression at the same time. With many special interest groups dictating standards not agreeable to all of society, we have no one unifying standard to rally behind.

The family as a unit has been all but destroyed. Women no longer live to raise their families, but freely compete in the work force with men rather than be a devoted section of society geared to the attention and rearing of the children. For that matter, if it is not a financial necessity for both spouses to work to make ends meet, there is nothing wrong with the husband staying home and raising the kids. The point is, today no one is staying home to raise the children. Most of our children are handed off to a government run school and instructed from a curriculum regularly deteriorating because of pressure to make education a fair experience for all children. This does not serve to raise the bottom levels of students, but on the contrary it has been repeatedly shown to lower the upper level's students. All this while we sit by and allow Christian expression to be removed from any educational setting so as not to discriminate against the non-Christian students.

We can see this tendency to remove any Christian expression invading our government buildings also. Plaques bearing the Ten Commandments have been removed from many city halls and courthouses where they had been displayed for as long as the buildings may have stood before being removed. Corruption, deception, and a lack of scruples are displayed on what seems to be a daily basis in our news. Prayer has been removed from our schools, and the same protagonists of such progress are attempting to have all broadcasts related to the scriptures taken off the radio waves and television transmission.

Ask the children of today who their idols or role models are, and do not be surprised to hear a sport star or the name of the current popular singer. It used to be the name of an American hero, one of our country's Founding Fathers, or a scientist, or writer. It seems the only apparent idols our children are allowed to see are earning a king's ransom playing some sport. It appears the only role models our children are presented with are wealthy by any standard, rather than displaying a great level of personal devotion or accomplishment for society's sake. The idols and heroes of the past, who represented personal sacrifice and devotion, have been supplanted by those of physical prowess and commanding positions of great income.

To further compound the problem and confuse the role of standards in our society, remember the two primary societal reasons contributing to the loss of our Warrior identity: loss of all initiations, and the disintegration of our patriarchal society. The role of males in society has become diluted and disturbed; consequently, men no longer know or understand a definite role as men in our society. This has disturbed the natural order of things, but the role of women has likewise been upset to the point many of them no longer understand what it is to be a Woman. Let men be Men, and women be Women.

There are identifiable traits we recognize as masculine and feminine. We are created as two distinct sexes with our own identifiable attributes. To try to completely level the playing field is as foolish as it is beginning to prove impossible, and with disastrous effects as well.

In the course of one generation, our society has shifted from one in which the children were instilled with proper attitudes, values, and character in school, home, and church, to one in which it is questionable if they actually receive any instruction in these matters. With our schools deprived of the power of discipline and a religious presence, the destruction of the family unit, and the watering down of instruction found in most churches, it should come as little surprise that our children fall prey to peer pressure and learn the worst lessons in life rather than the best. Our children are being left to their own design and choice, falling prey to peer pressure. We have in reality "The Blind Leading the Blind."

Standards have eroded from a very real external symbol which represented the spirit of those bearing it and serving a very real purpose as a symbolic model, to the internal and personal standards to which we commonly refer in regards to those principles which are supposed to shape and direct our actions. In the past, during times of war and conflict, it was traditional to "raise the standard" to lead an attack and serve as a point of rally if disarray were to occur. In the same sense today, in waging this new war, it is time to "raise our standards" again not to just lead in the attack against the many destructive influences in our world today, but to form that much needed rally point to come together and unite our efforts once again under a common standard. *^{27}Set ye up a standard in the land, blow the trumpet among the nations, prepare the nations against her, call together against her the kingdoms...* **Jer. 51:27.**

What standard are you flying today? Are you willing to take a stand under and for a True Standard? *When the enemy shall come in like a flood, the Spirit of the LORD shall lift up a standard against him.* **Isa. 59:19.** This takes courage and a noble fighting spirit in today's world. To be willing to share a standard, be an example, or better yet, take part in instilling values and standards in the lives of our children today, is a wonderful way to pinpoint any weaknesses you may have. Your own standards become clear as you begin sharing them with others. To be able to impart such knowledge means you have to know, without a doubt, where you stand under that same standard. *...every man in his place by their standards.* **Num. 2:17.** This can be a painful, or difficult experience, but always a strengthening one. Start small, working on faith, until you build up your wings and soon you will fly on the wings of an eagle.

APPEARANCES

A Warrior is trained to be ever vigilant to appearances, as the enemy will often times disguise himself to hide his efforts and intentions from the purview of the mildly observant, or the inattentive. The efforts of the enemy are often concealed or in some way misrepresent the actual number of their forces involved, their strength, how they are deployed, or what they may be up to. An example of this would be a military, strategist having innumerable campfires lit in the encampment to misrepresent the number of troops actually present. Alternatively, the fires and a handful of men making some noise around them may be employed to represent the presence of a force that had in fact moved away. Another example would be a detachment of the same troops being led on a repeatedly circuitous route to be seen as a multitude of troops on the move. The point is that appearances can be deceiving. How many of us thought we had bought the perfect car from a reputable car dealer only to find out within a short period the car was in fact a lemon and the dealer not as honorable as you had thought? Most of us have at some time made a great deal on jewelry, only to find later the real value of cheap plated base metal.

Deception and false appearances are all around us today. Think of the many marketing tools used to convince the unwary consumer some product will enhance their image or wealth. Tell me you have never received a letter attempting to sell you on some get rich quick plan. Better still; just remember a couple of the get rich plans you have been taken in by. The fact is successful marketing is designed to remove a portion of your money from you in a cleverly contrived fashion. This is not to say that all marketing is used for get rich programs, to the contrary, the best marketing is used by large corporations to get you to buy a product they have convinced you is either better than anything else on the market, or you simply can't live without it. The result is their marketing program has presented a product with a certain appearance to you, and you bought it.

I have heard reports that con games are one of the growing crimes in our country among the elderly today. A successful con relies on a convincing appearance to pull off the dupe. A very simple, yet puzzling, question of conflicting appearances may be had by simply holding in one hand a newly minted silver dollar, and in the other a "one dollar" Federal Reserve Note.† Both the American Eagle and the Federal Reserve Note say on them that they are "one dollar." They may both be used to purchase one dollar's worth of merchandise at a local convenience store. They will both render the same amount of change for the same purchase. To make it even a little more confusing, both forms of currency will be accepted on deposit at any bank for a one dollar credit to your account. However, you cannot purchase American Eagles from a bank. If you are baffled by these facts, consider the American Eagle silver dollars will cost you seven to fifteen Federal Reserve Note dollars, depending on where you purchase it. Now haven't you always heard that a dollar "is a dollar, is a dollar?" I will let the reader research what is going on with this particular example, as you will discover some very shocking information. You see, appearances can be very deceiving.

Historically, robes have been worn to conceal what was being worn beneath them. In medieval times, a Knight traveling incognito wearing robes may in fact have been traveling in full armor. The robes he wore to present himself as a monk belied his actual social position and capability. Although he may travel in this manner seemingly as a "Man-of-Peace" and be seen as such, his personal appearance would have misled any unwary observers of his true capacity.

Another rather good misrepresentation of one's identity can be found in the Bible's book of Revelation. We are told "the Beast" will appear as a man of peace, seeming as the Son-of-God in fact, doing all things that we expect of the Lord Savior, when in fact he is Evil incarnate. Think of appearances in reference to...***the second beast will issue from the EARTH...*** Rev. 13:11. What could this mean? Will it be a worm or a mole, or some freak of nature? Could it mean

---

† Let the reader be aware that the Silver Dollar being referred to for this example is the U.S. "American Eagle" being minted by the U.S. Treasury Dept. This is not the same as the silver clad or "sandwich dollars" which are in circulation today. These clad dollars have many different sizes and designs, but are easily identified as having a copper center. Yet even these clad dollars say they are "one dollar."

this beast would be made of silicon as in the computer chip?! It would then have the power to talk. There are software programs available which enable a computer user to talk to his computer and have it respond. The scriptures go on to say this beast will be empowered to do great wonders. I certainly think many of the things computers are capable of today are truly wondrous. The scriptures also say this beast will be empowered to call down fires of war from the heavens, and are not computers used to aim, launch, and direct missiles. Computers are also programmed to automatically decide if a launch response is necessary without the command of man. The doomsday device fits this description well. This is pointed out merely as an example of how appearances can be deceiving and how each of us needs to be wary in many ways. Remember a Warrior is trained to be discerning.

We are told later in Revelation the "Mark of the Beast" will be imposed on all—the great and small, rich and poor, slave and free alike. We are cautioned that shrewdness and discernment will be required to see it for what it is, and that many will be deceived. **Rev. 13:16-18.** I think it unlikely that any of us would accept the mark knowing before hand what it was. If our government were to implement and support this mark as a means of grand social reform, how many true Christian Warriors would be wary enough to see it for what it was, and stand against it?

Scriptures tell us that in the final days many believers will be deceived. This is clearly a warning that appearances will be deceiving. If this weren't so, then why would any God fearing intelligent Christian be deceived? What do you expect? Is the TRUE BEAST going to announce to the world having performed all his "miracles and divine deeds," "Oh...By the Way...I happen to be the BEAST you have all been warned about!?" Give me a break. Get with the program! The scriptures themselves tell us all that wisdom and discernment will be required to see this monster for what it is. The characteristics of the Warrior would keep us ever vigilant and alert to this form of deception. Let us see what the scriptures say about deception and appearances a little closer:

Let all who have ears, hear. **Matt. 11:15.** *...Everything covered up will be uncovered.* **Matt. 10:26.** In short, if you *Use* your ears to hear and your eyes to see, you may not be taken in by appearances.

Or are you more like the people Jesus refers to in Mark: ***Do you still not understand, still not realize? Are your minds closed? Have you eyes and do not see, ears and do not hear?*** **Mk. 8:17-18.** And what about God's own warning about being misled in Deuteronomy: ***[16]Take heed to yourselves, that your heart be not deceived, and ye turn aside, and serve other gods, and worship them…*** **Dt. 11:16.** And again, in Jesus' own words in Luke: ***[8]And he said, 'Take heed that ye be not deceived: for many shall come in my name, saying, 'I am Christ;' and the time draweth near: go ye not therefore after them.'*** **Luke 21:8.**

The weapons of the enemy include deception, lies, and all manner or falsehood; thus, the need to protect the mind, i.e. the Helmet of Salvation. The idle mind is the playground of the devil. Remember the cautions and warnings of Christ himself with the parable of the ten Virgins, which addresses the need to be ever mindful and attentive. Be aware, as attacks that bolster one's pride may cause us to become unwittingly full of self-pride, thus not alert. Remember a true Warrior is HUMBLE.

To put it simply, remember the story of *Little Red Riding Hood* and the Big Bad Wolf. Little Red Riding Hood was led to believe the Big Bad Wolf was her loving grandmother by the deception and disguise of the Wolf. We all know the ending of that story. A well trained Warrior will always be questioning of appearances, using wisdom and discernment to root out a "Wolf in Sheep's Clothing," or false prophets.

Now that we have a better understanding of a Warrior's character, his *mettle*, we can delve into the spiritual principles of his armor, his *metal*. These two aspects of a Warrior serve to bolster and add definition to each other.

Part Two

Metal:

The Warrior As a "Man of War"

Eph. 6:11 *Put on the Whole Armor of God.*

We all expect the next appearance of our Lord to be in the image that our Jewish friends have been expecting all along: That being in the image of the Just King and Slayer-of-Evil; A Warrior King, a Military Man, a King to lead an army. Take a moment and think of the image of Christ in His Second Coming. You may very well visualize Him riding a white horse and wielding a Flaming Sword. Christ's first coming exemplified the character of the Warrior as a Man-of-Peace,

His Second Coming will be an exemplification of the character of the Warrior as a Man-of-War.

Part One was intended to give you enough information about your warrior nature to cause you to reflect upon the state of the Warrior within you. I hope that you have taken measures to liberate your warrior's distinct nature. Once the nature and character of the Warrior within has been identified, recognized, and accepted as part of ourselves, it is time to train and condition our Spirit in the spiritual principles of the Warrior's "tools of the trade." Unless the Warrior is accepted and allowed to develop, training in his ways will likely prove fruitless and counterproductive. It is not in the nature of the other aspects of our character to take on the role of another. A Lover cannot do the job of a Warrior no matter how badly he or she may try. There is a reason we all have the Warriors' aspect of in our nature, and that is to fight the battles of life for God, our Higher Authority. To do so, the Warrior must now be trained in the principles that will imbue him with the full protection God assures us of. These principles serve to reinforce the various aspects of character discussed in Part One as well as to create the Armor of God about oneself.

Once an individual has made a compact within himself to go forth and declares himself a Warrior for the Kingdom of God, it is only natural the individual be made aware of the weapons and armor they are to claim as their own. These are referred to as the "The Whole Armor of God" (**Eph. 6:11, 13**). The balance of this book will be concerned with the whole armor of God, how it works, feels, and how we are to visualize it, as well as understand and apply its practical applications. It is then that the Christian Warrior may rely on and use them. Remember what the scriptures teach us about declaring oneself: *...[9] that if you declare with your mouth that Jesus is Lord, and if you believe with your heart that God raised him from the dead, then you will be saved. [10]It is by believing with the heart that you are justified, and by making the declaration with your lips that you are saved.* **Rom. 10:9-10**.

The following chapters deal with a separate piece of Spiritual Armor. This armor is a Spiritual Reality, one that God intends for us to recognize, develop, and rely upon. The Armor of God, although of a spiritual nature, will nevertheless manifest a physical effect when the principles are properly grasped and utilized. The spiritual principles which govern the development of the armor are every bit as sound as the protection which will be manifested by the armor. Through proper development and faith in the spiritual truths that govern these simple principles, the Warriors of God's army will manifest the power and might of our Lord, tread where others fear, and do the remarkable and impossible.

Never mind that the armor is seemingly allegorical or intangible as often presented by the uninformed or un-empowered. Anyone making this type of statement is simply speaking from an uninformed position. What they are testifying to is the simple fact that they have never experienced true spiritual warfare, or else they would attest to the protection they moved within, having laid claim to Gods assurances and relied on His protection.

The first time the spiritual principles governing the armor are relied on and acted upon by an individual, the reality of the armor becomes every bit as real and present as the shoes worn on your feet, or the clothes on your back. Experiencing the manifestation of the armor may range from absolute unawareness to absolute surprise. Can you feel the socks on your feet or the belt around your waist unless attention is directed to them? I will bet you have at one time in your life had a hat or helmet on which protected you from the rain or a falling object, and you may have commented at the time, "Gee, I sure am glad I had that on!" Thus, it is with our spiritual armor.

The simple reason that the protection of the armor often passes unnoticed is that it is being *relied upon*. When something is relied upon, it is to a measure taken for granted as being there. This reliance is the only way one can comfortably act with all the protection of the armor in place. To be preoccupied with whether or not it is present, or if it will provide sufficient protection, would constitute thinking and not doing, and often comes from the seeds of doubt and fear. Proper and diligent training serves to eliminate this form of distraction from the Warrior, enabling him to act in a moment and simply Do-What-Needs-to-be-Done. This is an element that was dealt with in the chapter on character.

I have had almost twenty years of experience with fighting in armor, exploring the traditions of medieval armored fighting forms. From my years of practical experience fighting in real armor, a very real and simple description may serve to illustrate the above point.

The most important individual piece of armor worn in heavy armored combat is the helmet. The helmet is worn expressly to protect the head from attacks, which are expected, though not always seen. This is not to say that I intend to have my head hit, on the contrary, I have trained to use my shield and sword to protect this one most vital and vulnerable target from the enemy. As good as I may be at protecting my body from attack with my shield, there are those moments when I find myself in a position such that my shield is in the wrong place, possibly pinned by the enemy, and a blow may force its way past my sword and still, regardless of my best efforts, strike my head. Let's face it…the enemy makes no guarantee that he will not strike my head, intentionally or not!

Now, I have written this book, so the attacks certainly have not been fatal. It is because of the protection offered by my helmet that I have survived. I relied on its protection, and it did not let me down. I was able to engage the enemy without fear of an injury to my head, not because I thought that I would not be struck there, but because of my reliance upon my protection such that if I were struck, I knew that I would not be harmed. Having endured repeated attacks to the head, first during training, then in combat, has developed within me an unshakable dependency and reliance on the protective ability of my helmet. This imbues me with an unflinching perseverance in facing the enemy. Even when I recognize a blow about to fall, I continue to press the attack because I have developed an unshakeable fearlessness towards bodily harm. This is a consequence of good training in the absolute protection afforded me by my armor. Its protection was tested in training and experienced in combat. Without having trained in it, and learned of its protective ability, I would not confidently engage the enemy in combat.

This is no different from how I trust and rely upon my Spiritual Armor. Just as with physical armor, training in its use and conditioning in the protective ability of our Spiritual Armor is essential to allow the Christian Warrior to confidently engage the enemy. Just as with the character of an individual, the "character" of my armor has been tested in "action" and developed. Remember, character develops by taking action. In much the same way, our spiritual armor develops with use and action (battle action). As separate and distinct as you may think the two are, character and our armor, you will see that they reinforce and develop together in a very direct and interrelated way. It is to this degree of understanding and acceptance that I hope you develop the practical applications of the spiritual principles discussed in Part Two.

Bear in mind that each of us is encouraged to see ourselves encased and supported by these spiritual realities, this Spiritual Armor, just as if it were a physical item. As mentioned in the first part of this book, it is this Spiritual Armor which will be portrayed in a very real way, in a physical sense, while actually being "physically" intangible(at least to many people). Each piece of armor will be depicted in such a fashion that the reader may imagine them realistically enough to visualize donning each piece as if they were literal accoutrements that may be held in the hand. It is only when the aware and spiritually alive Christian applies the following principles that the protections and fruits thereof may be fully appreciated. As an example: It is not enough to say one has faith, for faith must be acted upon and expressed or it will not serve to protect. On the contrary, acting in a purely trusting and faithful manner will manifest the protections derived by *Faith* in the most peculiar and unexpected manners. The principles are as real and sound as the protection derived thereof.

Each piece of Spiritual Armor serves to protect us and support the various aspects of our Warriors' character. In many instances, scriptural text will specifically address how the armor relates to certain aspects of character. I hope the reader will see how interrelated these spiritual truths are to character development and character expression.

As with real armor, wearing one individual piece may serve to offer some protection, but then who would choose to go into combat with only a helmet and no other weapon or protection, especially when the full set is available and ready to go. Real armor was designed to be used as a fully integrated system of protection which the warrior trained in the use and wearing of. With training and experience, there develops within the warrior a certain reliance and unconscious comfort in his armor and what it affords him. The same is true of our Spiritual Armor of God. The more we train in its use and applications, the more comfortable we become in using it. In time, it will become second nature to depend upon and utilize the beneficial aspects of our armor as mentioned above. At that time, one may say they have grown reliant upon it.

The strength of real armor, historically, was proven or proofed by testing under fire. In the late medieval period, this was accomplished by actually firing a projectile at the armor. This may have been an arrow, a crossbow bolt, or even later, a bullet. The actual "mark of proof" or "proof marks," of the armors protective value would be the mark left by the actual test. This proof mark served as a great selling feature as the protection availed by the armor had been verified as fireproof or bullet proof. It was literally tested under fire. It was only when the armor had been tested under fire and verified as fireproof that the armorer could sell his ware as armor proofed. As the protective value of the armor had been displayed, a great price would be commanded. In the same way, unless the protective value of our Spiritual Armor is proof marked, how assured of its protection can the wearer be? This means we should always test-proof our armor so that we may rely upon it when called to battle.

There are many small ways by which our spiritual armor may be tested. It is during a training period that these small tests help us to grow in confidence with the armor's true protective value. Once we can see the proof marks ourselves, confidence in its protection in combat can be achieved. Each of the following chapters will bear witness to the protective value of this Spiritual Armor we are to don and grow accustomed to. In a sense, these scriptures may be viewed as proof marks. It is in trusting in Gods word and His proof marks, that we may quickly learn to rely upon all of the protection His armor gives us.

Rom. 5:1-5 *[1]So then, now that we have been justified by faith, we are at peace with God through our Lord Jesus Christ; [2]it is through Him, by faith, that we have been admitted into God's favor in which we are living, and look forward exultantly to God's glory. [3]Not only that; let us exult, too, in our hardships, understanding that hardship develops perseverance, [4]and perseverance develops a tested character, something that gives us hope, [5]and a hope which will not let us down, because the love of God had been poured into our hearts by the Holy Spirit which has been given to us.*

From this, we can clearly see that it is the tests we endure which develop our character, as well as our spiritual armor. I suggest that you reread the above, and let it soak into your spirit and dwell upon the simple message. It speaks reams. As concerning those small tests mentioned above:

2 Cor. 12:9-10 *[9]'My grace is enough for you; for power is at full stretch in weakness.' It is, then, about my weaknesses that I am happiest of all to boast, so that the power of Christ may rest upon me; [10]and that is why I am glad of weaknesses, insults, constraints, persecutions and distress for Christ's sake. For it is when I am weak that I am strong.*

This may be a strange concept for many. I hope that it brings a certain amount of enlightenment to your spirit. If you have a reference or study Bible, you may want to do a little additional reading about the concept presented above. I will leave this for the reader to pursue.

Let us look at one more scripture that addresses testing and see if it can be made even clearer for the reader to understand:

Jam. 1:2-4 *[2]My brothers, consider it a great joy when trials of many kinds come upon you, for you well know that the testing of your faith produces perseverance, [3]and perseverance must complete its work [4]so that you will become fully developed, complete, not deficient in any way.*

So you see, it is through tests and tribulations we are being given an opportunity to improve ourselves. It is in dealing with the daily troubles and inconveniences we experience that we are given the opportunity to try our spiritual armor for effect and thereby improve and perfect our character. Think back upon the many troubles present in our society today. Think of the aspects of character presented in Part One, and how the problems of society can be corrected if each of us remembered the aspects of the warrior's character we are to practice and **DID** something rather than sit on the sidelines of life as an ineffective spectator. A kind word, a joke told to lighten someone's mood or load-of-life, a simple compliment for a job seen well done, not participating in gossip, and out-right confronting someone when we know they are doing something wrong-These are just some of the simple examples of the way in which each of us as Warriors may make an impact and help change the world for the better. Remember that even though a warrior may be involved in the destruction of an institution or a culture, what comes out of the destruction is not salted ground, but rather a fertile, tilled soil from which will spring a healthy society or civilization. If we are successful in destroying the abuses, evil, and corruption of our society of today, we will have created the fertile ground to give rise to a better society of tomorrow.

Simply put: to accept and learn from our hardships by PARTICIPATING in them, we will not only develop our character to its fullest, but in the process, have an effect on those around us. If we were all to take our individual stands on drug abuse, child abuse, sexual harassment, mean spirited people, corruption, selfishness, and the bullying actions of others, at least we could say we put an end to casual indifference. If we as Warriors were to listen to our children and the children of others, maybe childhood runaways could be spared from a life on the street. How many broken homes of today do you think may have been prevented if a warrior somewhere had taken a stand for principles earlier. Just some food for thought…

To accomplish these things, our Lord does not expect us to go into battle undeveloped or unarmed for a fight. On the contrary, He has made available to each of us all the protection and armor we need to resist the wiles of the enemy and yet to stand **(Eph. 6:11)**…this is how we are to visualize ourselves armed and accoutered daily to meet the difficulties of life and proceed with God's will.

Just how powerful a defense and valuable asset armor is, can be found quite readily by a simple reading into some of the conflicts of medieval Europe. If one reads any accounts of castle siege warfare, the feats performed by armor-encased knights abound. A further credit to the spirit of the Warrior, and the virtue of his armor, can be found documented in the mid to late medieval period. It is not unusual to find within the records from this period instances when one knight could stand braced in a doorway or in the breach of a wall and single-handedly hold at bay all but the most determined attacks of the enemy, without being dislodged or harmed. Such are the fruits of good stance, good protection, and diligent training.

To consider the effectiveness of armor historically is one thing, but when compared to the effectiveness and power of the armor we are entreated to wear, historical armor pales in comparison. To get a more accurate picture of the true awesomeness of our Spiritual Armor, I would direct the readers attention not to those situations in which one armored knight fought another, but rather consider the awesome devastation wrought by the armored knight against the *UN*-armored peasant. This is a much better comparison of the power and effectiveness the *enemy* sees *US* wielding in our Spiritual Armor! An armored knight could easily quell an entire village of peasants in rebellion. The peasants had no weapons that could affect the knight, and his actions could be taken with impunity. This, in fact, is closer to the situation the enemy is placed in when the true Christian Warrior pays attention and having learned his lessons well, faces the enemy filled with God's assurances and acting in faith and obedience.

Even if outnumbered, wounded and borne to the ground, we are entreated to keep up the fight, and having withstood all—yet to STAND! (**Eph. 6:13**).

Eph. 6:10-18 *[10]Finally, my brethren, be strong in the Lord, and in the power of his might. [11]Put on the whole armour of God, that ye may be able to stand against the wiles of the devil. [12]For we wrestle not against flesh and blood, but against principalities, against powers, against the rulers of the darkness of this world, against spiritual wickedness in high places. [13]Wherefore take unto you the whole armour of God, that ye may be able to withstand in the evil day, and having done all, to stand. [14]Stand therefore, having your loins girt about with truth, and having on the breastplate of righteousness; [15]And your feet shod with the preparation of the gospel of peace; [16]Above all, taking the shield of faith, wherewith ye shall be able to quench all the fiery darts of the wicked. [17]And take the helmet of salvation, and the sword of the Spirit, which is the word of God: [18]Praying always with all prayer and supplication in the Spirit, and watching thereunto with all perseverance and supplication for all saints...*

Would you have the strength of character to endure the following situation, and still hold the field:

Ps. 91:2-7 *²I will say of the LORD, He is my refuge and my fortress: my God; in him will I trust. ³Surely he shall deliver thee from the snare of the fowler, and from the noisome pestilence. ⁴He shall cover thee with his feathers, and under his wings shalt thou trust: his truth shall be thy shield and buckler. ⁵Thou shalt not be afraid for the terror by night; nor for the arrow that flieth by day; ⁶Nor for the pestilence that walketh in darkness; nor for the destruction that wasteth at noonday. ⁷A thousand shall fall at thy side, and ten thousand at thy right hand; but it shall not come nigh thee.*

A True Warrior would just be getting started...undaunted, unrelenting, with but one thought on his mind: doing the will of the Father!

For the following discussions of our Spiritual Armor, the long established and traditional sequence of arming oneself for combat will take us through our discussion of each piece of armor individually. The reader will find that this process of preparation, while historically accurate, is helpful in remembering the various pieces of armor and the symbology of them individually.

In each of the subsequent chapters, a scripture passage or two will introduce each individual piece of armor. This will be followed by a brief description of the particular piece of armor, how it was constructed and worn, and the typical extent of its protective abilities. Next will be a synopsis of our Spiritual Armor as promised in God's Word, how it serves to protect us, how we can strengthen each piece, claim its protection, and how developing each piece of armor will fortify our character as a Warrior in God's army. These points will be borne out by a sample of scriptures which hopefully will render a clear and easily understood grasp of the concepts of the spiritual principles involved. As it may help the reader to have their own Bible handy to reference to, all of the pertinent scriptures for the quotes will be stated with their chapter and verse cites for reference. Some of the versions available today may or may not carry as clear a meaning in regards to the purposes of the following chapters, so two versions in particular will be quoted from so as to render the clearest statements.

The two translations, which will be used to draw quotes from, are the King James version, and the New Jerusalem Bible. Passages from the King James version will contain superscripts on each line, while the New Jerusalem quotes will not. This should help clarify for the reader why certain passages may not read exactly the same in their own Bible version. The reader is encouraged to follow the references in their own concordances to find more scriptures that may be pertinent to the matter at hand. While the author has done a thorough inclusion of scriptures which address the particular subject of each chapter, the Holy Bible is a remarkable record, and it would take a tome many times larger than this book to completely reference each topic as a study guide. The enclosed quotes should be sufficient to serve as a study of their own, as each quote has been included for a particular reason to make a point clear. This is a MOST IMPORTANT aspect of this book, and the reader is encouraged to take his or her time to slowly read the scripture quotes contained within, and dwell upon them. These quotes, when committed to memory, will serve as a balm for troubled times, and will aid the Warrior in training to develop character and remain strong in the face of opposition. It is God's Word, and His Promises, which we as His warriors will rely upon. It is His Power and Might, which will become manifested though a careful study and incorporation of the scriptural principles discussed in each of the following chapters.

In the following chapter, chapter six, we will begin our study of the Spiritual Armor with that which is worn on the feet. This is a fitting place to start, as protection for the feet is typically donned first when preparing for combat. This stands in contrast to the typical order of dressing oneself today, as the slacks or pants worn today do not allow the feet to pass through the leg of the garment once the feet are shod—not so for a warrior preparing for combat. During the time of Christ, warriors often wore simple leggings, which could be fastened on the limbs once the feet were shod, and the body was typically covered with a tunic, which could be slipped overhead after the feet were covered. The protection for the feet will be held as symbolically representing our Willingness and Doing to spread the gospel of peace. It was also prudent to arm the feet first so as a speedy escape could be made if ample time to prepare for a general engagement with the enemy was not allowed.

After we look at the protection for the feet and legs, our attention will be directed on an interesting piece of armor, which today is not thought of as armor in the least fashion. Chapter seven will discuss the Belt of Truth as the second piece of armor we will look at. The way it was worn, the purpose it served, and the spiritual principle of truth for a Warrior in the army of God will be our study.

Following this will be a chapter on the Breastplate of Righteousness. The breastplate represents our right action, our rightness. The breastplate is seen by many as the most extensive piece of armor, and rightly so for it typically consists of the greatest amount of overall weight to be borne by the warrior. When following the dictates of right action, it will be shown how acting in such a fashion makes one a shining example.

Chapter nine will elaborate on the Helmet of Salvation. In later periods of history, the helmet was the most elaborate and technically difficult single piece of armor to be made. In comparison, while salvation and God's plan may be difficult for us to understand, grasping the fundamentals of His grace and our redemption and salvation is very simple. God loves us, and wants all to be saved.

Chapter ten concerns itself with the Shield of Faith. The power of faith, even the size of a mustard seed, stands as good testimony to the protective strength of this piece of armor. The many strengths and powerful warding ability of faith will be examined. It must be borne in mind that even though faith is capable of protecting us from all forms of attacks as thoroughly as a bastion, Faith is effortless to bear.

The last piece of armor to be discussed, in chapter eleven, will be the warriors only listed weapon, 'the Sword of the Word of God.' Understanding how to wield God's word to attack the enemy is crucial to the development of a Warrior in God's army. It is through studying the scriptures that His promises are revealed and understood, and it is by applying these principles that the absolute awesome nature of His protection and assurances can be personally manifested.

Chapter twelve will sum up some of the most important principles of the book, and will contain a few short stories from real life representing how some of the principles contained herein may be used to combat Powers and Principalities, and serve to protect the trained and disciplined Warrior. This chapter is followed by an epilogue containing autobiographical information about me and how I have seen God's hand orchestrate my life.

Knowledge is a tool that can be fashioned into a weapon, and for this reason, a little knowledge is a dangerous thing. With knowledge comes responsibility, the responsibility to use the knowledge one has gained. Make yourself a dangerous weapon in God's army, and remember not to hide your light! *¹⁴Ye are the light of the world. A city that is set on a hill cannot be hid. ¹⁵Neither do men light a candle, and put it under a bushel, but on a candlestick; and it giveth light unto all that are in the house. ¹⁶Let your light so shine before men, that they may see your good works, and glorify your Father which is in heaven."* Mt. 5:14-16. *²¹But he that doeth truth cometh to the light, that his deeds may be made manifest, that they are wrought in God.* Jn 3:21.

Chapter 6

Shod Your Feet

Eph. 6:13, 15 *¹³Wherefore take unto you the whole armor of God, that ye may be able to withstand in the evil day, and having done all, to stand...¹⁵And your feet shod with the preparation of the gospel of peace...*

Ps. 18: 35-38 *...you never cease to listen to me, you give me the strides of a giant, give me ankles that never weaken.*
I pursue my enemies and overtake them, not turning back till they are annihilated; I strike them down and they cannot rise, they fall, they are under my feet.

To the warriors of ancient times, the importance of good foot protection and the benefits thereof were foundational. Often, the troops would doff many pieces of their armor before resting for a period, but the protection for the feet was seldom removed. It was common for the foot soldiers to keep their campaign boots on for weeks at a time while in hostile territory. Even if caught unarmed and shield-less, a shod warrior could quickly outdistance an armed assailant, while one caught asleep and barefoot would be easily run down and killed.

Once his undergarments were donned, the preparation of the Warrior in donning the rest of his armor was traditionally and often ritualistically performed. Always beginning with the shoeing of the feet, and continued to the anointing of the shield and blessing of the sword, all preparations must be completed before reporting for duty. The armor was conscientiously put on in a specific sequence to assure that no belt would slip, nor straps free thus jeopardizing one's protection in a time of need. It is what a soldier wears on his feet that primarily determines whether or not he can continue to march, hold his ground, and confidently pursue the enemy over difficult terrain without fear of slipping or being harmed by rough or uneven ground, to say nothing of a battlefield prepared by the enemy.

Today when we refer to a "well-heeled gentleman" we refer to a man whose shoes are in good condition, showing little wear on the bottom. This term generally refers to someone of some social standing, typically in a position of authority and financially secure. This is a person "prepared to take on the world." Spiritually this could represent someone with "No holes in the 'Soul'." A well "Souled" Warrior is one able to stand his ground, do his best and, having resisted all, TO STAND. He can confidently withstand the enemy knowing he has been fully prepared for the fight. To engage effectively in combat, well-heeled boots are essential. This gives a certain "all terrain ability" to the Warrior to fight the battle wherever it may lead. The feet were shod in such a way so as not to hinder swift movement or speedy marching.

The bearing of Peace brings joy to the heart and a spring to the step. Rather than a burden, the bearing of Peace is a pleasure, as easy to bear as a comfortable pair of shoes.

The importance of good footing in time of conflict should be immediately apparent. Without gaining purchase on the ground you stand on, you may be easily shoved aside, or pushed over. A Warrior with poor footing is truly "a push over." No matter how desperate the situation, it would be impossible to hold ground or maintain your position. The problem is not unlike trying to ride a horse without stirrups. The simple addition to the saddle of the stirrups made it possible for a mounted rider to maintain balance better, control the horse better, and have greater impact upon the enemy. Until the Romans invented the stirrup, the force delivered in a cavalry charge was substantially reduced as the rider could not brace for impact and deliver a full blow. More often than not, it was the size and mass of the charging horse impacting and running down the unfortunate footman that did the job. Even if the rider carried a spear, as soon as he tried to thrust forcibly with it while mounted, he stood a great chance of being thrown from his horse, for he had no way to brace himself. It was common practice to thrust and release the weapon just before impact to avoid the possibility of one being thrown by the impact. The use of the stirrup gained a sound stature in the saddle for the rider, and allowed the force of impact of a charge to be carried through the saddle and tack to the horse. With the use of stirrups, the full charging energy of a horse and rider could be transmitted by the rider into the enemy, while the shock of impact was easily borne by the rider and transmitted to the horse through the saddle and tack. This changed things considerably, and the force of a cavalry charge gained a new respect. Even the wary foot soldier could not stand against such an onslaught. By direct comparison, he didn't have the "mount" or "support" to hold his ground against such an attack. It would take another mounted warrior to even up the stakes or "put things on an even footing."

Good footing is essential for a Warrior to hold his ground when pressed upon by the enemy. Think of how difficult it is to push a car on pavement if you are wearing slick soled shoes. You can push and push, and all that happens is that your feet slide out from under you. You cannot transmit any energy into the car thus pushing it anywhere due to the simple fact you are not gaining a good footing. If the situation were to face you while wearing sneakers, the result would be somewhat different. Actually, while you may require several people to help push the car if you all wore shoes, you may find that you could push the car alone while wearing sneakers. The simple explanation for this is the softer sole of the sneakers allows you to get

Awaken The WARRIOR

more traction with the pavement. You might say that good footwear "gains purchase" of the ground. Having gained purchase, one can "take more ground," or "purchase more ground."

For the above reason, a foot soldier's boots are typically covered with a pliable sole, with many ripples or ridges on it to gain more traction on a wide variety of surfaces. The Romans understood the importance of good footing, and how to achieve it. They developed for their Legionaries the first of the "campaign boots" to be worn by soldiers of their day. These boots, or "caligae" as they are called, were hobnailed so as the soldiers could gain a purchase on the sod underfoot.* The exposed knobby surface of the caligae allowed the soldier to dig into the surface of the ground he trod on and allowed him to easily climb up steep grades or hold back the force of the enemy on slick surfaces such as wet grass, or gore-covered ground. They offered the same types of advantages to the Roman soldiers as cleats on athletic shoes today offer athletes in sports such as football or baseball. In both of these sports, the ability of the athlete to stay on his feet is of paramount importance. Also, the hobnails could help prevent a soldier from being dragged away by the enemy (***Do not drag me away with the wicked, with evildoers… Ps. 28:3.***). Wearing footwear of this type imparted a tremendous advantage to a soldier.

The caligae were sandals cut from a single piece of leather, and were laced above the ankle. It was no simple matter to put these on or take them off for that matter, as the lacing would take several minutes to complete. Being so secured gave the Roman soldier confidence knowing that his boots would remain on his feet and not slip off or shift on his feet when he most needed a sound footing. They offered the soldier support for his ankles much as the combat boots of today do. Anyone who has ever attempted ice-skating can attest to the advantage gained by good ankle support. In hand-to-hand combat, it is very important to remain on one's feet, and good strong ankle support is a definite plus. ***So then, let us be always seeking the ways***

---

* Caligula was the Roman Emperor of the time who made the sandals fashionable, and by some accounts, had them designed for his troops to wear.

Philip Paul Sacco

which lead to peace and the ways in which we can support one another. **Rom. 14:19.**

Another protection offered by the caligae was gained by the multi-layering of the sole. These multiple layers of thick leather made it safe for the Roman soldiers to march over sharp rocky terrain without the fear of stone bruises to their feet. Surely, most of us at one time or another has experienced the difficulty of running on loose rocky terrain, or through the woods with many fallen limbs on the ground. The ankle support offered by good footwear could prevent turning an ankle under such conditions when a rock or piece of wood shoots out from underfoot. But what about that stub or sharp rocks projecting from the ground that you tread on? If this should happen while bare-foot or wearing anything but the sturdiest footwear, a stone bruise or worse is likely the result. *He pulled me up from the seething chasm, from the mud of the mire. He set my feet on rock, and made my footsteps firm.* **Ps. 40:2.**

It was common practice for the Romans to deploy caltrops on the battlefield to additionally handicap the enemy. A caltrop is a four pronged metal object much like a child's jack. When tossed to the ground, they always present a vertical prong. Another type of caltrop was a simple metal hook imbedded in a chunk of wood with a barb exposed and placed in a hole or depression in the ground. Caltrops were suitable for deployment against enemy foot soldiers as well as mounted troops. If the Romans were to deploy caltrops, it would be imperative not to handicap their own troops and allow them free movement on the battlefield at the same time. The Romans were the masters of battle field preparations such as these. The caligae was again the solution. Their enemies would occasionally fashion a surprise of their own, however, the solid supportive protection the Caligula offered the Roman soldiers often minimized the effects of these snares. *To you, Yahweh, I turn my eyes, in you I take refuge, do not leave me unprotected. Save me from the traps that are set for me, the snares of evildoers. Let the wicked fall each into his own net, while I pass on my way.* **Ps. 141:8-10.**

Following are a few examples of scriptures, which relate to the power of God's peace and the blessings that will follow those who carry our Lord's message. Being a bearer of God's peace may derive many more benefits, but these quotes will give the reader some excellent examples of the immediate blessings God will bestow upon the Warrior bearing His words of peace. Some scriptures refer to the gospel of the word as the gospel of peace or the gospel of Truth. Truth is a thing that is undeniable. It is stubbornly unshakeable and nothing can dislodge the Truth. The phrases "God's Word" and "God's Truth" are often used interchangeably. Truth, as a separate piece of armor, will be discussed in the next chapter.

Please bear in mind as you continue throughout the following chapters that the scriptures here included are not intended to be the complete compilation of pertinent scriptures, and as you continue, you are encouraged to continue each thread in your own reference Bible to find more revealing scriptures.

The principles at work here are the bearing of God's peace, the willingness to do so, and the actual act of doing so. With this in mind, the protections derived from this mindset and outward action would include sound footing, protection, strength, support, sure-footedness and speed. Let us look first at the assurances of peace and protection in bearing Gods peace and love.

1 Cor. 14:33 *...for God is a God not of disorder but of peace.* Note: Recognizing this makes His orders easy to hear and discern...a definite plus in the turmoil of battle.

Eph. 2:12-13 *...you that used to be far off have been brought close, by the blood of Christ. For he is the peace between us, and has made the two into one entity and broken down the barrier which used to keep them apart...* This is another form of mutual support which is gained by Gods peace...unity!

Ps. 25:10 *Kindness unfailing and constancy mark all Yahweh's paths, for those who keep his covenant and his decrees.* Our God is easy to understand, He is unchanging and dependable. Following His decrees, allow us the full and unlimited blessings of our Lord.

Phil. 4:6-9 *Never worry about anything; but tell God all your desires of every kind in prayer and petition shot through with gratitude, and the peace of God which is beyond our understanding will guard your hearts and your thoughts in Christ Jesus. Finally, brothers, let your minds be filled with everything that is true, everything that is honorable, everything that is upright and pure, everything that we love and admire-with whatever is good and praiseworthy. Keep doing everything you learned from me and were told by me and have heard or seen me doing. Then the God of Peace will be with you.* When our minds are filled in this manner rather than with worries and concerns, doesn't that put us at peace? Reread the first sentence of this scripture.

1 Thess. 5:14-24 *Be at peace among yourselves. We urge you, brothers, to admonish those who are undisciplined, encourage the apprehensive, support the weak and be patient with everyone. Make sure that people do not try to repay evil for evil; always aim at what is best for each other and for everyone. Always be joyful; pray constantly; and for all things give thanks; this is the will of God for you in Christ Jesus.*
Do not stifle the Spirit or despise the gift of prophecy with contempt; test everything and hold on to what is good and shun every form of evil.
May the God of peace make you perfect and holy; and may your spirit, life, and body be kept blameless for the coming of our Lord Jesus Christ. He who has called you is trustworthy and will carry it out. This is a powerful assurance. The above advice shows many of the hallmark characteristics of the Warrior.

Col. 3:11-17 *...the holy people whom He loves, you are to be clothed in heartfelt compassion, in generosity and humility, gentleness and patience. Bear with one another; forgive each other if one of you has a complaint against another. The Lord has forgiven you; now you must do the same. Over all these clothes, put on love, the perfect bond. And may the peace of Christ reign in* *your hearts, because it is for this that you were called together in one body. Always be thankful.* Bearing a heart willing to make amends will avail us of the goodness, which comes from forgiveness.

Rom. 16:16-18 *Greet each other with the holy kiss. All the churches of Christ send their greetings. I urge you, brothers, be on your guard against the people who are out to stir up disagreements and bring up difficulties against the teaching which you learned. Avoid them. People of that sort are servants not of our Lord Christ, but of their own greed; and with talk that sounds smooth and reasonable they deceive the minds of the unwary.* This is a lesson in discernment, as well as brotherly-love.

The above scriptures show us those bearing peace and love carry a responsibility to act in other ways as well, and that acting in such a fashion will bring blessings to us. In studying the actions called for in the above scriptures, it is apparent that many of the characteristics of the warrior are being called upon.

By following the above advice, there is the added benefit of strength being given to those carrying peace:

Ps. 29:11 *Yahweh will give strength to his people, Yahweh blesses his people with peace.*

Ps. 23:4 *Even were I to walk in a ravine as dark as death I should fear no danger, for you are at my side.* This is the strength of confidence from faith in divine protection and guidance.

Ps. 27:3 *Though an army pitch camp against me, my heart will not fear, though war break out against me, my trust will never be shaken.* No Worries…nothing but confidence.

Ps. 28:3 *Do not drag me away with the wicked, with evildoers, who talk to their partners of peace with treachery in their hearts.*

John 16:32 *…when you are going to be scattered, each going his own way and leaving me alone: and yet I am not alone. I have told you all this so that you may find peace in me. In the world you* *will have hardship, but be courageous: I have conquered the world.* These words of Jesus carry an additional element of perseverance and doggedness.

1 Sam. 2:9-10 *He safeguards the steps of his faithful but the wicked vanish in darkness; for human strength can win no victories. Yahweh, his enemies are shattered, the Most High thunders in the heavens.* We can rely on the power and might of Almighty God.

Isa. 43:5-6 *Why be so downcast, why all these sighs? Hope in God! I will praise him still, my Savior, my God. When I am downcast I think of you.* These words offer strength and an uplifting of the spirit for those times when we may despair or feel downtrodden.

Ps. 18:33-34, 36 *...who makes me as swift as a deer and sets me firmly on the heights, who trains my hands for battle, my arms to bend a bow of bronze...you give me the strides of a giant, give me ankles that never weaken.* This scripture speaks of the strength of position, support, discipline, speed, and brawn.

Now that we understand it is God's peace and love which directs our actions and offers us strength, it is important to realize His protection and "footing" will always be made available to us also. The following scriptures take the element of protection and guidance hinted at in some of the above scriptures and brings them more clearly to mind. These are powerful principles, and when acted upon, the following vantage points will be seen as invaluable:

Ps. 143:10 *Rescue me from my enemies, Yahweh, since in you I find protection. Teach me to do your will, for you are my God. May your generous spirit lead me on even ground.*

Ps. 116:7-8 *My heart, be at peace once again, for Yahweh has treated you generously. He has rescued me from death, my eyes from tears, and my feet from stumbling.*

Ps. 119:109-110 *My life is in your hands perpetually, I do not forget your Law. The wicked have laid out a snare for me, but I have not strayed from your precepts.* Thus, the snares will not catch me, if we stay mindful of God's precepts.

Ps. 91:10-13 *No disaster can overtake you, no plague come near your tent; He has given his angels orders about you to guard you wherever you go. They will carry you in their arms in case you trip over a stone. You will walk upon wild beast and adder, you will trample young lions and snakes.* Do you get the feeling of an indomitable spirit in these words?

Ps. 141:9-10 *Save me from the traps that are set for me, the snares of evildoers. Let the wicked fall each into his own net, while I pass on my way.*

Ps. 40:2 *He set my feet on rock, and made my footsteps firm.*

Prov. 4:18-19 *The path of the upright is like the light of dawn, its brightness growing to the fullness of day; the way of the wicked is as dark as night, they cannot tell the obstacles they stumble over.*

Ps. 17:5-7 *...my steps never stray from the paths you lay down, from your tracks; so my feet never stumble. I call upon you, God, for you answer me; turn your ear to me, hear what I say. Show the evidence of your faithful love, savior of those who hope in your strength against attack.* Here we see surefootedness and direction expressed.

I think it only fitting that spreading God's peace provide the spiritual armor for our feet and legs. In a time before postal service and mass transit, when one went most anywhere by foot, unless one was of such status to own a horse, we had just our two legs to take us where we wanted to go. Without the use of both of them, spreading God's peace can be somewhat difficult. Our two legs may be seen as representing "Willingness and Doing." It is not enough to have the *willingness to fight* the Lord's fights when directed-we must **Fight Them**. To be an obedient servant of the Lord, it is important *to do the doing*, and do so *happily and willingly*. An act of charity or compassion is much more productive when the heart of the Warrior is compliant and willing to do whatever directed. If willingness is absent, carelessness is bound to manifest itself. One's mind may not be on the task, and rather than be seen as one that is truly caring, one may be seen as disinterested and just going though the motions. *But you must do what the Word tells you and not just listen to it and deceive yourselves. Anyone who listens to the Word and takes no action is like someone who looks at his own features in a mirror and once he had seen what he looks like, goes off and immediately forgets it. But anyone who looks steadily at the perfect law of freedom and keeps to it—not listening and forgetting, but putting it into practice—will be blessed in every undertaking.* **1 John 3:18-19, 21-25.**

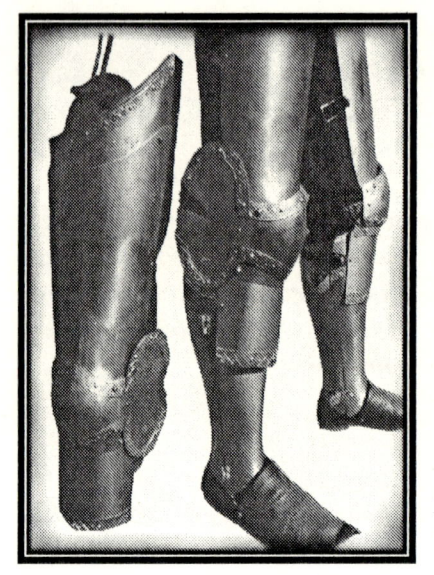

The aspects of character which will lend support and aid in developing the spiritual principles of spreading God's peace include: nobility, trustworthiness, humility, willingness and doing, doggedness/ persistence. Several secondary characteristics have already been shown to benefit from spreading the Gospel of Peace. When the following characteristics are developed and applied, additional support and strength will be added to bolster up the armor of our feet and legs.[†]

Noble is the warrior who professes peace, a cause much more beneficial than the cause of war. To bring peace about is always much more difficult than to start a war, for greed and discontent most

---

[†] By no means should the reader assume that the characteristics attributed to support our armor be limited to those discussed. Each of us are encouraged to study the scriptures and find any other attributes you feel may support our spiritual armor in addition to those mentioned in the text.

often direct the actions of man. The number of notable peacemakers around the world pales compared to the number of warmongers. After all, the Noble Peace Prize is awarded to an individual who has displayed extraordinary skills and ability to create peace. There are no rewards for those who start wars, no matter how good they may be at it, what good may come of it, or how noble the cause. The noble actions of the peacemakers make us all feel a little taller, a little prouder to be human. In the words of our Lord himself: *[9]Blessed are the peacemakers: for they shall be called the children of God.* Matt. 5:9.

Trustworthy is the Warrior who is willing to do what is bid of him, and does so. When called to action as a peacemaker and one fulfills the task, one is pronounced dependable, an aspect of character which serves to support trustworthiness. There is a certain amount of reliance that can be placed on one shown to be dependable, and trustworthy. To individuals such as this will fall the special duties and assignments for the King, for they have shown they can be relied on much as a warrior must learn to rely on his armor. *[21]His lord said unto him, Well done, thou good and faithful servant: thou hast been faithful over a few things, I will make thee ruler over many things: enter thou into the joy of thy lord.* Matt. 25:21.

A humble spirit is much preferred to haughtiness. The advice and words of one who is humble are much more likely to be given attention over one displaying arrogance. Humility shows an understanding of things which are above oneself, and is represented by a meek spirit. A Warrior, by not putting on airs and putting himself above others, shows a certain amount of humility and meekness. This is an extension of the devotion to a greater cause Warriors believe in and subject themselves to. Remember what our Lord said about a meek spirit: *[5]Blessed are the meek: for they shall inherit the earth.* Matt. 5:5.

Prov. 15:18 *The hot-headed provokes disputes, the equable allays dissension.*

Being shod with the protection, which emanates from carrying the message of peace, a Warrior is more disposed to pursue the cause of peace with dogged persistence and perseverance than an individual who questions his footing and whether he has the proper stance for an endeavor. If you were dashing barefoot through a field and came to the sudden realization that the field through which you were running was covered with broken glass, I doubt that you would continue to charge right on ahead without a care. Now, if you knew you were properly prepared for such a situation, your dash would be unimpeded. Just imagine being well shod, and in pursuit of the enemy who was barefoot when you noticed the glass-strewn field. Without a doubt, the enemy you pursue will be brought to heel. Being well-heeled undoubtedly lends much to the willingness of the spirit to pursue a task, and knowing the security, strength and protection with which you move serves to make the doing much less daunting.

Now how exactly do we don this fine protection, you may be asking yourself. It's not very hard at all. Reflect on the aspects of character just discussed and how they are reflected and related to the message of Peace. Developing and expressing these traits will bind you with the attributes of our Lord's Peace.

By being noble in spirit and being kind when you don't think you have to be, or just admitting you may have made a mistake rather than presenting a terse confrontational demeanor, you will not only go a long way towards promoting peace, but in the eyes of your peers you will be seen as a much greater person.

Keeping your word and keeping your promise is an excellent way of building up your trustworthiness in the eyes of those that know you, and keeping the peace. Holding your tongue rather than lashing out at someone, and not engaging in gossip are also good ways of showing a developed and disciplined character. Not only will it raise your self esteem, but you will gain the confidence of others. Likewise, keeping your confidence and not disclosing what has been placed in your care are also sure ways of showing you are dependable and reliable.

"Find the good in a bad situation," and "there is a silver lining in every cloud," are expressions we have all heard growing up, but have you ever really dwelt on what these words promote? Do you practice this sage advice? Have you ever suggested these comments to someone else in a time of trouble?

A kind word at a time when emotions are getting heated will serve to diffuse potentially volatile situations, and insisting that others raise themselves a little above the moment will show you to be thoughtful and concerned for all. *A mild answer turns away wrath, sharp words stir up anger.* **Prov. 15:1.** Placing the ideals you believe in above your personal agenda will define that which is truly most important to you. This will be apparent to those around you as well. In much the same way, when you have devoted yourself to an effort and expressed your willingness to do a certain thing, by following up without the prompting of others you will have shown yourself to be more than a mouthpiece. Who would ever have cause to come to you at a later time and say, "Put up or shut up" or "Put your money where your mouth is?" In other words, just do not say you will do something, ***DO IT***. It is important you do what you say you will, to the best of your ability. Just attempt, for you never truly know what you are capable of accomplishing unless you try. Failing doesn't matter; just do the best you can...always. If you fall short of the mark, try again. Although you may fail at an endeavor, at least it will be said of you that you tried. It is important to make the efforts even when there are no witnesses, YOU are there, and so is our Lord. *The eyes of Yahweh are everywhere: observing the wicked and the good.* **Prov. 15:3.**

These are just some of the ways that you can apply the spiritual principles of peace. You may never know the impact these simple acts have on others, or who may come to your assistance in a time of need just because you followed these principles at some time. I am sure you have been affected by such actions on the part of others at some time in your life. Reflect on one, and what influences it had on your life.

With the Lord's peace directing us and willingly acting under His direction, we shall not stumble, our journey will be swift, our way always brightly lit, and we shall not fail. What better bedrock is there to STAND FIRM on?

This is but the first piece of God's armor we are to don. With our feet securely protected, we can confidently continue to arm ourselves resting in the comfort and knowledge that our ways are directed and protected from the ground up. Once the feet are secured, the preparations of the Warrior continue with the belting of the undergarments and securing of the straps leading to the harness.

The topic of the next chapter is:

"The Belt of Truth"

Chapter 7

The Belt of Truth

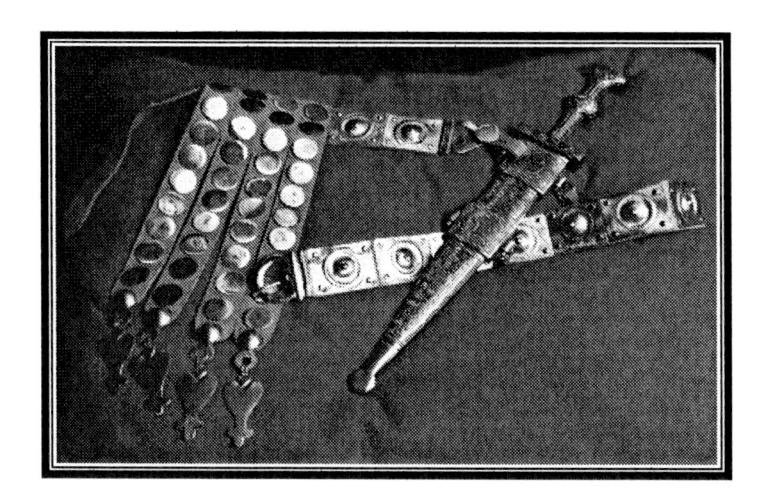

Eph. 6:14 *Stand therefore, having your loins girt about with truth...*

To the warriors of the Roman Empire, girding one's loins meant much more than comes to mind today. This act today consists of using a simple leather belt to hold our pants or slacks up. For Roman soldiers, the belt worn to gird the loins served to support the back as well as provide protection for the soldier's soft underbelly, in addition to the loins. Historically, there have been typically three different belts involved in the arming of a Roman soldier, and later the knights of Europe. One belt served as a girdle and was worn in a manner that would bind the undergarments and protect the privates. The second belt was worn as an additional form of protection for the kidneys and belly and supported the body armor, or served as a point of attachment for the protective armor of the lower extremities. The third type of belt was worn to carry and support the warrior's side arms. Some may understand the various applications of a belt as armor, but the manner in which Truth serves in this capacity as our spiritual armor is a concept few understand.

The analogy of relating truth to the functions of a warrior's belt is simple to remember. Think of truth protecting the most sensitive part of your body in much the same way as a belt worn for protection. Actually, this is exactly how practicing truthfulness will serve to guard and support you. If we are truthful about those most sensitive parts of our being, we can never become confused concerning our statements, or lost in a web of lies. The truth we have told will guard us from the reproach we may otherwise suffer if caught in a lie. Ironically, it is typical of human nature to, at times, replace the protection derived by truth with the 'protection' we may feel telling a lie may give us. This is a true self-deception. A falsehood can never replace truth, and can never offer any real protection. Lies have a way of being discovered or making their effects known in our lives.

There are many reasons for which we transgress against truth. Sometimes it may be to take advantage of a situation or in some way derive a personal gain. Or, we may tell a lie to protect the feelings of others. For some people, telling the truth is just not in their makeup for whatever reason. You may know someone whom you may call a chronic liar. For these individuals, telling the truth is simply not possible. In some instances, this condition may be caused by childhood trauma. It may be their choice of action is a habitual continuation of improper past actions (remember, character develops from actions we take, be they good or bad). Repetitive proper action leads to the development of a good, well-rounded character. Poor or improper actions, which remain uncorrected, foster poor character. People who are chronic liars typically require counseling to uncover and correct their behavior. Some people who suffer from a lack of self-esteem choose to lie to add an element of mystery about them and thus feel somehow important. For others of us, we may feel lying in some way allows us to live out a different reality than is our life, or give a false sense of meaning or accomplishment to our life. This is truly tragic. Use of this type of logic to direct a course of action is obviously imbalanced, and will result in a life built like a house-of-cards. At the first breeze of truth, a life such as this will fall apart.

There are many reasons we may tell a lie. Simply put, it is hoped a certain pain or loss to our most personal agenda or security may be avoided by the simple lie we may tell. Interestingly, it is typically out of a desire to protect our self-image, or to safeguard the respect of others for us, that results in our telling a partial truth or an outright lie. Rather than rely on the protection of the truth, we find it easier to hide behind the pseudo protection we feel a lie will provide. It may be that we have done something we are not especially proud of. It may be we have done something that we never intended others to scrutinize. Another rather typical reason for telling a falsehood is that it is just easier to tell a lie and avoid all the embarrassing questions the truth may lead to. This way of thinking, or course of action, may itself be a consequence of previous lies in our life.* There is a certain element of **PRIDE** involved, generally speaking, which may compel us to depart from the truth. We will come back to this point at the end of this chapter. The point to be stressed here is the fact we must practice truth to protect the most sensitive aspects or our being.

The first type of protective belt, most commonly called a girdle, can be found detailed in the history of the early Romans. By some accounts, the Romans on some occasions would "tuck" their privates within their pelvic bone, and wear a girdle of thick leather between their legs and fastened about the waist. This would all but eliminate their fear of castration in combat, and offer protection to the abdominal area, the soft underbelly. This type of belting was typically found in use among Gladiators. Gladiators would not generally be furnished with extensive armor for combat in the gladiatorial arena, and the use of a girdle offered much in the way of protection to a very vulnerable part of the body, easily and inexpensively.

The Roman Legionaries were practiced in making deliberate attacks to the soft underbelly and privates of their adversaries. They were aware not only of the poor degree of protection most of their adversaries had in this area of the body, but they understood the devastating effect of a well-executed attack to these portions of the body. Given the poor level of medical understanding and trauma treatment available, a groin or abdominal wound would prove to be not only exceedingly painful, but also ultimately deadly. A stab to the stomach or intestinal area was almost certainly a killing wound. It

---

* If you would like more insight into why we tell lies, I suggest the reader get a copy of Scott Peck's book, *People of the Lie*.

may take a number of days for this type of wound to kill, but peritonitis is bound to set in and a slow death is the typical fate for anyone so wounded. Additionally, a successful attack to an adversaries groin assured his bleeding to death rapidly.

To portray the level of understanding the Romans had for the devastating effects of lower body and groin attacks, a brief description of a strategy used on at least one occasion paints the picture clearly. Upon closing with the enemy, the Romans would typically unleash a volley of uniquely designed javelins or "pilum" to force the enemy to protect themselves with their shields, or be struck by the spears. The barbed head of the pilum would embed in the shield making it difficult to remove, especially in the heat of combat. The enemy had specially designed the shank of the weapon so once thrown, it would either bend or break thus denying its use. To further complicate the situation for the defender, the pilum typically had a rather long iron shaft by which it was affixed to its wooden staff. This feature made cutting the head of the weapon free an impossibility. Generally, the effect of a volley of pilum would be to render the enemies shields useless, if not cumbersome, at best. This tactic in itself won the Romans many a fight at the onset. After closing with the enemy in this fashion, the front line would serve to engage the enemy, keep them occupied and distracted with immediate threat. While engaged, a special unit formed for just this purpose would engage the enemy from below, attacking their lower extremities and unguarded underbellies with small headed axes. It is not difficult to understand how demoralizing and devastating such an attack would be.

To whatever extent the belt worn under the armor may serve as protection, another principal purpose for this belt was to bind the undergarments and padding worn under the external, primary armor. Suffice it to say, symbolically, this may be taken to represent how truth is required to hold right action together and support it. In addition to this, it is not uncommon for this type of belt to carry the weight of the armor protecting the legs also. To offer additional protection for this supportive belt, the belt was most often found worn under the outermost protective layer of armor. Symbolically, this can be seen as truth supporting our "willingness to spread the gospel of peace," as well as how correct action may safeguard truth. When our willingness and doing are supported by truth, are not our burdens lighter, our tasks accomplished more readily? When we act in a righteous fashion, is it not easier to be truthful?

It is a common practice to gird oneself with a strong belt in preparation for arduous labor or strenuous tasks. This offers support and strength to the body by supporting the back. Wrist bracers or arm cinches may also be used to protect muscles from becoming overly strained. In this sense, truth is supportive of doing hard tasks, and is capable of sustaining you. A belt is also useful in removing any hindrances of clothing by allowing one to cinch them up, and keep the legs and arms free to move unimpeded. *And ye shall know the truth, and the truth shall make you free.* Jn. 8:32. Being well girt in truth, one may freely move as needed without fear of reprisal. The spiritual analogy to this is simple: truth keeps us clear in mind and undistracted by lies and deceit. Just think about the many alterations in one's thinking required to sustain one lie, while the truth is simple to remember and is always consistent. Discernment of truth is a valuable tool available to a Warrior in God's army. *With so many witnesses in a great cloud all around us, we too, then should throw off everything that weighs us down and the sin that clings so closely, and with perseverance keep running in the race which lies ahead of us. Let us keep our eyes fixed on Jesus, who leads us in our faith and brings it to perfection…* Heb. 12:1-2.

The second type of belt, worn externally for support as well as protection, will come to mind readily when any typical representation of a Roman Legionnaire is recalled. An example of this type of external belt would be the belt typically depicted being worn by the Romans known as a "sporran" or "cingulum militare," or military belt. It was fashioned of leather straps upon which were riveted small plates of metal. The sporran hangs vertically down from the front of the military belt. This belt served to protect their privates as well as add to the formidable impression of the Roman unit as a whole when in formation or on the march. The swinging and shining bits of metal would catch the eye, and to some degree cause the enemy to reflect upon the totality of the protection of the approaching Romans. When contrasted to their own relatively unarmored level of protection, the psychological effect of this very visible impression had to have been disarming for any enemy facing the advancing Romans.

The military belt not only served to protect the loins, but could also double as additional protection for the kidneys, and when securely cinched, would help support the weight of the body armor by allowing a large portion of the armor to be distributed to the hips. During those periods of history when body armor was constructed of fabric, leather, scale, or chain mail, a thick leather belt worn externally was a simple addition to one's protection. When I am fully suited up in preparation for martial combat, I wear a chain mail shirt that weighs close to fifty pounds. I find it to be a tremendous advantage to wear a heavy leather belt on the outside of the body armor to aid in the distribution of this weight. Without the belt, all of the weight of the chain shirt drags on the shoulders. This can quickly tire the muscles of the upper back and shoulders as well as the neck, especially when you consider the weight of the sword and the shield that must also be carried by the muscles of the arms and shoulders. When the support belt is well cinched, over half of the weight of the chain shirt is transmitted to the hips, and is thus much easier to bear. The thickness of the belt also helps distribute the force of any blows that may fall on the lower torso, as the rigidity of the belt itself is backed by the chain mail under it.

If one considers the relationship of the protective belt and the body armor it is worn over, many similarities can be seen in this relationship and that of truth and right action. Truth makes right action easier to bear, and acting in a correct fashion aides in being truthful, as nothing need be covered up by a lie. Where there has been a transgression by poor action, or a lie is told, we are often left naked and unprotected by the true nature of what we have done or said. In effect, we have a hole in our spiritual armor. As the Breastplate represents right action or "righteousness," symbolically this represents that truth supports right action and sustains it. Isn't it easier to be Righteous when you are well girt in TRUTH? When one is surrounded by truth, are they not beyond reproach? Without its protection, isn't one vulnerable to attack and ridicule? To be well covered in truth symbolically covers our soft underbelly or that part of our being without other support. Think of the many political and public figures of today who are not being seen surrounded in the light of truth, and what this does to our confidence in them when truth is shed on them.

When a professional soldier wears a protective belt, it would often be reinforced with bits or plates of metal and would help protect the lower ribs in addition to the kidneys. Mercenaries, highwaymen, and brigands would often encrust their protective belts with jewels. This served as a sort of advertisement of their worth and prowess. It was practical and not uncommon for the belt to be layered with shingles of coinage. There are many examples of entire body armor made of coinage. It was certainly a simple way of keeping up with ones money! This concept, to make armor with coinage, adds a new twist to today's expressions such as "protected by one's assets," or "to put one's money to work for oneself." In the medieval period, armor such as this was truly a prize to gain in combat if one could overpower the wearer. I am sure it served to spur the defensive actions of the owner considerably as well. Spiritually this can be taken to show the value of truth, and how valuable investing in truth can be. Those things we consider valuable today are things of worth which expire or erode with time. With this in mind, consider how valuable God's Truth is. *^{5}For the LORD is good; his mercy is everlasting; and his truth endureth to all generations.* **Ps. 100:5.** *^{1}O praise the LORD, all ye nations: praise him, all ye people. ^{2}For his merciful kindness is great toward us: and the truth of the LORD endureth for ever. Praise ye the LORD.* **Ps. 117.**

What can be more valuable than the price of a man, or the price of freedom? For those whom the price is paid, be it a ransom paid to gain freedom from captivity, or a redemption price paid to liberate one from slavery, it is worth the world. With this as a measure, consider the following scripture, and do read it in your Bible, for it relates specifically to a sort of bondage or slavery. *^{31}Then said Jesus to those Jews which believed on him, If ye continue in my word, then are ye my disciples indeed; ^{32}And ye shall know the truth, and*

the truth shall make you free. **Jn. 8:31-32.** To know God's truth is to be made free from bondage to sin and worldliness.

Spiritually, what can be more fitting to represent that protection for our most sensitive and vital areas but Truth? Truth is often referred to as being felt in the guts, and as truth is the ultimate spiritual cleanser, it is fitting we envision being girt by truth to serve as protection for those areas of our body which themselves serve to purify and cleanse our body. When worn as protective armor, a belt as armor covers the kidneys-and as the kidneys are the body's purification centers, the Spiritual symbolism of this is beautiful. The kidneys are the organs responsible for the purification of the blood by removing toxins from our blood. This leaves good clean blood (the "Pure Bloods" of olden days were referred to as "Blue Bloods." They had clean blood lines of heritage. There was no outside breeding into their bloodlines. Their lineage was pure. Perhaps you know someone today you would call by this.). Blue-blood is non-oxygenated blood. It is blood that has served its purpose, and is returning to the heart and lungs to be charged with oxygen again so it may once more serve to clean and feed our body. Blood only turns red when exposed to or carrying oxygen. It is blue-blood that courses to your heart and then your lungs to receive the life-sustaining essence of life for your body.

The oxygen carried in the blood is used to exchange with the toxins found within the tissue of the body and allow the toxins to be carried away in the blood to the kidneys for removal. The oxygen carried in the blood may be seen symbolically to represent the Spiritual Truths, which must be carried in our blood to seek out the toxins in our body. These toxins may be viewed as the residue of sin. The Spiritual Truth being carried in the blood would be responsible for removing this residue of sin, and allow for their purging. **[6]*Then flew one of the seraphims unto me, having a live coal in his hand, which he had taken with the tongs from off the altar: [7]And he laid it upon my mouth, and said, Lo, this hath touched thy lips; and thine iniquity is taken away, and thy sin purged.* Isa. 6:6-7.** From this scripture may the efficacy of truth be seen.

In a certain regard, our kidneys may be seen as the allegorical "confession center" of the body. Confession is the act by which we purge the residue of sin from our body. This is made possible by the Spiritual Truth which is at work in our bodies to make us clean again.

***⁵I acknowledged my sin unto thee, and mine iniquity have I not hid. I said, I will confess my transgressions unto the LORD; and thou forgavest the iniquity of my sin. Selah.* Ps. 32:5. *¹⁶Confess your faults one to another, and pray one for another, that ye may be healed.* James 5:16.**

Bear in mind, spiritually, it is in the blood that the Spirit or "soul" of a creature is to be found. As an analogy, our blood may be taken to **be** "Spiritual Truth." In a sense, it is Spiritual Truth coursing through our body, much as blood, which serves to seek out the poisons or residues in our bodies left behind by sin, our ultimate contaminant. God's Spiritual Truth then carries these poisons out of our body through our "confession center," our kidneys. It is here the poison of sin is removed, having been purged by God's Truth. Once this is done, we are again Blue Bloods, restored or cleansed in God's eyes. ***By mercy and truth iniquity is purged: and by the fear of the LORD men depart from evil.* Prov. 16:6.**

There is a term that has been used specifically to identify a natural born American. I am sure we have all at one time heard the expression, "Red-Blooded American." While the bloodline of most Americans may not allow them to be called "Blue-Bloods" in the traditional sense, the symbology of referring to Americans as "Red-Blooded" is interesting. The term generally defines a revolutionary, or a radical. It is the true "Red-Blooded Americans" who, historically speaking, have a tradition-or rather blood carried drive-to hunt down corruption and evil in society or "high places" so as to make it possible for true freedom and liberty to survive. Allegorically speaking, this can be related to removing corruption or poison from a political system or society. If nothing else, the two terms "Blue-Blood" and "Red-Blooded" in an allegorical sense, certainly seem fitting for the purpose of reflection upon the purpose of Truth as our spiritual armor.

Think of the many applications of using Truth to gird oneself in the spiritual sense. Protecting the loins with truth may be taken to speak of fidelity, or honesty in regards to one's sexuality or sexual activity. A man or woman found to be indiscriminate, unfaithful, or untruthful in regards to their fidelity or sexuality, will suffer in many different ways from this form of untruthfulness. If this aspect of one's being is not covered in truth and honesty, a man may suffer a social form of castration: that being the loss of trust, or in a general sense the loss of "a part of his masculinity." A woman seen as untruthful in this regard, or being wanton, will typically suffer a social stigma of a different nature. Her character takes a brand somewhat differently than a man. "Loose," or "slut" are typical brands placed on a woman of indiscreet behavior. In effect the end result is the same for the individual concerned. By not protecting this very vulnerable and sensitive part of one's person with truth, castigation and social castration are typical results. This occurs because of the lies which typically follow an act of indiscretion. *...[14]they commit adultery, and walk in lies...* **Jer. 23:14.**

The third general type of belt to be discussed is best thought of as the belt worn externally during the "Age of Plate Armor." In later periods of history, when the soldiers wore plate armor, the external belt was relegated almost exclusively to supporting the soldiers side arms. In regard to the Spiritual Armor of God, the Warrior's sidearm is described as the "Word of God." While this will be discussed in detail in chapter eleven, it will suffice to say here allegorically that Truth supports God's Word, and often God's Word itself is often referred to as "God's Truth" or "God's Law." We are to understand from the scriptures Truth forms the bedrock of understanding and leads to wisdom, the very thing we are encouraged to allow guide our path in life. *From your precepts I learn wisdom, so I hate all deceptive ways. Your word is a lamp for my feet, a light on my path.* **Ps. 119:104-5.** *But you delight in sincerity of heart, and in secret you teach me wisdom.* **Ps.51:6.** *Any of you who lacks wisdom must ask God, who gives to all generously and without scolding; it will be given. But the prayer must be made with faith, and no trace of doubt, because a person who has doubts is like the waves thrown up in the sea by the buffeting of the wind. That sort of person, in two minds, inconsistent in every activity, must not expect to receive anything from the Lord.* **James 1:5-7.** This relationship between Truth and God's Word is just another example of how the spiritual principles of our Armor of God work to support each other. This integration is remarkable, and is found to operate between each piece of armor.

The symbol of truth being so closely tied to a weapon relates truth to a function that we normally do not associate it with. Truth alone may be used as a weapon. In this function, it can serve very well. Truth is well suited for the task as a weapon for it always strikes home, is undeniable, and is unstoppable when presented. You may not generally think of truth in use as a weapon, but after all, Truth is used to combat lies and deceit, is it not? We even have a phrase to describe the cold reality of being *confronted* by Truth: "To get slapped in the face by the Truth of the Matter," "The Truth slapped him in the face like a belt," or "The Truth struck as a cold glass of water." Often, when caught in a lie, Truth is capable of making cold chills run through one's body.

As an interesting aside, consider most belts are made of leather, sometimes reinforced with metal. Unlike other pieces of armor, the belt required a different kind of care and upkeep. Rather than to prevent rust, care was to prevent dry rot. This is interesting if one considers a lie or being untruthful as a type of corruption, which affects the armor. Think of a lie as forming a spot of rust on one's armor. Although a lie, or rust, cannot affect the truth, its effects can be as devastating on every other aspect of one's armor as unchecked rust can be to real armor. Ultimately a lie, when thought of as rust, has the capacity to rust, or corrupt, every aspect of a Warrior's armor, including his only true fashioned weapon: The Word of God. If one is found to be dishonest in one's words, one cannot expect to use the Word of God to secure God's promises or bolster up oneself with God's might in time of need. Such a person can be discredited to the point that any witnessing he may perform would be discounted or disavowed. There is no shortage of formerly well renowned evangelists whom have been discredited by the discovery of their lies. It is significant that most of their indiscretions have been sexual in nature. *Liars' lips are a cover for hatred, whoever utters slander is a fool.* **Prov. 10:18.** *The honest have their own honesty for guidance, the treacherous are ruined by their own perfidy.* **Prov. 11:3.**

Consider this: When confronting someone we find to be a liar, what other adjective usually comes to mind? I am sure you have heard: "Why you *lying*, rotten so-and-so..." Just as the effects of a lies may act to blemish and corrode the other pieces of our spiritual armor, the substance of truth, *as our spiritual armor*, can be made to ROT or evaporate as a consequence of a lie. Whereas a leather belt is subject to rot and decay, one of the greatest qualities of Truth is, Truth endures to all generations for it is unchanging. A lie can never change or destroy the truth, only the protection we would otherwise have is destroyed. Knowing TRUTH can never be blemished or destroyed allows us to see it serve as a stable bastion to rest and rely on. *For the LORD is good; his mercy is everlasting; and his truth endureth to all generations.* **Ps. 100:5.** *For his merciful kindness is great toward us: and the truth of the LORD endureth for ever. Praise ye the LORD.* **Ps. 117:2.** *He that speaketh truth showeth forth righteousness: but a false witness deceit...The lip of truth shall be established for ever: but a lying tongue is but for a moment.* **Prov. 12:17, 19.**

When fully armed for combat, the author wears three belts about his waist, each serving separately to protect, support, and reinforce the body. All three of these features are found served by Truth in a Spiritual sense. *All scripture is inspired by God and useful for refuting error, for guiding people's lives and teaching them to be upright. This is how someone who is dedicated to God becomes fully equipped and ready for any good work.* **2 Tm. 3:16-17.**

Let us now take a look at some specific scriptures which deal with these characteristics of Truth as Spiritual Armor: Supportive, Protective, and Strengthening. Remember to follow some of the references in your own Bible and see what other scriptures you can find to support these aspects of truth and how it can serve us as our Spiritual Armor. This first scripture below has various elements of all three characteristics of truth in it. See if you can identify them yourself.

Ps. 25:2, 5, 8, 15, 19-21 *But in my trust in you do not put me to shame, let not my enemies gloat over me. Encourage me to walk in your truth and teach me since you are the God who saves me. Integrity and generosity are marks of Yahweh for he brings sinners back to the path. Permanently my eyes are on Yahweh, for he will free my feet from the snare. Take note how countless are my enemies, how violent their hatred for me. Unless you guard me and rescue me I shall be put to shame, for you are my refuge. Virtue and integrity be my protection, for my hope, Yahweh, is in you.*

These next couple of scriptures speak specifically of the supportive nature of Truth and what devoting oneself to Truth can gain us individually.

Ps. 119:153-161 *Look at my suffering and rescue me, for I do not forget your Law. Plead my cause and defend me; as you promised, give me life. Salvation is far from the wicked, for they do not seek your will. Your kindness' to me are countless, Yahweh; true to your judgments, give me life. Though my enemies and oppressors are countless, I do not turn aside from your instructions. The sight of these renegades appalls me; they do not observe your promise. See how I love your precepts; true to your faithful love, give me life. Faithfulness is the essence of your work, your upright judgments hold good for ever. Though Princes hound me unprovoked, what fills me with awe is your word.*

Jn. 8:32 *...you will come to know the truth, and the truth will set you free.*

Ps. 30:11-12 *You have turned my mourning into dancing, you have stripped off my sackcloth and clothed me with joy. So my heart will sing to you unceasingly, Yahweh, my God, I shall praise you forever.*

This last scripture does not specifically speak of "truth" in the way it has been presented in the previous scriptures you have just read. Bear in mind when we sing praise and glory in thanksgiving to God, the *Truth* of the matter is He will lift up our spirits and console the bereaved. This is perhaps not as obvious an aspect as some of the more apparent ones discussed herein, but that just goes with the territory. We are discussing matters of spiritual concern, and it is not always the obvious that must be considered. As you can see, Truth is very liberating. It allows joy to reside in the heart. Truth will keep one from the assaults of those who find fault, for Truth is irreproachable.

It can be difficult sometimes to separate the supportive and protective aspects of Truth as Spiritual Armor. The next two scriptures have this dual nature to them, sharing both the attributes of support and protection:

Ps. 33:1-3, 16-22 *Shout for joy, you upright; praise comes well from the honest. Give thanks to Yahweh on the lyre, play for him on the ten-stringed lyre, Sing to him a new song, make sweet music for your cry of victory.*

A large army will not keep a king safe, nor his strength save a warrior's life; it is delusion to rely on a horse for safety, for all its power it cannot save.

But see how Yahweh watches over those who fear him, those who rely on his faithful love, to rescue them from death and keep them alive in famine.

We are waiting for Yahweh; he is our help and our shield, for in him our heart rejoices, in his holy name we trust; Yahweh, let your faithful love rest on us, as our hope has rested in you.

2 Cor. 6:4-10 *...So [that] no blame may attach to our work of service; but in everything we prove ourselves authentic servants of God; by resolute perseverance in times of hardships, difficulties and distress; when we are flogged or sent to prison or mobbed; laboring, sleepless, starving; in purity, in knowledge, in patience, in kindness; in the Holy Spirit, in a love of affection; in the word of truth and in the power of God; by using the weapons of uprightness for attack and for defense: in times of honor or disgrace, blame or praise; taken for impostors and yet we are genuine; unknown and yet we are acknowledged; dying, and yet here we are, alive; scourged but not executed; in pain yet always full of joy; poor and yet making many people rich; having nothing, and yet owning everything.*

As a clear and present reminder specifically of the protective nature of Truth, keep these scriptures in mind. These are just a taste of the wonderful and revealing scriptures that teach us of the protective nature of Truth.

Ps. 91:4 *...His truth shall be thy shield and buckler.*

Ps. 138:7 *Though I live surrounded by trouble you give me life—to my enemies' fury! You stretch out your hand and save me, Yahweh will do all things for me.*

Jn. 17:15-17 *I am not asking you to remove them from the world, but to protect them from the Evil One. They do not belong to the world. Consecrate them in the truth; your word is truth.*

Ps. 37:14-15 *Though the wicked draw his sword and bend his bow to slaughter the honest and bring down the poor and the needy, his sword will pierce his own heart, and his bow will be shattered.*

Just as the various characteristics of a Warrior all lend to support and strengthen each other, so it is with the protective nature of God's Spiritual Armor for us. The last attribute derived from Truth is strength. Now as it is difficult at times to separate that which serves to protect us and how it strengthens us, the next scripture has both of these elements in it:

Ps. 18:32-34 *This God who girds me with strength, who makes my way free from blame, who makes me as swift as a deer and sets me firmly on the heights, who trains my hands for battle, my arms to bend a bow of bronze.* Reread this scripture and dwell upon it for a few minutes.

This God who girds me with strength... This speaks of truth which is being worn, and as such, shows itself to be directly supportive in the nature of a belt worn to brace oneself for arduous work. It is the next phrase which clears this point up very well: ***...who makes my way free from blame.*** Here is a sense of the belt securing loose garments as mentioned earlier as a function of a girding belt. Blame may interfere with the course of action a Warrior would like to take, much in the same way as loose clothing or untied shoes may hinder one's movement. This is coupled with the virtue of blamelessness, and as mentioned earlier, this is a consequence of truth. When one is blameless, he is free to pursue any action. ***...who makes me as swift as a deer and sets me firmly on the heights.*** Here can be found an element not only of the liberating effects of truth, but relative to the supportive nature truth has in regards to the first piece of spiritual armor discussed; that which is worn on the feet. In the previous chapter, we looked at how that piece of armor affords a Warrior a solid stance and position of power or strength. An important aspect of our spiritual armor, each piece of our spiritual armor supports and enhances each other piece, a facet which must be pointed out and kept in mind. ***...who trains my hands for battle...***God's truth can prepare us for any situation. ***...my arms to bend a bow of bronze...*** It would take a truly stalwart Warrior to draw a bronze bow. Here we find it is God himself who gives us the strength to accomplish this feat. The entirety of **Psalm 18** deals with the might of God, and it is generally handled in the light of truth, or certainty. I find this to be very revealing and foundational, and encourage the reader to read the Psalm in its entirety.

Let us now venture into the scriptures and find a couple of scriptures that serve to show specifically how Truth may serve to strengthen us. I personally find these to be powerful quotes to remember. They can bolster the Spirit, and remind us of our duty:

Ps. 45:3-5 *Warrior, strap your sword at your side, in your majesty and splendor advance, ride on in the cause of truth, gentleness and uprightness. Stretch the bowstring tight, lending terror to your right hand. Your arrows are sharp, nations lie at your mercy, the King's enemies lose heart.*

Ps. 18:39 *You have girded me with strength for the fight, and bent down my assailants beneath me, made my enemies retreat before me; and those who hate me I destroy.*

1 Pet. 2:1-2 *Rid ourselves, then, of all spite, deceit, hypocrisy, envy and carping criticism. Like new-born babies all your longing would be for milk-the unadulterated spiritual milk—which will help you to grow up to salvation...*

2 Sam. 22:40 *You have girded me with strength for the fight, bent down my assailants before me...* See what other scriptures you can uncover which deal with the benefits of truth. I know you will find many references as I found over 200 myself.

Always remember to don Truth as a garment of protection, for without it you may find yourself wandering in the dark, unprotected, unsupported, ranged about by the enemy, with no refuge to turn to, and no strength to put up a fight.

Once acceptance of God's Truth/Law/Word is confirmed and confessed, we become free to act without fear of reproach and with a light and joyous heart. Our ways will be supported and protected from lies and deceit, and all we say and do are strengthened and supported by the untarnishable Truth!

Upon reflecting on the aspects of Truth as Spiritual Armor, there are several characteristics that prove helpful in reinforcing and developing the principles, which will imbue the Warrior with the protections derived from Truth. The characteristics of being Trustworthy and Strong are both enhanced by the protection derived from Truth, and likewise these two characteristics are helpful to maintain truth about oneself. These characteristics support and develop the spiritual armor and vice-versa. In addition, the characteristics of Honor and Justice both serve to support the principles of Truth.

Honor is brought upon oneself when identified as being an adherent to Truth. It is easy to fall prey to the ease and temptation of telling a falsehood, but to stand up and be courageous enough to admit to the truth is an honorable thing. Generally speaking, when we tell a lie, we are protecting our ego in some fashion. This is directed out of a sense of self image and pride. *[12] For the sin of their mouth and the words of their lips let them even be taken in their pride: and for cursing and lying which they speak. Ps. 59:12. [21] For from within, out of the heart of men, proceed evil thoughts, adulteries, fornications, murders, [22] Thefts, covetousness, wickedness, deceit, lasciviousness, an evil eye, blasphemy, pride, foolishness...[23] All these evil things come from within, and defile the man. Mrk. 7:21-23.* If it were not for our ego and pride, telling the untarnished truth would be easy.

As "God's Truth" is often equated with "God's Law," can there be any question *truth* and *justice* are integrally bound and supportive of each other? If Justice is not founded on Truth and Mercy, there can be no standard to rely on, no justice regularly issued. As the laws of man have departed in a large measure from the fundamentals of the laws of God, it is easy to see the injustice of our current system of "Law" or "Justice." Trying to make sense of many of the rulings and decisions being made in our courts today clearly shows what happens when justice and truth aren't written with the same words, or in the same book. Justice is determined on truth, and it is impossible to have one without the other. A legal system in which truth is ignored is anything but Just. The very heart of our justice system relies on those testifying to "tell the truth, the whole truth, and nothing but the truth..." and it is upon what is accepted as truthful statements that justice is meted out. When lies are presented, no just judgment may be forthcoming. *[14]Justice and judgment are the habitation of thy throne: mercy and truth shall go before thy face.* **Ps. 89:14**. *[14]And judgment is turned away backward, and justice standeth afar off: for truth is fallen in the street, and equity cannot enter.* **Isa. 59:14.**

From the above, it is obvious it is that what we ***Do*** and ***Say*** that is contrary to truth, which can bring the most reputable of characters to ruin. It takes a certain type of character to tell the truth. Likewise, telling the truth and learning from it will develop the type of character that is supportive of the truth, the true character of a Warrior.

The next chapter will deal specifically with actions we may take, and just as we may be prompted to lie because of pride, we often do certain things out of a sense of pride. Pride can effect not just what we ***Say*** or ***don't say***, but it can effect what we may ***Do*** or ***not do.*** Pride certainly can get us in a lot of hot water, if not just complicate our lives. Read over the following scriptures to see what God has to say specifically about pride and its pitfalls. They will show a relationship between pride and lies, as well as wisdom and prudence.

Prov. 8:13-14 *Fear of Yahweh means hatred of evil. I hate pride and arrogance, wicked behavior and a lying mouth. To me belong good advice and prudence, I am perception: power is mine!*

Prov. 11:12 *Whoever looks down on his neighbor lacks good sense; one of intelligence holds his tongue.*

Prov. 16:18 *Pride goes before destruction, a haughty spirit before a fall.*

Prov. 29:23 *Pride brings humiliation, whoever humbles himself will win honor.*

Isa. 16:6 *We have heard about Moab's pride, about how very proud it is, about its arrogance, its pride, its rage, its bravado, which will come to nothing!*

Acting out of a sense of bravado, arrogance or haughtiness may certainly make for putting on a great show, but to act *honorably*, with *justice* and *fairness, speaking the truth*, while not the easy way to act, will certainly gain the respect of others. This is what we are to strive for as the true nature of a Warrior in the Army of God.

Truth is a formidable piece of armor for the Warrior in the Army of God! Not only will it serve to support the previous piece of armor- The Willingness and Doing of spreading God's message of Peace, but Truth will also serve to support, protect, and strengthen correct action, or Righteousness. This is the next piece of armor we shall don in route to total preparation and the topic of the next chapter:

"The Breastplate of Righteousness"

Chapter 8

The Breastplate of Righteousness

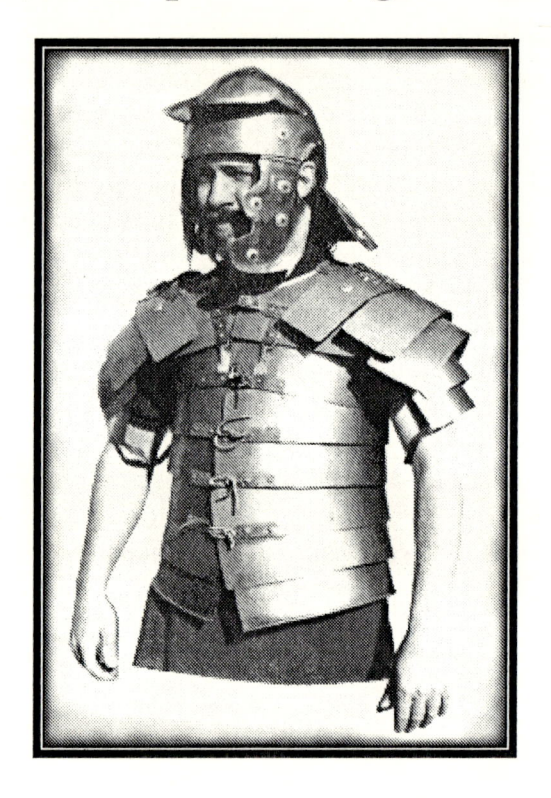

Eph. 6:14 *So stand your ground, with truth...and uprightness a breastplate...*

Isa. 59:17 *^{17}For he put on righteousness as a breastplate...*

2 Tm. 3:16-17 *All scripture is inspired by God and useful for refuting error, for guiding people's lives and teaching them to be upright. This is how someone who is dedicated to God becomes fully equipped and ready for any good work.*

Once the feet are shod, and the undergarments and protective padding belted in place, a warrior next begins donning the body armor. This part of his armor is the most often thought of distinguishing feature of a knight of olden days that sets him apart from the common foot soldier. Throughout history, various forms of protective garments were fashioned and worn by combatants, including simple hides, treated leather, and elaborately stitched multiple layers of cloth and padding. None compared to the formidable encasement worn by the professional warrior, or knight. The armor worn on the body of the Roman Legionaries and the knights of medieval Europe was sufficient to defend against the most sophisticated weapons of their day and all but the most deliberate and determined attack.

As we have seen in our study of the character of the Warrior, there is a certain dependability of behavior, which can be expected from a well-trained Warrior. This is presented clearly when the Warrior is acting right, or correctly, displaying the full manifestation of his training. Uprightness or righteousness may be defined as acting in a just, upright manner; doing what is right, virtuous, and doing what is morally right. The full character of what constitutes uprightness or righteousness may be better understood if one considers nobility, fairness, honor, saintliness, devotion, reverence, religiousness, godliness, spirituality, zeal, and worshipfulness as well in the definition. *For us, right living will mean this: to keep and observe all these commandments in obedience to Yahweh our God, as he has commanded us.* **Deut. 6:25.** *Your saving justice is for ever just, and your Law is trustworthy. Though anguish and distress grip me your commandments are my delight. Your instructions are upright forever, give me understanding and I shall live.* **Ps. 119:142-44.** You see, there are a lot of requirements upon one to be truly upright or righteous. The absolute measure of uprightness is ultimately God's Law. It is the measuring stick by which our actions are measured. If this measurement is all one concerns themselves with, there can be but one result; we are all found to fall short, to be imperfect and sinful. The scriptures tell us that none are righteous; therefore, all are unworthy of God's grace (**Rom. 3:20**). This being the case, you may wonder how any of us may claim this Breastplate of Righteousness to serve as any sort of defense. We all accept that we are imperfect creatures in God's eyes due to sin. However, through confessing our sinful nature and accepting God's love and grace through the sacrifice of His Son, our righteousness in His eyes is no longer a question. ***No distinction is made: all have sinned and lack God's glory, and all are justified by the free gift of His grace through being set free in Christ Jesus.* Rom. 3:23-24.** Accordingly, what is of concern here is our acting correctly, or acting "right." For a Warrior, this can be interpreted as simply following orders. To use this as an analogy, to do what one is told and expected to do, is, in a sense, acting right. As a Warrior in God's army, we are expected to do as we have been instructed. As we will see, acting in such a manner, we become a "shining example" for all to see by our uprightness and the shining Breastplate we shall spiritually display.

    The scripture quoted at the opening of this chapter from **2 Timothy** is specific in telling us that God's recorded word provides us with a ready-made checklist against which our actions may be compared for correctness. As the scriptures are helpful in refuting the errors one may make, they most certainly are valuable as a guide from which proper action may be learned. The manner in which God would have us behave is certainly no secret, and the rewards for acting in the proper fashion are specifically discussed in the first part of this book and throughout the remaining chapters. While it may be impossible for us to perfect our every action, we can rest assured that as long as we try and do our best, and acknowledge our failings, God's grace will provide for our "perfection." In a sense, it is every proper and good action we take which will be noted and rewarded, while our failings are forgiven when we try our best in a contrite spirit to do better, and ask for forgiveness. God is a truly loving and forgiving King to serve. *[32]And be ye kind one to another, tenderhearted, forgiving one another, even as God for Christ's sake hath forgiven you.* **Eph. 4:32.**

    Bearing the above in mind, that God's Law finds us all sinful, God's grace makes up for our deficiency, and we will derive the protection of the Breastplate of Righteousness by our right actions. We may not be perfect, but some times, we get it right, and when we do, we are imbued with the protection of this piece of armor—"The Breastplate of Righteousness." The more fully we embrace correct action and act accordingly, the more absolute and habitual will be the Breastplate's protection. Just as a warrior of days gone by were accustomed to wearing one, and would not think to engage in combat without it, so it is with our spiritual protection derived from our correct actions. As our correct behavior becomes habitual and unconscious, we become more accustomed to the burden of our Breastplate of Righteousness. This type of conditioning is not that much different than the conditioning one would have in wearing such a weighty piece of armor daily.

In the proceeding chapter, we concerned ourselves with the "Belt of Truth" and how it relates to the belts worn by a warrior for protection. Among the purposes served by a belt, it was pointed out how belts have been useful in binding the under padding and garments of warriors throughout the ages. In much the same way as a belt serves in conjunction with the body armor, let us take a moment, and consider the importance of truth in serving correct action.

Historically, warriors typically wore a padded or quilted garment, a gambeson, under their main body armor. This under-padding was necessary to absorb the blunt trauma they would otherwise be subjected to from the blows they received. Severe bruising and even broken bones can be sustained even while wearing armor, and it is the padded undergarment that principally served to protect the warrior from this trauma. While it was generally completely unseen, this padding was of utmost importance for total protection. For this reason, it was an integral component of the body armor worn for protection. Historically, soldiers of a low station in life typically considered themselves fortunate to have even this simple gambeson to wear as protection. Spiritually, it must be remembered that a belt, or truth, is essential to hold this primary level of protection, our correct action, together. For a Warrior of God, just as a belt may be required to hold the undergarment tight about the body, truth is essential to bind those actions which are measured for correctness or to display righteousness. When one considers that truth is equated to God's Law, and it is God's Law that serves as the measure by which our actions are judged, there exists a strong relationship of support between the two-truth and righteousness. Often it can be seen in our lives and the lives of others that as one departs from the way of truth, one's actions will depart from correct, or righteous, action.

Two very simple mental images should serve to help visualize the relationship between truth and right action. One is to imagine the body covered with all the belts and straps required to hold all the armor on, without the armor. This, spiritually, could be seen to represent what honesty and truth would afford us without any action being taken in light of truth. The protection of the belts and straps alone is incomplete. The other image to fix in your mind is how all the various pieces of armor would be secured to the body without the many belts and straps required to hold them in place. This spiritually displays how difficult it is to act rightly without truth. As can be seen from this analogy, it is just as difficult to support correct action without the application or utilization of truth, as it is impractical to wear armor without securing it without belts. In either case, it is when truth and correct action are combined that we derive the total package of protection. One without the other is almost pointless.

To carry the analogy a step further, consider this: when completely suited for combat, the author will have secured twenty-one various straps and belts to make fast all of his armor.[*] In the spiritual sense, this is a simple reminder of how every correct action has a truth associated with it, and each particular truth would typically be pointless without some action to support or associate with it. Recall how belts, or truth, support the armor for our feet-our willingness and doing. These analogies are important to stress the interwoven nature of the individual pieces of our spiritual armor. While each individual piece affords some degree of protection, when worn in conjunction with the other pieces of armor, protection becomes complete.

---

[*] I personally find a quiet significance in the number of belts and straps required for the proper securing of my armor. Heraldry, or the study of the symbols used in the identification of a knight by his coat-of-arms, is an integral and fascinating study related to medieval history and the history of warriors and knights throughout the past. In heraldry, certain significance is placed on objects and symbols used in association to a person or lineage. Not that I am by any means promoting numerology, but iconologically and symbolically speaking, the number 3 relates to God as the Trinity, and 7 is considered to be His Holy number. As my armor has 21 straps and belts, I find a constant reminder of His presence in each and every piece of my armor. 21 is a simple multiple of 3 and 7, 3x7=21. Magnify His name! **Ps 30:3** *³O magnify the LORD with me, and let us exalt his name together.*

This should call to mind the relationship of mutual support and amplification that exists between the various aspects of character and character development as discussed in part one. Just as each piece of our spiritual armor shows an integral relationship with the other pieces of our spiritual armor, our armor and our character are intimately woven together, one supporting the other. I hope the mental pictures drawn of historical armor help to clearly show this relationship of each piece of armor, one for another. Bear these relationships in mind as you reread the various sections of this book, and you will begin to see how they function and show themselves in your life and the lives of those around you.

The relationship between our character and our spiritual armor merits closer inspection. Certain weaknesses in character will carry with them certain "missing links," or points of vulnerability, just as if the person where missing a piece of armor. With just a little practice, various aspects of this interrelationship between character traits and our spiritual armor will become obvious. Concerning correct action, the weaknesses expressed by a lack of complete character development will become apparent, and timely action, or rather the lack thereof when called for, will at times become glaringly obvious. Just remember that, as none of us is perfect, we will all show some shortcomings. Do not be *too* hard on yourself. It is for those moments of imperfection, or character flaws that we observe, for which we must develop an understanding and compassionate nature. This is not just to be shown towards others, but us as well. Our Lord Christ's perfect patience and forgiveness serve as a model for us. The point is there is a direct association between the development of good character traits and the manifestation of strong spiritual armor.

Now let us look into the scriptures for a closer look at what a breastplate is and how it may serve to protect us in both a physical and spiritual sense.[†] If you were to do a word study concerning the breastplate as referred to by Paul in his letters to the Thessalonians (**1 Thess. 5:8**), you would find the word Paul uses refers to a specific

---

[†] While the word "breastplate" typically refers just to that armor worn on the torso, in a general sense it may be taken to refer to the armor covering the torso, and limbs.

Philip Paul Sacco

type of body armor known as a coat-of-mail, or "mail hauberk." The original language written by Paul reveals the specific armor. This form of body protection, chain mail, was typical for a Roman Legionary and remained a very prominent form of body protection throughout the Middle Ages, primarily for the landed lord or wealthy soldier. In Paul's time, the sight of mail-clad Romans would have been as accepted and typical as a policeman carrying a gun is viewed today. In virtually every area of the world, this form of body protection is found when the required metallurgical skills are acquired by society.

Chain mail was fashioned by linking metal rings together in such a manner that, typically, each ring was linked to four other rings of iron. In this way a metal garment, or "shirt," could be woven. In its simplest form, the mail-shirt was sleeveless and waist-long. In later periods, full sleeves' complete with mittens were added, and the overall length was extended in some cases to the knees. Complete mail-stockings could be additionally worn, as was a mail-hood to cover the entire head and neck. To round out the complete armored harness or "kit" as a suit of armor may be referred to, a helmet was typically worn in addition to the chain mail cover, in most cases. This brings us today the phrase "cap-a-pie," or head to foot, in describing the total coverage of the armor (And today, we refer to *insurance* as coverage—not in my book).

Chain mail is a type of armor known for its tremendous flexibility, and that it did not appreciably impede the movement of the soldier wearing it. Mobility and flexibility are a welcome benefit with this form of armor, even when considering the additional weight which it entailed carrying. A mail-shirt serves as exceptional protection against edged weapon attacks, as well as protection from projectile attacks, especially when worn in conjunction with a leather jerkin or "jack."

During the time of the Romans, chain mail was the absolute epitome of body protection. Wearing a chain-shirt would afford a warrior a high level of invulnerability to bodily harm from anything but the most determined attacks. Generally, a mail-clad warrior was most susceptible to severe puncturing weapons and heavy cleaving weapons, such as an axe or a crossbow bolt. Even full plate-armor gains little protection from such weapons, although protection from blunt trauma is increased with the wearing of plate. The plate tends to transmit the blow over a larger area than would otherwise be experienced as in the wearing of chain or leather. If worn without the under-padding, the plate armor will still allow the shock of a blow to transmit into the body, potentially causing injury in itself.

Paul uses the analogy of mail to describe how Faith and Love are meshed together to become a garment of protection...***let us put on faith and love for a Breastplate...*** **1 Thess. 5:8.** Just as faith and love lie close to our hearts, chainmail lies very close to the contours of the body, hugging the body with its weight. It therefore moves very well with every movement of the body, just as love is to be incorporated in our every act. This is analogous to the fact that acting right is a requisite placed upon the entire body. Just as the chainmail would conform to the body, every action of the body needs to conform to right action. Symbolically this tells us that right action should fit to every part of our being, conforming to our every motion and action we take. Spiritually faith and love are to direct our every action.

In **Eph. 6:14,** Paul uses a different word, one meaning a cuirass or close-fitted armor plate (see also **Isa. 59:17**) in referring to the breastplate. A cuirass was a custom crafted piece of armor that was typically fashioned for an individual at a considerable sum. While the front-piece of the cuirass, the simple breastplate, could be worn alone, it was typically worn secured to a backplate. In this way, the entire torso was completely encased in this close fitted armor. A cuirass would generally include both pieces as a unit, not unlike the bulletproof vests worn today by police and the military. The cuirass was reserved for persons of military honor or rank among the Legions of the Romans. In later periods of history, the wearing of full plate armor was typically reserved for landed Lords and knights. In addition to serving to protect the noblemen of the day, limiting the use of such protection served another purpose as well...it made sure that the Nobles did not have to worry about an uprising of an armored peasantry. When armored nobles fought with a code of conduct, warfare was engaged safely, rather than embracing the dangers of armored rabble in open warfare.

As pointed out above, chain mail was a type of armor renowned for its flexibility. When we think of a knight wearing full plate armor, we tend to think of him as being rather limited in mobility and flexibility. This, however, is an unfounded image, due chiefly to the impressions we have from the stylized armor and movement of knights as depicted in Hollywood movies. Quite to the contrary, a well-made suit of full plate armor would have more flexibility in each joint than the body it covered. The drawback of full plate in comparison to chain mail was principally in the bulkiness of the armor. Whereas chain mail would lie close to the body, plate armor was often contoured to maximize its protection, and by the Late Medieval Period, plate armor became quite heavy and grossly contoured.

By recalling the body armor of the Greeks or Spartans, a very clear picture of a cuirass may be called to mind. In its earlier forms, the cuirass was typically fashioned with full anatomical features such as a navel, muscles, and nipples, and was often embellished with bronze, silver, or gold inlays, or appliqués depicting various motifs. The motifs may depict scenes of glorious past victories, or the likeness of pagan gods worshiped at the time. Whether the primary material comprising the cuirass was specially treated leather or metal made little difference in the degree of embellishment it sported. If made of leather, the cuirass would typically be colored a bright color such as white or gold to stand out from the background. The metal cuirass was typically highly polished to attract attention. This also helped to single out the leaders during the confusion of combat.

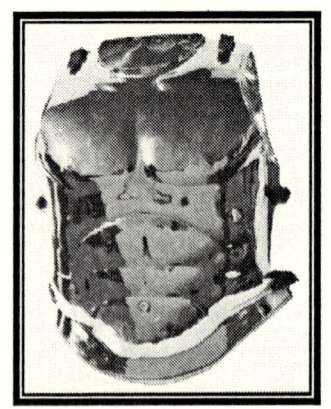

In this sense, you might say that the spiritual breastplate of right action makes one a "shining example." As the cuirass was also a symbol of the Legionary Centurions, or leaders, the figure in this armor during battle was conspicuous and was looked to for guidance and as an example to follow, if not literally, at least ideologically. The wearing of such a noticeable and bold piece of armor would make conspicuous acts of valor easier to identify, as would be acts of a lesser character. The thought of wearing a cuirass of this type would serve to remind the wearer that his every action was on review, and his actions would serve as an example to those he led. A leader in the forefront was sure to express a bold and most noble presence on the battlefield for the benefit of his men, as well as to enhance his reputation.‡ To do otherwise was certain to tarnish one's character. Besides, to fall in the face of the enemy while acting in a valorous way was to ensure one's place in "the hall of the gods" for many pagan societies such as the Romans and the Vikings.

The fictitious Klingon Spiritual Warlord, Kahless, from the popular sci-fi television series *Star Trek: The Next Generation*, summed this sentiment up quite nicely. If I may quote, "Today is a good day to die!" served as his battle cry. To be slain by the enemy while acting in anything less than a heroic fashion was to be condemned to the underworld of woe not just by this fictitious race, but many races throughout history. The Romans, Vikings, Celts, and warriors of Islam are among the most notable historical examples of a warrior race following this belief. This shows even historically speaking, correct action has always been intimately related to the actions of a warrior. Considering that when Paul wrote the words

---

‡ The visible presence of a unit's leader in the front lines instilled great confidence among the soldiers under his command. His visibility was a tremendous asset. If a leader was rumored to have fallen in combat, or worse yet, deserted the battle, the effects of the news could be devastating for a unit. For this reason, on many occasions, a popular commander may have had one or two subordinates wear similar armor to confuse the enemy, and increase the confidence of his troops. On some occasions, a charismatic commander has been recorded as being in two places at the same time performing acts of heroism. This, no doubt, was due to subordinates wearing similarly distinguished armor so as to protect and preserve the true leader.

relating righteousness to a breastplate predated the medieval Celts, the Vikings, and "the Age of Chivalry," I find his choice of words insightful as well as significant. His words truly speak a Spiritual Truth.

The breastplate serves primarily to protect the heart. Now consider the symbology of correct action, or righteousness, serving as our spiritual armor to protect the heart. The scriptures tell us all actions come from the heart. Any truly significant endeavor must be acted upon with a heartfelt desire or drive to be accomplished. For this reason the endeavor may be said to be rewarding, as a sense of accomplishment is achieved. A Warrior must act out of Rightness-of-Heart, always acting out of heartfelt **truth**, not personal desires, or for a personal vendetta. We must endeavor to wage battle for only the purest of reasons and for a higher cause. It is this simple heartfelt "belief" which we will contrast with the "Believing" which comes after we have subjected our heartfelt belief to our will and thinking.[§] Acting in this way, our spiritual breastplate will serve to protect our heart, our center of action.

A story of a Japanese Samurai following the code of "Bushido" (or the Japanese code of chivalry) may illustrate this principle. A samurai, having witnessed the murder of his Lord, is sworn to avenge his Lord's death. He spends his entire life hunting the murderer. Finally, after many trials and tests, he is able to corner and confront his Lord's murderer. At the last moment, while the samurai is poised for the final blow, the murderer spits in the samurai's face in defiance. The story goes that the samurai warrior slowly lowers his blade, and sheathing it, turns and walks away. You see, in that instant the samurai's heart is filled with a personal insult and he is no longer able to complete his mission for lack of rightness. If he were to dispatch his Lord's murderer in that moment, he could not say his motivation was pure, for his actions would be confused with personal impulses.

Whether one considers a chain mail hauberk or a metal cuirass, the breastplate typically covered the front, sides and back of the body. This offered protection to the vital areas from all directions, from

---

[§] This is a concept, which we shall look at a little more closely in the next chapter.

attacks both seen and unseen. You see, Right-Action, when supported by Truth, creates a veritable bastion of protection.

In its construction and design, a plate armor breastplate would not significantly inhibit the free motion of a warrior. While its weight was easily endured on the body, chaffing and pinching are typical complaints, as the rigid armor tends to rest and rub on specific areas of the body such as the shoulders and hips. The undergarments minimized these effects. The gambeson, which I spoke of earlier serves to prevent chaffing as well as to absorb the impact of blows. Spiritually, this can be taken to represent that a little correct action (the gambeson), supporting and underlying all of our actions, may reduce the amount of "chaffing" or difficulty experienced by acting right. It is much more difficult to do what should be done when there has been no support for such action previously. As an analogy, a known thief who turns to an honest life is much less likely to be accepted as an honest man than a person who has always acted honestly.

Whereas a chain hauberk was form fitting and easily cinched to the body, plate armor typically relied on hanging from some point of attachment. When the weight is evenly distributed around the body, the armor is easier to bear and less difficult to carry. In comparing the manner in which the weights of chain mail versus plate armor is borne, consider carrying a weight of 100 pounds. When carried in a backpack, chaffing of the shoulders and hips is typical. This type of discomfort is found in a poorly fit set of plate armor. Now consider carrying the same weight distributed in pockets over the entire body. The same weight may be borne, but as it is evenly distributed over the body, it is more easily carried, and there are no pressure points to produce sore spots. This is more typical of the fit found when wearing chainmail. Symbolically, when correct action is borne by our whole being, no "sore spots" develop. As the entire body supports each action, the burden of continued action is reduced, and continued correct action is easier to maintain.

Through all the ages, the one type of attack that could compromise body armor, regardless of whether it was plate or chain, has been a stabbing or piercing type of attack, as from a pick, or a powerful projectile weapon such as a crossbow. Even today, the greatest challenge for body armor worn by the President, law enforcement officers, or our armed forces is a simple stab from an ice pick. While today's body armor is capable of protecting one from bullets, a simple stab from an ice pick still renders a bulletproof vest defenseless. It is this type of pointed or thrusting attack that is most dangerous to the body of a Warrior, for the armor is susceptible to penetration from a hard penetrating attack. In simple terms, a pointed, direct attack can render harm.

Ironically, it is the pointed, or "needling" attack that causes us the most pain in our heart. It is the cruel slurs directed at our character, our heart if you will, which may offer us harm. It is common for this simple, yet effective, means of attack to be experienced in everyday life. It is easy to fall into the trap of attacking someone's character or their actions with callused and mean spirited words when inflamed by emotion. As adolescents, this is perhaps the first lesson we learn to apply offensively. We all learn to use harsh words early in our development, whether it is as a defense mechanism, or a tool used to "put someone in their place." I am sure anyone who has raised children has experienced the pain and agony of harsh words as the adolescent learns to define their self-image. The term "the terrible teens" sums up this situation very nicely.

Understanding just how damaging our words can be should direct one to consider what one says to a brother or sister in Christ. Because of our years of unchecked, unthinking use of this damaging attack so often plied in retaliation, we often hurt those we love with our words. Remember, character is not taught, but rather learned by actions taken. Lashing out at others when hurt or frustrated is often simply the sign of an ill-disciplined character. It takes control and discipline to guard what we say to others. To do so shows character; character displayed by choices made and expressed, character shown through right action. Acting in this fashion represents a shiny surface of our breastplate of righteousness and serves to protect one from the very type of action refrained from, or not condescended to. Remember the expressions: "Two wrongs don't make a right," and "I won't descend to your level to make a point." Both of these expressions concern themselves with a choice of action, or right action, and show character when acted upon in daily life. When we lash out at others with harsh or cruel words, we often incite the other person into a defensive mental posture and we may suffer a retaliation. After all, it is one of the first methods of behavior we learn. If we temper what we say, and speak accordingly, we increase our chance of being met with, at worst, a neutral stance. "Like breeds like."

As mentioned at the opening of this chapter, the scriptures provide us with a clear set of guidelines that should stand as rules for living and acting "uprightly," or right. The following scripture quote contains several admonitions concerning how we are to speak and act towards one another: *Intellectually they are in the dark and they are estranged from the life of God, because of the ignorance, which is the consequence of closed minds. Their sense of right and wrong once dulled, they have abandoned all self-control and pursue to excess every kind of uncleanness.*

...you were taught what the truth is in Jesus. You were to put aside your old self, which belongs to your old way of life and is corrupted by following illusory desires. Your mind was created on God's principles, in the uprightness and holiness of the truth.

So from now on, there must be no more lies. Speak the truth to one another, since we are all parts of one another. Even if you are angry, do not sin: never let the sun set on your anger or else you will give the devil a foothold.

No foul word should ever cross your lips; let your words be for the improvement of others, as occasion offers, and do good to your listeners...

Any bitterness or bad temper or anger or shouting or abuse must be far removed from you—as must every kind of malice. Be generous to one another, sympathetic, forgiving each other as readily as God forgave you in Christ. Eph. 4:18-19, 21-26, 29-32.

From the above scripture, we see that by keeping our minds open we may leave ignorance behind and find closeness with God. "To keep one's head in the sand," so to speak, develops a dulled sense of right and wrong, and invites one to become involved in pure self-indulgence. This certainly does not remind you of anyone in particular, does it? We are reminded that our minds are created on God's principles, and adhering to this, correct action or uprightness will follow. We can rise above our own selfish desires by putting our mundane concerns aside and concerning ourselves with the principles instilled in us by our Creator. Reread the last half of the above scripture and note the many examples of ways in which we defile ourselves by that which we speak. We are told elsewhere in the Bible that it is, in fact, that which comes from our mouth which makes us unclean. ***Can't you see that whatever goes into the mouth passes through the stomach and is discharged into the sewer? But whatever goes out of the mouth comes from the heart, and it is this that makes someone unclean.* Matt. 15:17-18.** It is from the heart that evil intentions come and take form in murder, adultery, fornication, theft, perjury, and slander to name a few (**Matt. 15:19**).‖

Remember, it is the Breastplate of Righteousness that we are to train ourselves with for protecting our heart. If this is not done, all the evil actions listed above are clearly allowed to usurp our goodness and give us the appearance of anything but upright. I do not find this coincidental. Consider the above in addition to the simple statements to be found in the following Psalm. Remember that God's principles are instilled in all of us, and it is recognizing this and acting in accord with it which allows His principles to operate in our life.

Ps. 15 *Yahweh, who can find a home in your tent, who can dwell on your holy mountain? Whoever lives blamelessly, who acts uprightly, who speaks the truth from the heart, who keeps the tongue under control, who does not wrong a comrade, who casts no discredit on a neighbor, who looks with scorn on the vile, but honors those who fear Yahweh, who stands by an oath at any cost,*

‖ I find no lack of coincidence between the removal of God's simple presence in our schools and the lack of control and common sense shown by so many of our children today. What role models are our children exposed to that teaches them values and standing up for principles? More typically they are trained to be "good little boys and girls, and rather than learn to deal with their adolescent energy, they are doped up with Ritalin and Prozac. 'Just stay in the box and do what you are told' exemplifies the type of conditioning our children receive today, rather than teaching them to become freethinking individuals. This form of education sounds more fitting of a Communist or Socialist society rather than a free society directed by the Laws of God. Is it any wonder what we find being produced more often than not is a society of "cookie-cutter characters" rather than individuals molded by a sense of God?

who asks no interest on loans, who takes no bribe to harm the innocent. No one who so acts can ever be shaken.

From the above we find a simple assurance that by acting in accord with God's principles, we fortify our resolve. When you think of becoming unshakeable, think of a fortress carved out of solid rock. No amount of shaking will bring it down. When we become unshakeable, we also become fearless, a secondary attribute of acting right. When we know our actions are beyond reproach, we can stand by our actions with absolute resolve. This may sound to be a simple thing, but when looking around at the people we have daily dealings with, how long must we search before we find anyone standing up for any ONE principle, let alone a set of them? This is a major problem in our society today. Far too few people show willingness, or the ability, to take a stand and act on their convictions, if they have any convictions at all.

A lot has been said about how we are to act, but lest we gain a big head by our virtuous actions it is brought to our attention that we are not to call attention to our manifest actions. A simple directive about boastfulness is in order to keep us straight on this point. *As the scripture says: If anyone wants to boast, let him boast of the Lord.* **1 Cor. 1:31.** Boasting of one's wonderfulness and virtuous action is self centered and self serving, and is contrary to the character of Humility.

The next scripture shows that in acting right, we gain wisdom and understanding. Some issues of moral concerns are brought up, and how we are to act when confronted by situations such as these are made clear. When we do so, we have certain assurances in return for our efforts.

Prov. 2:9-22 *Then you will understand uprightness, equity and fair dealing, the paths that lead to happiness. When wisdom comes into your heart and knowledge fills your soul with delight, then prudence will be there to watch over you, and understanding will be your guardian to keep you from the way that is evil, from those whose speech is deceitful, from those who leave the paths of honesty to walk the roads of darkness: those who find their joy in doing wrong, and their delight in deceitfulness, whose tracks are twisted,* *and the paths that they tread crooked. To keep you, too, from the woman who belongs to another, from the stranger, with her wheedling words; she has left the partner of her younger days, she has forgotten the covenant of her God; her house is tilting towards Death, down to the Shades go her paths. Of those who go to her not one returns, they never regain the paths of life.*

Thus you will tread the way of good people, persisting in the paths of the upright. For the land will be for the honest to live in, the innocent will have it for their home; while the wicked will be cut off from the land, and the faithless rooted out of it.

So you see, it is simple understanding that keeps us from the pitfalls of those who follow the way of the enemy. Understanding helps make our appropriate actions clear when confronted by situations such as those above. There is no need to pause and consider what is the correct thing to do. In our hearts, we understand the deceptions for what they are and we are not taken in by them and led astray. We simply know better. Always remember we are engaged in war, a spiritual war, and the path to our ultimate defeat is typically a very enticing one. As understanding lights our path, we can think of the darkness of our past way of acting to be behind us, and we may move forward as children of the light. The army we serve in is "The Army of Light." As such, consider every action you make as though it were in broad day light, for all to see. When thought of in this way, that our actions may be scrutinized by anyone as if illuminated in the full light of day, a different choice of action may come to mind as being prudent. Prudence is mentioned in **Prov. 2** above as watching over us, and this is a good way to think of it. The following scriptures are a perfect compliment to the above situations, and spell out clearly how our conduct may best be classified.

1 Thess. 5:5-9 *No, you are all children of light and children of the day: we do not belong to the night or to darkness, so we should not go on sleeping, as everyone else does, but stay wide awake and sober. Night is the time for sleepers to sleep and night the time for drunkards to be drunk, but we belong to the day and we should be* *sober; let us put on faith and love for a breastplate, and the hope of salvation for a helmet.*

Rom. 13:12-14 *The night is nearly over, daylight is on the way; so let us throw off everything that belongs to the darkness and equip ourselves for the light. Let us live decently, as in the light of day; with no orgies or drunkenness, no promiscuity or licentiousness, and no wrangling or jealousy. Let your armor be the Lord Jesus Christ, and stop worrying about how your disordered natural inclinations may be fulfilled.*

"And stop worrying about how your disordered natural inclinations may be fulfilled." That says it all. You see it is our **natural inclinations**, which if not controlled, will simply turn our life into that of an animal, rather than a thinking, caring, concerned and loving **Human-being**. Generally, it is our natural inclinations that form the root of many of our sins. Paul addresses this quandary well in this verse: *We are well aware that the Law is spiritual: but I am a creature of flesh and blood sold as a slave to sin. I do not understand my own behavior; I do not act as I mean to, but I do things that I hate. While I am acting as I do not want to, I still acknowledge the Law as good, so it is not myself acting, but the sin which lives in me. And really, I know of nothing good living in me- in my natural self, that is—for though the will to do what is good is in me, the power to do it is not: the good thing I want to do, I never do; the evil thing which I do not want-that is what I do. But every time I do what I do not want to, then it is not myself acting, but the sin that lives in me.*
So I find this rule: that for me, where I want to do nothing but good, evil is close at my side. In my inmost self I dearly love God's law, but I see that acting on my body there is a different law which battles against the law in my mind. So I am brought to be a prisoner of that law of sin which lives inside my body. **Rom 7:14-23.**

Now this is not to give us an excuse to do what we know we should not do, knowing what is asked of us by the Law. What Paul was saying was *Identify* that part of our nature as sin, and deal-with-*It* as we know we should. The closing two verses in **Rom. 7** and the opening of **Rom. 8** address this dilemma head on, *What a wretched man I am! Who will rescue me from this body doomed to death? God-thanks be to Him-through Jesus Christ our Lord.*

So it is that I myself with my mind obey the law of God, but in my disordered nature I obey the law of sin. Rom. 7:24-25.

Thus, condemnation will never come to those who are in Christ Jesus, because the law of the Spirit which gives life in Christ Jesus has set you free from the law of sin and death. What the Law could not do because of the weakness of human nature, God did, sending his own Son in the same human nature as any sinner to be a sacrifice for sin, and condemning sin in that human nature. This was so that the Law's requirements might be fully satisfied in us as we direct our lives not by our natural inclinations but by the spirit. Those who are living by their natural inclination have their minds on the things human nature desires; those who live in the spirit have their minds on spiritual things. And human nature has nothing to look forward to but death, while the spirit looks forward to life and peace, because the outlook of disordered human nature is opposed to God, since it does not submit to God's Law, and indeed it cannot, and those who live by their natural inclinations can never be pleasing to God. You, however, live not by your natural inclinations, but by the spirit, since the Spirit of God has made a home in you. Rom. 8:1-9.

Paul completes this very instructive lesson by explaining exactly how this works. *Indeed, anyone who does not have the Spirit of Christ does not belong to him. But when Christ is in you, the body is dead because of sin but the spirit is alive because you have been justified; and if the Spirit of him who raised Jesus from the dead has made his home in you, then he who raised Christ Jesus from the dead will give life to your own mortal bodies through his Spirit living in you.*

So then, my brothers, we have no obligation to human nature to be dominated by it. If you do live in that way, you are doomed to die; but if by the Spirit you put to death the habits originating in the body, you will have life. Rom. 8:9-17.

This reiterates what was mentioned earlier in this chapter concerning our actions as measured by the Law, and how God's grace redeems us. *...give yourselves to God, as people brought to life from the dead, and give every part of your bodies to God to be instruments of uprightness; and then sin will no longer have any power over you-you are living not under law, but under grace.* **Rom. 6:13.** Basically, we are reminded we serve an allegiance that is above our personal desires. This is a principle supported by the aspect of our devotion to a higher cause. You see, we as Warriors of God have a higher mark to measure our actions by. It goes beyond conscience: it is simply, *"Rightness..."*

Job 29:14 *Uprightness I wore as a garment, fair judgment was my cloak and my turban.*

Acting in accord with this higher principle comes with its rewards. This next section of scriptures will enlighten us as to the benefits of correct action beyond simply "being a good person." They will also help define somewhat the protections and securities provided by the Breastplate of Righteousness beyond our actions being above reproach.

Ps. 37:16-17 *What little the upright possesses outweighs all the wealth of the wicked; for the weapons of the wicked shall be shattered, while Yahweh supports the upright.*

Prov. 21:15, 21 *Doing what is right fills the upright with joy but evildoers with terror. Whoever pursues uprightness and faithful love will find life, uprightness and honor.*

1 Tm. 6:11-12 *...You must aim to be upright and religious, filled with faith and love, perseverance and gentleness. Fight the good fight of faith and win the eternal life to which you were called and for which you made your noble profession of faith before many witnesses.*

In effect, when we act according to God's Law, we inflict terror upon the enemy, shattering all their weapons and leaving them defenseless, while being supported by the hand of God—not bad for a demonstration of power and protection to be found within the

Breastplate of Rightness. Therefore, this acting enriches our life with the promise of joy, love, perseverance, gentleness, and eternal life. These are wonderful blessings; I know you will agree.

Equally as clear as the blessing derived from right action is the condemnation, that will be leveled upon evildoers. The following scriptures point this out as well as some more of the rewards for those acting right:

Prov. 12:21 *No harm can come to the upright, but the wicked are swamped by misfortunes.*

Prov. 11:8 *The upright escapes affliction, the wicked incurs it instead.*

Prov. 10:16 *The wage of the upright affords life, but sin is all the wicked earns.*

From these scriptures, we can see that adversity will beset those acting out of wickedness. Indeed, there is one definite end for those who follow the way of evil. The following two scripture quotes point this out very clearly:

Prov. 12:28 *In the way of uprightness is life, the ways of the vengeful lead to death.*

Prov. 10:2 *Treasures wickedly come by give no benefit, but uprightness brings delivery from death.*

These are clear assurances. There are few things as certain, nor as definite, as death. As an additional note, **Psalms 34** and **37** contain an interesting historical point of interest. When battles were lost, the vanquished were often held for ransom or they faced the grim prospects of a slow and tortured death, or starvation in the dungeons of the victors if ransom was not forthcoming. In our spiritual war, we have no fear of being captured and placed in this situation as our King will always come to our aid.

Ps. 34:21-22 *But to the wicked evil brings death, those who hate the upright will pay the penalty. Yahweh ransoms the lives of those who serve him, and there will be no penalty for those who take refuge in him.* **Ps. 37:39-40** *The upright have Yahweh for their Savior, their refuge in times of trouble; Yahweh helps them and rescues them, he will rescue them from the wicked, and save them because they take refuge in him.*

In addition, the following scriptures carry immense protection and assurances, if we hold on to them:

Isa. 32:17 *...and the product of uprightness will be peace, the effect of uprightness being quiet and security forever.*

Ps. 37:1-4 *Do not get heated about the wicked or envy those who do wrong. Quick as the grass they wither, fading like the green of the fields. Put your trust in Yahweh and do right, make your home in the land and live secure. Make Yahweh your joy and he will give you your heart's desires.* From this we can rest assured that we will always be provided our hearts content, and will live securely without fear.

1 Tm. 4:7-10 *Train yourself for religion. Physical exercise is useful enough, but the usefulness of religion is unlimited, since it holds out promise both for life here and now and for the life to come; that is a saying that you can rely on and nobody should doubt it. I mean that the point of all our toiling and battling is that we have put our trust in the living God and he is the Saviour of the whole human race but particularly of all believers.* Religion in this context is taken to mean the devotion and desire of things of God, and the entire Christian attitude.

Matt. 6:33 *Set your hearts on his kingdom first, and on God's saving justice, and all these other things will be given you as well.*

Rom. 1:17 *...As it says in scripture; Anyone who is upright through faith will live.*

Rom. 4:8 *How blessed are those to whom the Lord imputes no guilt.* Therefore, acting in a right fashion imputes no guilt.

2 Tm. 2:22 *Turn away from the passions of youth, concentrate on uprightness, faith, love and peace, in union with all those who call on the Lord with a pure heart.*

Right action serves to shore up the defenses of the heart, the center of our emotions, the target of deceit and lies. Guarding our center of being, our heart, can be just as difficult as not acting in a manner to wound another. This is due to the simplicity of the careless word, an unthinking act. The very nature of unthinking behavior makes for a very dangerous attack, and defending against it can be a daily endeavor because of its prevalence in our interactions today. This simple form of lashing out is easily perfected in our youth, and is as difficult to change in our behavior as it is to defend against. *[29]Let no corrupt communication proceed out of your mouth, but that which is good to the use of edifying, that it may minister grace unto the hearers.* **Eph. 4:29.**

Right action is as impervious to ridicule as telling the truth. When one's actions are right, they are easily explained and often beyond reproach. The honesty, integrity, and nobility of the action is plainly obvious and beyond reproach. Rather than having to face the frontal assault of the enemy when one is acting rightly, the right acting Warrior is often beleaguered with backbiting, deception, and rumors. The enemy knows better than to attempt a frontal assault against one acting rightly, and they are forced to move under concealment, or in a hidden fashion.

This should present no trouble for a Warrior, however, for even if surrounded and hounded by an enemy not wanting to recognize right action, our Heavenly Father always sees what we have done. The above scriptures contain many of His promises to us for acting consistent with His will. Any enemy offering attack against our rightness will see their weapons smashed.

In wrapping up this chapter, let us consider some of the aspects of character, which assist the fortification, and the development of right actions in a Warrior and the development of the Breastplate of Righteousness. If you study the scriptures above, you will find devotion, nobility, honor, justice, discipline, and strength represented in the actions which comprise righteousness.

Devotion to the principles of God's Law is fundamental to becoming a Warrior in His army. Having this higher code of conduct as a model for our behavior gives us a model of behavior that is above the normal inclinations of our normal sinful nature. As our self-interest will not direct us, we will be singled out as following a higher calling. By following a code of conduct such as directed by God's Law, our actions are noted as following a higher dictate than self interest and there is a certain Nobility seen in acting in such a way. When we perform an action for the right reason—in the right way—there is typically someone else who benefits from our correct and selfless deed. When others see the merit of our selfless acts, it is felt in a very ennobling way. Acting in this way not only elevates us, but most importantly those others effected as well.

When we allow our devotion to God's cause to direct our actions, we pay Honor to God by following His tenets. This represents a sort of "homage" paid to God by those actions taught to us to be desirable to God. When we have taken to heart the precepts of God, bearing in mind His saving justice and we act in accordance with them, we display our conscious effort to follow instructions, thereby honoring His precepts, and displaying discipline.

In many of the above scriptures, Justice is tied to right action. I hope that true Justice follows a higher code of conduct than self-interest. In acting in a right manner, we perform actions in accordance with a higher code of conduct as defined by God's Just and Holy Laws. Character of integrity will be noted in acting correctly, doing what is just, and following what we know to be true.

Discipline and Strength are both displayed by taking actions that may not be the simplest course, but the best or most correct in light of our instruction. By following the dictates of discipline and good training, and acting with true strength of character, we display a moral inclination towards the correct path and not the easiest form of action. Speaking out against injustice or confronting the ill actions of another when they have harmed an innocent or defenseless person are simple examples of how strength and discipline may be shown. When displaying these character traits, it is also typical to be placed in a position to bear the brunt for someone else's error. Rather than lash out in defense when we know we have done no wrong, we are in a position to point the error out without recrimination. Apologies typically follow.

Often, we are placed in a position to know an act was performed with the best of intentions, although the results may not show this to be the case. By studying those individuals involved in an incident such as this, it becomes clear one person typically has their feelings involved and they are not in an intellectual position to consider what may have been intended. When we are caught up in our emotions, it is extremely difficult to think clearly and rationally. This is a difficult position to understand when we assume we have been the subjects of the direct actions of another. It is important to be able to set our emotions aside and objectively look at any situation we find ourselves in. To do so shows strength and discipline. This is not to say we should ignore how we feel. Think of our feelings and emotions as a temperature gauge or barometer. Our emotions function for much the same reason as the temperature gauge on our car. When we notice the gauge showing the engine to be running hot, it is time to stop and see what may be wrong. Often it is the thermostat that is stuck or not operating properly resulting in an indication there may be a problem with the engine while this is not the case. Our feelings and emotions operate in much the same way. They indicate something may be wrong, and we are well advised to "take a look under the hood" and see what the facts of the matter are. It may be that our feelings are misplaced, or we may have assumed to understand the actions of another and pass judgment without having all the facts. Assumptions can lead to some rather unpleasant results. Remember this mnemonic device: When we assume something, we oft-times make an "ass"—out of "you" and "me"—"Ass-u-me."

We have been given a heart to feel with and a brain to think with. The two organs can not function in any other capacity. Let them each work in the proscribed manner, and many actions of impulse may be avoided. While our brain and heart each have a specific function, it is important to let them work in conjunction with each other. Always keep tabs on why you make the decisions you do, and be aware of how you feel because of them and the actions of others.

Bearing God's Law in our heart is a great way to protect our heart and encourages the development of our "Breastplate of

Righteousness." This ensures our security, well-being, and serves to disarm our opponents. In a larger context, it should be borne in mind that the fully developed "breastplate" can be taken to cover the entire body, inclusive of the limbs, in one complete suit of protection.

Chapter nine will involve the crowning of our body armor with:

"The Helmet of Salvation"

Chapter 9

The Helmet of Salvation

Eph. 6:17 ...*Take the Helmet of Salvation*...

Isa. 59:16-17 ...*So he made his own arm his mainstay, his own saving justice his support...on his head the helmet of salvation.*

1 Thess. 5:8 ...*let us put on faith and love for a Breastplate, and the hope of salvation for a helmet.*

This chapter brings us to our last piece of armor worn directly on the body: our helmet. The helmet covers a significant area for defense: our head. Unchecked physical attacks to the head can obviously impart severe harm, but in spiritual warfare, we often fall prey to nonphysical attacks. The head is the center for our ***mind and our thoughts***. Spiritual attacks upon our head, or our mind, include attacks upon our way of thinking, rationalizing, or our understanding and beliefs. Often a successful attack of this nature will render a Warrior unable to act, or paralyzed to action by indecision or ***FEAR***. Our mind is the center of our **Fear**, and an area most susceptible to attack. Remember: ***Fear*** is nothing more than **F**alse **E**xpectations **A**ppearing **R**eal. The principal defense against fear is a staunch belief in God. *[1]The LORD is my light and my salvation; whom shall I fear? The LORD is the strength of my life; of whom shall I be afraid? [2]When the wicked, even mine enemies and my foes, came upon me to eat up my flesh, they stumbled and fall. [3]Though an host should encamp against me, my heart shall not fear: though war should rise against me, in this will I be confident.* **Ps. 27:1-3.** Attacks, which render false expectation real, come in many guises. Typically, this type of attack is made through false appearances, deception and lies, the only real weapons the enemy is equipped with. Another attack of fear is self-doubt, or falsely believing we know the outcome of our potential actions before we ***act***. Think of it this way, Fear is a four-lettered word. We should act toward fear as we would any foul four-letter word; shun it as foul.

The principal goal of a helmet from any period of history would be to provide protection for the top and sides of the head. The typical Roman helmet had several additional design advantages over not just the helmets of its time, but helmets in general throughout all of history. These specific characteristics serve to distinguish a Roman helmet from helmets of any other period of history, placing them in a classification almost distinct unto themselves. Several hundred years after the demise of the Roman Empire, the same elements found in the early Roman helmets were revived in later creations. Since its earliest form of construction, the Roman helmet was forged from a single piece of bronze or steel depending on the ore available in the region and the skill of the metal-smith. While it required a great deal of expertise to fashion a helmet in this way, the resulting helmet was rendered stronger by design, as any riveted or jointed areas prove to be weak spots in armor. In its creation, the Roman helmet was superior to all contemporary designs of its day, and all but the finest of helmets constructed later in history.

Other than the technique of its construction, three principle design characteristics typify a Roman helmet. One is the wide flared skirt that protrudes from the rear of the helmet. This characteristic has been preserved in the traditional fireman's helmet of today. The flanged piece affixed to the rear of the helmet provided the Roman Legionaries with protection from blows to the rear of the neck and upper shoulders in addition to protection from falling debris. The second prominent characteristic of a Roman helmet, in all but the earliest of examples, is a metal brow, or rim, which was affixed to the front of the helmet's foreplate. This brow prevented a blow from falling directly on the front of the helmet, thus dispersing the blow's impact over a greater area. This would aid in preventing damage to the helmet, to say nothing of the wounding or death of the soldier from a well directed and penetrating blow. The third characteristic of a Roman helmet, which sets them apart from other helmets, can be found in the creatively designed hinged flaps, which served to protect the face and chin. What began as a simple metal skullcap saw the later addition of these cheek pieces that became identified as being typically Roman.[*]

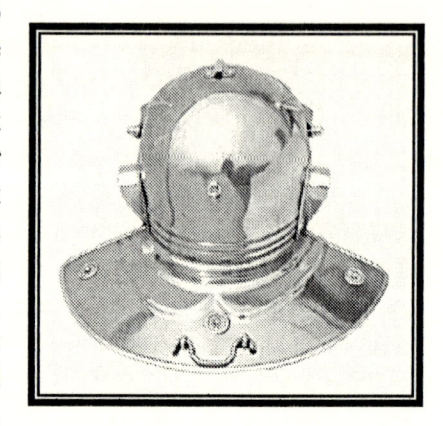

Later, these supplemental flaps saw the addition of iron cross braces across the face and on top of the helmet to offer more protection for the head and reinforcement for the helmet.

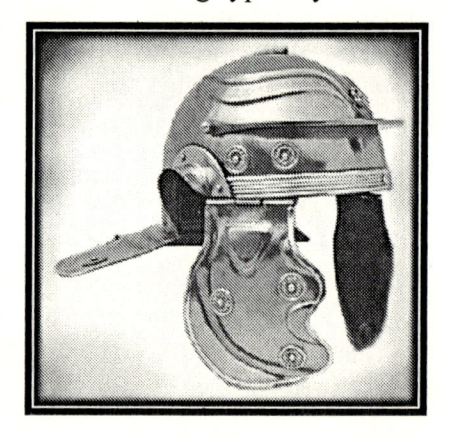

As time progressed and the skills and weapons of the day dictated, the eventual development of the full enclosing helmet was imminent. The

---

[*] Among all helmets of antiquity, there is one other characteristically unique design that I find as interesting and singularly distinctive as this. It is the faceplate of the Japanese Samurai Helmet. This faceplate rested directly upon the face and was a separate piece from the rest of the helmet being held in place by ties and the fit of the helmet itself. They were lavishly decorated and typically featured a fully detailed face, usually sporting a grimace, and sometime bearing teeth.

helmet's ingenious padding and strapping made them impossible to remove in combat and additionally provided the all-important absorption of impact from blows. Being in this way so well secured to the head, unless one was trapped helplessly on the ground and therefore prey to being pried open or impaled through the eye-slots, the head was very well protected from all but the most crushing of blows, or attacks from piercing types of weapons such as a pike or crossbow bolt.

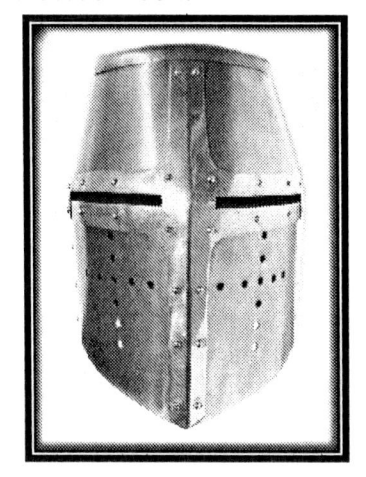

Let us refer back to an expression I spoke of earlier in the book, "The idle mind is the playground of the devil." In a simple way, what this means is the devil will entertain himself by distracting your attention to those things which bring him enjoyment. If you do not keep your mind at work on thoughts of the Lord's work, the devil can preoccupy your thoughts. I assure you that in the end, what he finds entertaining, you will not. For this reason it must be remembered that salvation is all enclosing, as is a helmet for combat. Once we are able to grasp with our mind and understand the full encompassing nature of salvation, this belief will be as sound as bedrock. It will fill our minds and allow the Warrior to be undisturbed with the state of his salvation. **[47]*The LORD liveth; and blessed be my rock; and exalted be the God of the rock of my salvation.* 2 Sam. 22:47.** Think of it, when do we typically question things as concerned with our life, when our mind is idle. Can you say you have never questioned your state of salvation? This serves as an example of how readily the enemy is provided with the opportunity to use our idle thoughts or doubts to weaken our defenses. Unless we stand on the bedrock understanding of God's redemption of us by the sacrifice of His Son, our doubts, and personal concerns provide a regular avenue of weakness or potential attack by the enemy. Any questions or concerns about God making good on His promises should normally be seen as a waste of energy, for who would question God and His Word…Quite simply, any of us would; it is part of human nature. It is part of what we are. It has a lot to do with the simple fact that fundamentally, none of us is worthy of God's grace, as discussed in the last chapter. It is the measure of His perfect love for us that allows any of us to stand in His presence. For the simple fact that none of us can truly fathom the unfathomable, we are at times beleaguered by random, unsolicited, destructive thoughts. These can and will often be used against us. It takes an act of volition to declare and profess your belief in the saving redemption found in Jesus Christ. ...*if you declare with your mouth that Jesus is Lord, and if you believe with your heart that God raised him from the dead, then you will be saved. It is by believing with the heart that you are justified, and by making the declaration with your lips that you are saved.* **Rom. 10:9-10.**

The enemy's assault on our mind can typically begin when we entertain thoughts we consider self-analytical, or reflective. Thoughts along this line will typically begin with three words that generally lead us from reflection to remorse, or regret. These three words which tend to lead one to confusion or feelings of misgiving are: **Would've, Could've,** and **Should've.** When we use these three words, we sap ourselves of our confidence and our ability to make decisions. We use these three words in reflecting on our past actions, and we typically end up questioning our actions, or our ability to perform useful service. Such is the power of words. These three words are used specifically to compare a result or action to an alternative result, which in retrospect, may be more desirable. It seems obvious, but I will guarantee, you have never considered it before. Reflect on those times you have used these three words, and I am sure you will remember many instances in which you ended up questioning your abilities, or confidence in some respect. This is not constructive. These three words lead to the denial of possibilities. When we use them, we tend to not bother trying, and rather than practicing doing, we become inactive and ineffective. Don't quit when you should ***"Keep on keepin' on!"***

Correcting this very destructive thought process is a simple matter. Using the three regretful words tends to lead one to dwell on actions, which cannot be taken back, wasting the present when we ***are*** able to ***take action***. This wasted mental anguish robs us of the present, and undermines our ability ***to take action*** when we need to. When discussing things of this nature one day with a friend of mine,

Tracy Wilson, he quoted a very simple adage, "I only concern myself with today, the present. I don't dwell on yesterday or tomorrow-these are "God's Days" and dwelling on them drive men crazy." Tracy's simple statement carries a lot of wisdom. It is in concerning ourselves with the issues and matters at hand, the present, which will lead to constructive action. It is fundamentally much more powerful to say *"I will," "I will not," "I did,"* or *"I did not"* do this or that. It is also more fun to think in this more positive way, and these statements lead one to take constructive action. Considering what one *will do*, is empowering and directing. The word fundamental can be looked at in this way..." fun-(*for*)da-mental." It is fundamentally more constructive to have a positive, forward thinking, goal oriented form of expression, rather than one founded on regrets.

When we feel "our plate is full," and we become concerned for the choices we face, worry and trepidation often fill our minds. Just remember, "Even the longest journey begins with a single step." No matter what the obstacle we need to overcome, when we focus on the moment, we realize that however insurmountable it may appear, any obstacle becomes a series of grips and handholds, each one bringing us closer to the summit of our dilemma. After all, it was a countless series of small steps that finally landed man on the Moon.

Once we fall prey to regrets and remorse, it is usually not long before we have become sufficiently weakened to spend countless fruitless hours filled with worry. At such times, two simple rules should be called to mind, 1) Don't sweat the small stuff, 2) It's all small stuff. Be a Warrior and think of this-The victory is already ours! We just have to endure the struggle for a short time. [57]***But thanks be to God, which giveth us the victory through our Lord Jesus Christ.*** **1 Cor. 15:57**. When we study the Shield of Faith, we will study the tools essential for conquering two principle weapons of the enemy-fear and doubt, which are closely related to worry. Worry is a stepping stone to fear, and by first understanding how to deal with worry, a lot of fear will be circumvented. When we reflect on past action with regret using the three *"ould'ves,"* we have set a mental trap for our self. When considering possible consequences of our actions, we must remember God is on our side. We must not leave Him out of our considerations. We have been admonished to turn all of our worries and mundane concerns to God. We all have a choice-

"Become a Warrior, or be a Worrier." The two are mutually exclusive. A Warrior filled with worry cannot act as a Warrior must. When filled with the full character of a **Warrior**, *Worry* cannot enter the mind.

Phil. 4:6-7 *Never worry about anything; but tell God all your desires of every kind in prayer and petition shot through with gratitude, and the peace of God which is beyond our understanding will guard your hearts and your thoughts in Christ Jesus.*

Consider this: What have any of your worries ever amounted to or accomplished? How many of your worst fears and worries were ever really materialized? Knowing that we are prone to worry all the time over countless things, it should not be hard to bring some of our worst worries and fears of the past to mind. However, how many of your worst fears of the past can you truly recall? Probably not many, unless they are recurring; it is because they are "shadow monsters" that we cannot remember them. Only our current condition and our immediate concerns of the day are material for our daily worries. A quick and simple immediate cure for moments of worry is to simply give praise to God and thank Him for all we have been blessed with. When we set our mind on the blessings of God, our spirits are raised, and our worries are relegated to the garbage bag they belong in.

Worry follows low, or depressed, spirits. Anything we can do to raise our spirits will eliminate worry, but singing praise to God's power and might, His holy name, will far remove our worry. When in good spirits it is a wonderful time to remember God's blessings. However, when our spirits are low, and we are susceptible to worry and concern, it helps to be more accepting of ones being, and to not dwell on the immediate condition we find ourselves in. When you feel overly burdened, remember these words of our Lord, Jesus: [28]*Come unto me, all ye that labour and are heavy laden, and I will give you rest.* [29]*Take my yoke upon you, and learn of me; for I am meek and lowly in heart: and ye shall find rest unto your souls.* [30]*For my yoke is easy, and my burden is light.* **Matt. 11:28-30.** Share your concerns with Him, He cares and will alleviate your concerns.

When you fill your mind with devotion to God's higher cause, worry and concern take a back seat. Our thinking and understanding are limited when it comes to understanding the timing and plans of God. Set your mind at ease, sit back, and expect the unexpected. When we act in this fashion, we remove the our restraints from God, and allow Him full rein to coordinate and implement His plans. We are instructed to *[7]Ask, and it shall be given you; seek, and ye shall find; knock, and it shall be opened unto you: [8]For every one that asketh receiveth; and he that seeketh findeth; and to him that knocketh it shall be opened.* **Matt. 7:7-8**. A life without worry is a life of blessings and fulfillment. If we dwell on fear, doubt and worry, that is simply all we get more of! Buck up, take courage, and DO that which God directs to be done. When we act in this manner, we *take charge* of the fear which otherwise binds us, and we can then claim the *Victory*, which is already ours. We have been given the victory already; all that remains to be done is for us to claim it. If in our minds we know the victory is ours, **then act like it!** There is true power to be harnessed through positive action and a positive mindset. Try it, you'll like it.

On the greater scheme of things, how can our individual concerns stack up with the stakes of the world? It is the victory over the entire world, which we are guaranteed through our Lord. *[4]For whatsoever is born of God overcometh the world: and this is the victory that overcometh the world, even our faith. [5]Who is he that overcometh the world, but he that believeth that Jesus is the Son of God?* **1 Jn. 5:4-5**. This should help put our worries into proper perspective, and help us recognize Rule 2: "It's all small stuff!" As a Warrior for God, there can be no more specific instruction than that found in the following scripture: *[3]Thou therefore endure hardness, as a good soldier of Jesus Christ. [4]No man that warreth entangleth himself with the affairs of this life; that he may please him who hath chosen him to be a soldier.* **2 Tm. 2:3-4**. You see, being solely concerned with the matter at hand, taking the first step, we keep things simple, and an otherwise overwhelming concern is dealt with easily. Jesus told us specifically how to deal with our daily worries: ***So do not worry about tomorrow: Tomorrow will take care of itself. Each day has enough trouble of its own.*** **Matt. 6:34**.

The Helmet of Salvation serves primarily and most obviously to protect our "head" by spiritually safeguarding our mind against doubt, worry, and fear.[†] As the many questions we may have concerning our state of salvation are due to our mind and thinking process, it comes as no surprise that *Salvation itself* serves to protect the mind. Our salvation comes from our "Head" our Father-God. The scriptures are clear on this point, that we must *Believe* to be saved: **[2]*By which also ye are saved, if ye keep in memory what I preached unto you, unless ye have believed in vain.* 1 Cor. 15:2. [31]*And they said, Believe on the Lord Jesus Christ, and thou shalt be saved, and thy house.* Acts 16:31. [12]*Those by the way side are they that hear; then cometh the devil, and taketh away the word out of their hearts, lest they should believe and be saved.* Lk. 8:12.**

If you consider the point raised in Luke, it also serves to illustrate the interrelated nature of our spiritual armor. In this instance, the breastplate which serves to protect our heart and the helmet which protects our mind. In having the Word of God in our heart, or serving as our breastplate, we additionally don the helmet. An illustration may help make this point better understood. While we generally relate *"belief"* with a heartfelt-realization, or an emotional state which may be served and protected by our spiritual breastplate, our conviction (*Believing, or Belief*) comes from a conscious decision to follow a certain observation, or fact, as our creed. Conviction comes after we have submitted our heartfelt belief to scrutiny and study. In a deeper sense of the word, *"Believing"* comes after we subject our *will* to a decision to follow a tenet or an understanding of faith. Heart-felt belief then becomes a conviction. Think of "Believing" in this fashion. While we tend to refer to a belief as something heartfelt, in a larger sense, when we subject our belief to a conscious decision, it

---

[†] I find an interesting play on words when relating to Salvation. Think of the symbolic representation of "the head." The leader of a coalition or body politic may be referred to as its "head," just as God the Father may be taken to be our "Head." It is by the divine plan of our "Head" that we are provided a way to redemption and salvation, and this is what serves as the spiritual protection for our head.

becomes a conviction, or a—big "B"—Belief.[‡] It is upon this type of settled conviction that salvation may rest in our mind. It is important to understand this point in order to develop our Helmet of Salvation. It makes the difference of a helmet made of jointed plates, or one hammered from one piece of steel.[§]

When we grasp our salvation and devote ourselves to the King, the terms of our life become clear and there is a certain joy in having that understanding. *I exult for joy in Yahweh, my soul rejoiced in my God, for he has clothed me in garments of salvation...* Isa. 61:10. During the late age of Chivalry, it was common to find a knight competing in a joust with his helmet secured rigidly to his breastplate and backplate. Having the helmet fastened in such a fashion added rigidity to one's defense, as the breastplate and helmet were rigidly affixed to each other, making them function more like one piece. When we relate the matters of our heart and actions with the matters of our conviction and devoted will, we create this form of defense about us spiritually, between our helmet of salvation and our breastplate of right action. Right action then supports our belief and convictions, and our convictions direct our actions.

Consider what may have happened to Lazarus after being raised from the dead, had he believed what everyone must have been saying in the room. Everyone knew Lazarus was dead, and when he miraculously awoke, the disbelief must have been extraordinary. Now, if Lazarus had simply believed "you are dead, and have been for three days!" as everyone must have been stating, he would have just laid back down, and by lack of belief in his own experience, died again. The point is not whether or not this would have really happened in the presence of our Lord, but that we must each submit our belief to our own conviction and experience, or observation, otherwise we would believe everything we heard. There are things

---

[‡] It is this form of training which leads to self-change, and when we change on the inside, we can effect change on the outside, or around us.

[§] Either you will follow a uniform and a fully developed belief system or you will put together your belief from separate belief systems and form a "helmet for your salvation" from many different pieces, like a piecemeal helmet.

know from our own experience, and while our gut feelings tell us otherwise, sometimes we must simply act on our conviction. To a large measure, this is where faith enters the picture, showing yet again the incredibly interwoven relationship of our armor.

To contrast the subtle difference in this understanding, consider this. At some point we have all confronted someone with a heartfelt emotional position, or "belief." It is not long before we see just how difficult or obstinate they may be. An individual such as this is a welcome friend in time of crisis, and welcome support. They may prove to be difficult to dissuade, as they rely on how they feel about an issue. However, when put to a concerted line of questioning, they may come unglued, as they do not have the answers to your questions. Contrast this type of individual with those you know have subjected their heartfelt belief to thorough study. Not only do these individuals become bastions of solidarity, they are capable of articulating their beliefs more so than simply stating, "this is just the way I feel." They can give a clear and full explanation to defend their stance. This type of person poses a terrible adversary, or a powerful ally. An individual such as this can present a compelling argument for their position. They are able to rationally discuss their position, and often will be able to convert others to their way of seeing things. A belief structure that is well versed and fundamentally sound extends beyond the emotional realm is solid ground to stand on. This level of conviction serves as a better definition of *"Belief."*

Here is another way to physically illustrate the relationship between a simple heart felt belief and the conviction of the mind in terms of our spiritual armor. In the previous chapter, we discussed the breastplate and it was related that a chain mail hood (coif) was often worn with the chain mail body armor to supplement the helmet. While the hood does cover the head, it is generally only worn if body armor is worn. A helmet may or may not be worn with any other form of body protection. There are not rules for the wearing of a coif, and if you had one you certainly would wear it regardless of any other armor you may have. So you see, it may be very difficult at times to separate the two forms of protection as to whether it is part of the body armor, or serving as head protection. The helmet and breastplate are as interrelated as salvation and true righteousness. As correct action, and expression, needs to conform to every aspect of our being as a chain shirt and hood does, our unshakable understanding and belief in our salvation serves to "cover" all of our actions as a helmet would cover a hood. Understanding the elements required to claim salvation helps to guide, direct, and check our actions. Remember, it is only through salvation that we become redeemed in God's eyes and meet the measure of "righteousness."

While the two aspects—right action and salvation, or the breastplate and helmet—may be difficult to separate, they are two distinctly different things. Right action will never get you salvation, and salvation is no guarantee of right action. If this were not true, then we would not find many lessons in the Bible concerning this point. *[16]They profess that they know God; but in works they deny him, being abominable, and disobedient, and unto every good work reprobate.* **Titus 1:16.** Each piece serves a separate purpose, and operates independently in support of each other. This is a valuable lesson to us in how we are to fulfill our purpose and relate with others.

It is easy to see the distinction between a heartfelt desire and a conviction when put in a military context. For a Warrior to be successful in battle, one must apply thought to derive a decisive action, rather than act on compulsion. An emotionless and calculating opponent is to be feared as they will act in a more concerted way, always focused on the result. This is clearly different from one who acts compulsively as fitting the moment and their whim because of how they feel. This is the difference between reacting and responding.

A mind of solidarity represents a strong castle, a stronghold. Now think of doubt or fear as a spy within that stronghold. With the gates closed and the drawbridge up (our mind made up and settled), the stronghold is virtually impregnable to simple assault. However, if the enemy can place one of their own within, the situation changes drastically. At a time of their own choosing, the enemy may have the gates flung open and the bridge lowered. Now compare your Helmet of Salvation to the stronghold in this sense. Fear and doubt open up our defenses from the inside, much like a spy within the stronghold. To root out this enemy within, it is imperative to use understanding and self-acceptance. Understanding Paul's statements concerning our human nature, sin, and God's grace as discussed in the last chapter will help to serve as a springboard toward self acceptance and holding on to God's assurances of salvation and redemption.

We can undermine any beliefs we may hold with self-deception; that is—trying to rationalize the way we may think or act. Self-deception cancels any amount of understanding in this regard, and is just another form of deceit, a tool to render our defeat by the enemy. We fall into a trap when we attempt to rationalize our actions, as our guidelines of correct action are clearly laid out for us to follow by our King. There should be no question within our mind as to how to think about our salvation or our actions. When we accept the truth of God's Word, we will clearly hear His voice within us, directing the way we should consider any course of action. In regard to combating the unwanted and seemingly uncontrolled doubts and fears which may find a way into our mind, the next chapter on faith will present some very powerful instruction. *Any of you who lacks wisdom must ask God, who gives to all generously and without scolding; it will be given. But the prayer must be made with faith, and no trace of doubt, because a person who has doubts is like the waves thrown up in the sea by the buffeting of the wind. That sort of person, in two minds, inconsistent in every activity, must not expect to receive anything from the Lord.* **Jam. 1:5-8.**

On the field of combat, knowing what to do is often determined by the orders we are given to follow. These orders can be difficult to hear because of the noise of battle around one's self even when not wearing a helmet. When enclosed within a helmet, knowing what we are to do according to orders can become a very real problem. Hearing is to a large measure affected because of the padding and the enclosing nature of the helmet.[||] On an actual battlefield, this could

---

[||] An additional advantage of the typical Roman helmet is the fact that the

present some problems in not hearing the approach of unseen danger, or not hearing life saving orders or warnings when issued. In the Spiritual sense, the Helmet of Salvation can be seen to function as a defense against the lies and deception of the enemy for much the same reason. To some degree, the Helmet of Salvation may protect us from what may otherwise be heard or dwelled upon. Whether this is by filtering lies we may hear and knowing them for what they are, or disarming destructive thoughts that may present themselves before they become a preoccupation and distraction, salvation serves to calm our mind and keep us focused. When the question of one's personal salvation is not present in the mind of the Warrior and the lies and deceit of the enemy fall "on deaf ears," the helmet of salvation has done its job. When doubt and fear are not present in the mind of a Warrior, no "spy within" exists to do harm.

Orders on the ancient battlefield were generally taken from the blare of the trumpet and beating of the drums. Listening and being aware of this form of command is distinctly different from listening for or responding to verbal commands. The rhythm or cadence of the drum, or the trumpet's blare is much easier to hear over the din of battle than orders shouted vocally. In the confusion of battle, many voices may be shouting out, but none resound like a trumpet or drum! It should also be pointed out there is a danger in taking verbal commands: there is no time to concern one's self with verifying the validity, or source, of the orders. For much the same reason, it should be borne in mind that our Lord's commands are clear, easily understood, and unmistakable. It is up to us to be quiet and listen for God's wisdom. This can only be heard when our mind is clear and uncluttered by senseless concerns and worry. God's orders are heard within and are always clear and nondisruptive. *You shall not commit adultery, you shall not kill, you shall not steal, you shall not covet, and all the other commandments that there are...you must love your neighbour as yourself.* **Rom. 13:9.** *...stop sleeping and wake up, because by now our salvation is nearer than when we first began to*

---

ears were ingeniously left exposed, yet protected. Even in the later forms of helmets, the Romans typically left an ear-opening to facilitate hearing commands.

***believe...Let us live decently, as in the light of day; with no orgies or drunkenness, no promiscuity or licentiousness, and no wrangling or jealousy. Let your armour be the Lord Jesus Christ, and stop worrying about how your disordered natural inclinations may be fulfilled.* Rom. 11, 13-14.** For this reason, the mind game assaults on our reasoning and beliefs by the enemy should be easy to disregard in light of the assurances and promises of our Lord, which are clear and felt deep within a Warrior.

The Romans had an additional unique method for the conveyance of commands on the battlefield. The Romans' use of battle standards was unique for their time. Each unit had its own standard to follow and use as a focus during attack, and a point of rally and reorganization after the confusion of battle. The fact that the Romans had a standard to follow made a great difference. The importance of a standard to be followed is mentioned again here to stress the importance of having *"Standards."* Evaluate the standards you follow in your life, and if you have trouble identifying them, this should point you to a possible reason for pointless, meandering indecision found in one's life.

Num. 2:17, 34 *The order of movement will be the order of encampment, each man under his own standard...The Israelites did exactly as Yahweh had ordered Moses. This was how they pitched camp, grouped by standards.*

Another aspect of wearing a helmet is that it focuses the concentration of your vision on what lies directly in front of you. This serves to concentrate efforts on the task, or the adversary immediately opposing one's self. At the same time, the helmet protects the Warrior from attacks from the unseen quarters. In much the same way, the Helmet of Salvation serves to keep our concentration and energy focused, while serving to protect us from the unseen attacks of the enemy. To derive the protection of salvation, it is required that we speak our faith, and assert our acceptance of our Lord's sacrifice for our behalf. This is the first step in donning the Helmet and allowing salvation to serve as a protection for us. We are then better able to focus on the duty at hand and not become distracted or rendered paralyzed by peripheral attacks of the enemy because of an otherwise unsettled, wondering, wandering, or idle mind.

Once we have come to terms with our salvation, we will have come into relationship with our King and Creator, and thus be able to take commands and direction of a higher order...*for of all the names in the world given to men, this is the only one by which we can be saved.* **Acts 4:12.** Our decisions become clear, as our best interest is always a concern of our King; however, we must allow Him to direct us, so our actions become in accord with a divine plan. While taking correct action as directed by our King may not always be easy, the choice is clear. *Your minds, then, must be sober and ready for action; put all your hope in the grace brought to you by the revelation of Jesus Christ. Do not allow yourselves to be shaped by the passions of your old ignorance, but as obedient children, be yourselves holy in all your activity...* **1 Ptr. 1:13-15.** This scripture also serves to remind us a Warrior is always prepared to act on a moment's notice. Preparedness is a by-product of following the direction of a higher cause and being "dead to one's self."

Let us now look at some scriptures and see how salvation and conviction may serve and protect us:

Ps. 62:1-2, 7 *In God alone there is rest for my soul, from him comes my safety; He alone is my rock, my safety, my stronghold so that I stand unshaken. ...In God is my safety and my glory, the rock of my strength.*

Ps. 140:7 *Yahweh my Lord, my Saving strength, you shield my head when battle comes.* What could possibly be more indomitable than the protection of our King for our head?

Ps. 20:5-8 *So that with joy we can hail your victory and draw up our ranks in the name of our God. May Yahweh grant all your petitions. Now I know that Yahweh gives victory to his anointed. He will respond from his holy heavens with great deeds of victory from his right hand.*

Ps. 38:22 *...those he blesses will have land for their own, and those he curses be annihilated.* This is a simple assurance and support for believers and condemnation for the enemy.

While the above scriptures are certainly supportive and encouraging, one of the greatest enemies to be faced is Fear (and his friend Doubt) as mentioned earlier. The following two scriptures deal directly with this element of attack and what we are to combat it with: Faith and Salvation. When you feel beleaguered and set upon by any travail, reflect on the following scriptures. I am sure when you reread them slowly a few times, you will find your spirit will accept these words as refreshing as a mint-julep in July and as invigorating as a cold splash of water on a hot August day:

2 Chron. 20:15, 17 *...Yahweh says this to you, 'Do not be afraid, do not be daunted by this vast horde, for the war is not your affair but God's. ...Take up your position, stand firm, and see what salvation Yahweh has in store for you... Be fearless, be dauntless; march out against them tomorrow and Yahweh will be with you.'*

Ps. 91:2-8 *...saying to Yahweh, 'My refuge, my fortress, my God in whom I trust!' He rescues you from the snare of the fowler set on destruction; He covers you with his pinions, you find shelter under his wings, His constancy is shield and protection. You need not fear the terrors of night, the arrow that flies in the daytime, the plague that stalks in the darkness, the scourge that wreaks havoc at high noon. Though a thousand fall at your side, ten thousand at your right hand, you yourself will remain unscathed. You have only to keep your eyes open to see how the wicked are repaid, you who say, 'Yahweh my refuge!' and make Elyon your fortress.*

The above scripture points out the depth to which Doubt and Fear may be removed from one's thinking. Now I am sure we all suffer from arrows by day and the threat of the scourge at noon and witness the loss of thousands daily, and all this may seem "old-hat" for the true veteran, but should your condition seem as desperate as all that, remember these words. They have been intended for our assurance since long ago. I do say this in a light-hearted way, but we all need to remember we are in fact engaged in a spiritual war, and while you may not "see" the arrows by day, I am sure you feel their effects in the office-place or whenever your character comes under callused ridicule. Arrows of another sort, but arrows none-the-less. And as for the thousands falling by your side-just look around you...I believe you will now recognize them every day in the dejected spirits of coworkers and the unsatisfied grumbles of loved one's whose value seems overlooked or unappreciated. Anyone who suffers a major setback and has life get them in a tailspin is just as much a casualty as one lanced in the thigh by a spear. Anyone not functioning to his or her potential could be counted as a casualty. Anyone not doing the work of the Father certainly can be counted as one as well—after all, they are removed from the front lines where the enemy is being confronted, and perhaps even enlisted with the enemy.

Let us now consider those traits of character that serve to develop and support our Helmet of Salvation. God and His Son have given us ample examples to follow. Some of the characteristics showing support and which develop the spiritual protection of our salvation include: compassion, selflessness, mercy, courage/fearlessness, and discipline. The following scriptures are a good representation of this relationship.

2 Kings 13:23 *[23]And the LORD was gracious unto them, and had compassion on them, and had respect unto them, because of his covenant with Abraham, Isaac, and Jacob, and would not destroy them, neither cast he them from his presence as yet.* Although God has the power to do away with the recalcitrant people, he honors His covenant with them and stays His hand.

Ps. 78:38-39 *[38]But He, being full of compassion, forgave their iniquity, and destroyed them not: yea, many a time turned He his anger away, and did not stir up all his wrath. [39]For He remembered that they were but flesh; a wind that passeth away, and cometh not again.*

Mk. 9:23-25 *'...have pity on us and help us.' 'If you can?!' retorted Jesus, 'Everything is possible for one who has faith.'* At once the father of the boy cried out, 'I have faith. Help my lack of faith!'

1 Jn. 3:16 *For this is how God loved the world: he gave his only Son, so that everyone who believes in him may not perish but may have eternal life.*

Matt. 26:38-39 *[38]Then saith he unto them, 'My soul is exceeding sorrowful, even unto death: tarry ye here, and watch with me.' [39]And he went a little further, and fell on his face, and prayed, saying, 'O my Father, if it be possible, let this cup pass from me: never-the-less not as I will, but as thou wilt.'*

This last scripture shows that even our Lord ultimately had a choice in accepting His orders to fulfill God's plan, and rather than direct His actions with His own desire in mind, He subjects Himself to God's plan. This not only stands as an example of selflessness in subjecting Himself to the will of the Father, it stands as a testimony of discipline as He fulfilled God's plan for Him: *No one can have greater love than to lay down his life for his friends.* **Jn. 15:13.**

The above scriptures reveal the level of compassion and love our Lord has for us and should in themselves serve as a model for our behavior. However, some people may not take the lesson from this and my need a more direct and personal directive for their behavior. The following scriptures point the way for us and are explicit in how we are to reveal our character:

Matt. 18:33 *[33]Shouldest not thou also have had compassion on thy fellow servant, even as I had pity on thee?*

1 Ptr. 3:8-9 *[8]Finally, be ye all of one mind, having compassion one of another, love as brethren, be pitiful, be courteous: [9]Not rendering evil for evil, or railing for railing: but contrariwise blessing; knowing that ye are thereunto called, that ye should inherit a blessing.*

Matt. 6:14-15 *¹⁴For if ye forgive men their trespasses, your heavenly Father will also forgive you: ¹⁵But if ye forgive not men their trespasses, neither will your Father forgive your trespasses.*

With this understanding of compassion and love, does it come as any surprise where the principle directing several of our "Golden Rules" come from, "Do unto others as you would have others do unto you," and "Turn the other cheek." Both of these rules for life will speak reams to our spirit once we have reached this level of understanding of compassion, selflessness, and discipline.

It is when we deny our "self" for the sake of others that we reveal a greater part of our true nature; a part that typically requires a giving of one's self to be shown. This is the nature of the principle. For example, we are all familiar with the expression, "You don't get something for nothing." What few people realize is the simple principle that if a statement is a real truism, its converse must also be true. If it is true that we do not get something for nothing, then the opposite is also true: "You can't give something away without getting something in return." Strange as it may seem, this is a fact seemingly borne out by spiritual principles found in the Bible. When one studies the principles of giving and receiving found in the scriptures in this context, the point is clear.

First, consider the simple statement that as we receive freely, we are to give in like fashion:

Matt. 10:8 *...freely ye have received, freely give.*

Remember what was just mentioned above, if a statement is a real truism, the converse must also be true. Therefore, if you freely give, you will freely receive. God has set the example. It is by God's selfless giving that we may receive freely. Now, consider the following: Do you think you can out-give God?

When we follow this simple principle, giving freely, we are being faithful in a small thing. Once we have shown our disposition to do so, God will honor our actions in a specific way:

Matt. 25:21 *²¹His lord said unto him, Well done, thou good and faithful servant: thou hast been faithful over a few things, I will make thee ruler over many things...*

Lk. 6:38 *Give, and there will be gifts for you: a full measure, pressed down, shaken together, and overflowing, will be poured into your lap; because the standard you use will be the standard used for you.*

In addition to this, by giving we receive a blessing, a fact, not just a principle, and this is also borne out by the scriptures:

Acts 20:35 *³⁵I have showed you all things, how that so laboring ye ought to support the weak, and to remember the words of the Lord Jesus, how He said, 'It is more blessed to give than to receive.'*

As a matter of fact, God goes even further to show His disposition to continually show His giving nature as an example for us:

Matt. 7:7 *⁷Ask, and it shall be given you...*

Our Creator, who sacrificed His only begotten Son on our behalf, is making this assurance for us. What greater example is there of giving?

These principles are simple to understand and take on a new dimension when the following is understood:

Rom. 11:36 *Everything there is comes from Him and is caused by Him and exists for Him.*

So you see, being a good steward of what we commonly refer to as "ours" and following a simple principle laid out for us to give freely and generously as this is the example we have been given; we are in a sense, merely redistributing God's property in the manner He wants us to. Pray on it, better yet, try it...you will be surprised, I am sure. While the return is typically not in like-for-like, the returns are generally magnified.#

The following scripture from **Malachi** serves to point out the generosity of God's return, and the spiritual importance of tithing in regards to giving freely:

Mal. 3:7-12 *⁷Even from the days of your fathers ye are gone away from mine ordinances, and have not kept them. Return unto me, and I will return unto you, saith the LORD of hosts. But ye said, Wherein shall we return? ⁸Will a man rob God? Yet ye have robbed me. But ye say, Wherein have we robbed thee? In tithes and offerings. ⁹Ye are cursed with a curse: for ye have robbed me, even this whole nation. ¹⁰Bring ye all the tithes into the storehouse, that there may be meat in mine house, and prove me now herewith, saith the LORD of hosts, if I will not open you the windows of heaven, and pour you out a blessing, that there shall not be room enough to receive it. ¹¹And I will rebuke the devourer for your sakes, and he shall not destroy the fruits of your ground; neither shall your vine cast her fruit before the time in the field, saith the LORD of hosts. ¹²And all nations shall call you blessed: for ye shall be a delightsome land, saith the LORD of hosts.*

Many people do not practice tithing. They then incur a curse. Rather than getting into the many shallow reasons people prefer to justify their not tithing, it is suggested the reader consider the very way they think of tithing, instead. When one considers tithing, it is generally thought that one tenth of your earnings are to be given, or tithed, to God. Rather than think of it in this fashion, consider this: Everything is God's. You do not "own" your life, your health, your prosperity, your children, or any of your possessions. Everything is God's, as pointed out above. Therefore, **God** only requires one tenth of the earnings, and He **gives you—ninety percent!**

If thought of in this way, it should make more sense that God considers being faithful in tithing, being faithful in a small thing, and

---

Having done a search using Strong's Index, the author found over 900 instances in which giving was involved in the scriptures.

then returns to you in multiple. Moreover, God will accept a tithe of your time, your energy, not just a portion of "your" paycheck. Giving money to the church is a great way to support the programs of the church, but someone still has to carry out the programs. Volunteers are always needed and welcomed. If you do not believe this, just go to your church and volunteer to help, see if you are ever turned away.

One final thought, to close this chapter with. Earlier in this chapter, we mentioned the intertwined nature of righteousness and salvation, or the breastplate and the helmet. The interrelated nature of Faith and Salvation (our Shield and Helmet) can also be easily found in the scriptures. The next few scriptures have an element of both aspects in them. When we examine the following scriptures, we shall see it may at times be very difficult to separate salvation and faith because of the nature of their relationship. Let us see what words of enlightenment the scriptures may have on this combination:

Isa. 12:2 *²Behold, God is my salvation; I will trust, and not be afraid: for the Lord Jehovah is my strength and my song; he also is become my salvation.*

2 Sam. 22:2-7...*Yahweh is my strength and my fortress, my deliverer is my God. I take refuge in him, my rock, my shield, my saving strength, my stronghold, my place of refuge. My Savior, you have saved me from violence; I call to Yahweh, who is worthy of praise, and I am saved from my foes. With Death's breakers closing in on me, Belial's torrents ready to swallow me, Sheol's snares on every side of me, Death's traps lying ahead of me. I called to Yahweh in my anguish, I cried for help to my God, from his Temple he heard my voice, my cry came to his ears!*

14-15 Yahweh thundered from the heavens, the Most High made his voice heard. He shot his arrows and scattered them, his lightning flashed and routed them.

17-19 He reached down from on high, snatched me up, pulled me from the watery depths, rescued me from my mighty foe, from my enemies who were stronger than I. They assailed me on my day of disaster, but Yahweh was there to support me...

Ex. 15:6-7 *Your right hand, Yahweh, wins glory by its strength, your right hand, Yahweh, shatters your foes, and by your great majesty you fell your assailants; you unleash your fury it consumes them like chaff.* While this scripture seems to be more related to purely faith alone, it must be remembered that to claim this faith, one must believe *in the salvation of our King.*

Rev. 12:11-12 *They have triumphed over him by the blood of the Lamb and by the word to which they bore witness, because even in the face of death they did not cling to life.* It is by this confidence in the saving bloodshed by Jesus leads the Warrior to be selfless.

Ps. 40:11 *You, Yahweh, have not withheld your tenderness from me; Your faithful and steadfast love will always guard me.*

Ps. 71:1-2 *In you, Yahweh, I take refuge, I shall never be put to shame. In your saving justice rescue me, deliver me, listen to me and save me.*

To beseech our God in this fashion, one must have a personal relationship with Him. This is only possible when one knows the author of our salvation.

This will serve as a good introduction to our next chapter:

"The Shield of Faith"

Chapter 10

The Shield of Faith

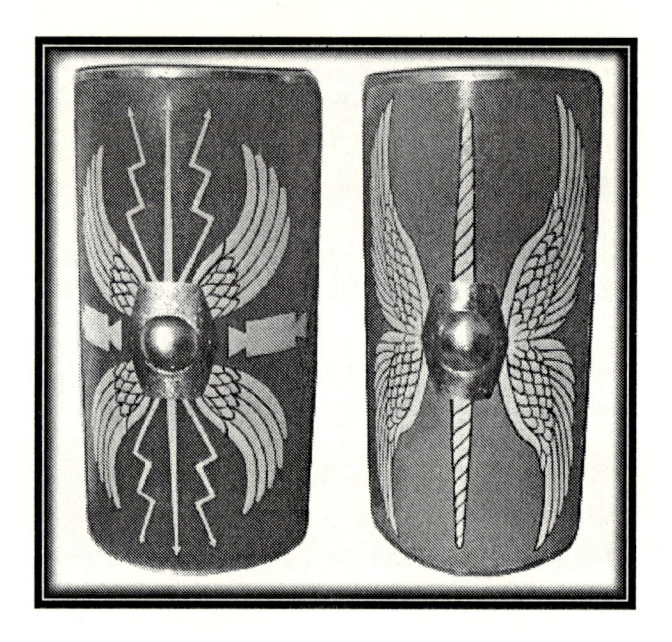

Eph. 6:16 *So take you the shield of Faith with which to quench the enemies fiery darts...*

Deut. 33:29 *Who Is like you, O victorious people? Yahweh is the shield that protects you and the sword that leads you to triumph. Your enemies will try to corrupt you, but you yourself will trample on their backs.*

The use of a shield certainly seems easy enough to master. It is picked up, grabbed by the straps, and held in front of the body. While a shield is certainly an instrument that can readily be picked up and handled, Faith is altogether a different thing. In times of need and confusion, we are so often counseled to pick up, or rely on, our faith to see us through a trying time or dilemma. For many of us, while we are so often directed to do this seemingly simple feat, *How* to do this eludes us. This principally is due to the simple fact that, while we are instructed to use our Faith, we have never really been instructed in what **Faith** is, let alone how to rely on, or use it.

It is interesting that Faith should be described as our spiritual armor in the form of a shield. In many ways, this symbolism well associates the use of faith with the function and use of a material shield. Just as a shield must be *applied* to serve as an aggressive defense or offensive arm, it is our *Faith* that we are taught must often be *exercised* or applied in those situations calling for other than simple solutions. When confronted with a situation, dilemma, or decision which we cannot, or do not understand, it is our *Faith* on which we are called upon to rely. As it is typical for a shield to be held before oneself when in use, in much the same way, our *Faith* best serves us when we allow it to precede us in times of uncertainty.

To come to a point of understanding about Faith, and then be able to apply it, let us start with the basics. In the Bible, Faith is commonly referred to as a shield. Thus, we shall first look at the history and use of a shield to get a better feel for how a shield is to function for us, then we will take a closer look at Faith itself, how it is defined, and how it may be applied.

The earliest shields were simple wooden frameworks covered with hides, or wood planks. Later, a metal frame, or banding, was used to hold the wooden slates of the shield together as well as serve to protect the edge of the shield from the hacking blows of the enemy. The wooden shield could be covered with hides, leather, or cloth, upon which designs or emblems believed to confer some magical protection may be displayed. In later periods, the shield was constructed mainly of metal. We tend to think of a shield as a thing indestructible. We have good reason to believe our spiritual shield of faith to be far more resistant than even a metal shield. We have this assurance from God Himself: ***You give me your invincible shield (your right hand upholds me). Ps. 18:35.*** I will leave it to the reader to decide which shield would be stronger: one provided by God, or one constructed by man.

Shields ranged in size from the small hand-held "buckler" that could be as small as nine inches in diameter and was easily carried hung on the belt, to the large Roman "scutum," which extended from the chin to the shins and was typically carried slung over the shoulder by a belt. When Paul referred to the Shield-of-Faith, he uses the word "Thureon," which relates to the scutum used by the Romans. This substantial shield was some 2 ½ feet wide, 4 feet long, and in some instances, up to 3 inches thick. It incorporated a metal rim, and the wood construction was of laminated layers of wood affording it much more resistance to penetration, or being chopped through. When not in combat, this type of shield could be used for shelter, or as a break against the elements.

Vikings were fond of a large round shield, sometimes in excess of forty inches in diameter. Standing shoulder to shoulder, these large round shields where overlapped to present what came to be known as a "shield wall," affording the defenders a considerable bulwark of defense. During the period of the Norman conquests, mounted knights often carried an elongated shield with a curved or rounded top and a long, tapered bottom designed to protect the left leg while fighting mounted on horse-back. The curved upper edge allowed additional protection for the head. This was essential, as helmets of this time were generally open-faced and not as generally protective as in later periods. As body armor became increasingly more protective and complete in its coverage of the body and limbs, and helmets became more protective and totally encasing, the shield saw a steady decline in its size, and general use. The development of the "heater" shield was introduced, providing us with the classic "shield" shape generally identified with today. This shield was typically twenty to thirty-six inches long, ending in a blunt or tapered point, curved across the face, and flat across the top. This particular shape was essentially all that was needed for general protection from blows as the body was then fully covered by steel, and the head was encased in a fully enclosing metal helmet.

This decline in the need for protection from a shield continued until the shield was no longer carried. Society today is generally deemed safe enough to preclude the use of even body armor, but think again. While our society may be safer in a physical nature, it is far more deadly in the spiritual context. As we have moved away from the use of shields, we have lost sight of their use in this context, and this has contributed to our cloudy understanding of the use of faith as a shield. For this reason, understanding the use of faith as a shield is of vast importance. To be without faith is to be without God, as our belief relies on our faith for its existence. Such is the nature of believing in a redeeming Creator. Our faith relies on our trusting in the Word of God, and accepting it as true. This can only be done through faith, with perseverance. Without it, we are lost: ***…and do not forget, I say, that you were at that time separate from Christ and excluded from membership of Israel, aliens with no part in the covenants of the Promise, limited to this world, without hope and without God.*** **Eph. 2:12.**

During the transitional period of armor development, which saw combatants become completely concealed by their armor, a means of identifying friend from foe became important. The use of "Heraldic Displays" on the shield and mantle of the knights gave rise to what we refer to today as the "Coat-of-Arms." The simplest example of a coat-of-arms generally recognized today would be the white shield and red cross which identified the Crusaders who fought to reclaim the Holy Land.[*] While noblemen would have their own distinctive coat-of-arms which identified them or members of the same family, large fighting-units would collectively wear a distinctive coat-of-arms to distinguish them from the enemy as well. This simple means of identification worked well to distinguish members of various units from each other, as well as helping to coordinate troop movements in

---

[*] One interesting development of the Crusades was the development of the religious fighting orders. Two in particular may be familiar to those students of the crusades: the Knights Templar who displayed a white mantle emblazoned with a red cross, and the Knights Hospitaler who displayed a black mantle emblazoned with a white cross.

the field.‡ In the spiritual context, we may consider the blood of Christ as our coat-of-arms. Some may represent this by displaying a crucifix, or cross, some a fish, a dove, or a pair of praying hands. However, it is the blood of Christ which covers us as a mantle, and which serves to shield our sins from the eyes of God. When God looks upon us, He sees the redeeming blood of His Son, and not our sin, and we are recognized as righteous in His eyes by virtue of His Son's blood, we are seen as co-heirs to the throne, Children of God. ***Thus He chose us in Christ before the world was made to be holy and faultless before Him in love, marking us out for Himself beforehand, to be adopted sons, through Jesus Christ. Such was His purpose and good pleasure, to the praise of the glory of His grace, His free gift to us in the Beloved, in whom, through His blood, we gain our freedom, the forgiveness of our sins.* Eph. 1:4-7.**§

This should sound familiar as these elements of redemption and righteousness were elaborated on when we discussed the Breastplate. It is in our being identified by the blood of Christ, which singles us out as being of God's army.∥ *...and from Jesus Christ, the faithful witness, the First-born from the dead, the highest of earthly kings. He loves us and has washed away our sins with His blood, and made us a Kingdom of Priests to serve His God and Father...* **Rev. 1:5-6.** In wearing the heraldic display of our Lord, we have been declared as members of God's army, and entry into His camp may be

---

‡ The shoulder patch worn by our service men today is a carry-over from this form of unit identification, as is the badge worn by policeman—still called a "Shield" today.

§ For a fuller reading of how we may be identified as children of God, bearing the mark of His household by His Holy Spirit, I refer the reader to **Rom. 8:1-16**. This is a fairly long writing of how the Spirit marks us as sons of God, by the sacrifice of Jesus on our behalf.

∥ There is also a later reference to the sealing (or identifying) of God's people with a mark to set them apart—Rev. 7:3-4 ³Saying, Hurt not the earth, neither the sea, nor the trees, till we have sealed the servants of our God in their foreheads. ⁴And I heard the number of them which were sealed: and there were sealed an hundred and forty and four thousand of all the tribes of the children of Israel.

made fearlessly, and with joy, for we know that the King will see the people He has claimed and marked with His blood when we are brought before our God. *In Him we are bold enough to approach God in complete confidence, through our faith in Him;...In the abundance of His glory may He, through His Spirit, enable you to grow firm in power with regard to your inner self, so that Christ may live in your hearts through faith, and then, planted in love and built on love, with all God's holy people you will have the strength to grasp the breadth and the length, the height and the depth...* **Eph. 3:12, 16-19**. There should be no doubt in your mind that we are citizens of heaven, as this is rightfully our Kingdom when we are redeemed by the blood of our Lord. *...our homeland is in heaven and it is from there that we are expecting a Saviour, the Lord Jesus Christ...* **Phil. 3:20**.

With a shield covered in leather and soaked in water, great protection could be found from fiery assaults. This was especially important when one may be confronted by boiling oil, flaming bombards, pitch, or fiery darts. Bear in mind we are told we are supplied with our spiritual shield to **Quench** the fiery darts of the enemy (**Eph. 6:16**). This is more than poetic phraseology. Remember that it is the penetrating attack to which our body, or heart, is most susceptible. Now, unless you are expecting to be shot at by flaming arrows, you may find it makes more sense to consider fiery or heated words of aggression, or refute, as "flaming darts" which may be directed at us. This form of assault, verbal assault, is very penetrating, and undoubtedly affects our heart. This is where we typically describe the pain we feel when targeted by the abusive taunts of another. Faith quenches this form of attack on our person and spirit. You may say Faith "rains on the parade" of evil contemptuous words and quenches them. Just *how* faith does this is not commonly understood. Faith protects us from false statements and words damaging to our character simply by virtue that we believe and have *Faith* that these things are not true. We know in our hearts that the words we hear are untrue and do not speak of our true nature or character, and thus we are immune to their effect. Our faith puts us in touch with the Truth, and it is unmistakable, and clear.

A dear friend, Lou DeBroux, brought to my attention a particular phrase some time ago, and I would like to share it with you. I dwelled on this phrase for a full week before I came to a full understanding of the lesson it teaches, and I would ask the reader to dwell on these words and come to their own understanding of them:

"A person who takes offense when no offense is intended is a fool; a person who takes offense when offense is intended is probably a fool."

When you have come to an understanding of this statement, you will have a better understanding of how *Faith* operates within us.[#]

An example is in order. Let us suppose you have words with a coworker. You may have made an error in some paperwork, and they have taken the opportunity to demean your abilities or job performance. If you had discovered the error yourself, it would have no doubt been corrected. The difference at this point, however, is that you have been "targeted" for assault by someone with a grudge or bone to pick with you and the world. These are two separate issues. Having any confidence at all in your ability to do your job, no thought would normally be given to making the correction. But in this instance, you are made to feel bad because of a simple error. It is in being able to separate two issues that we may remain nonplused by the confrontation. On the one hand, we have the belief, or faith, in our ability, and make a simple correction. On the other hand, we recognize the pain or anger someone else is misplacing, or venting on us. If we allow ourselves to be caught up in the words of the moment, often what will result will be many hurt feelings. *My dear friends, do not be taken aback at the testing by fire which is taking place among you, as though something strange were happening to you; but in so far as you share in the sufferings of Christ, be glad, so that you may enjoy a much greater gladness when His glory is revealed. If you*

[#] If simple, flagrantly inflammatory statements are all that are required to "get your ire up," this would not speak well of your balanced and disciplined character. Control is essential at a time such as this, and a true Warrior sees the intent of his adversary and does not fall into the trap. This is most especially true when the comments directed at our character, while not necessarily flattering, are true.

are insulted for bearing Christ's name, blessed are you, for on you rests the Spirit of God, the Spirit of glory. **1 Ptr. 4:12-14.**

Maybe a little closer to home, consider this situation: a loved one dies in a tragic car accident. In remorse, we typically question God for this seemingly senseless tragedy. "How can God let this happen," or "Why…God Why…?" are expressions often uttered from the pain of loss. In attempting to console the bereaved, friends and family pretty much all respond in the same way, "It was their time," "God called them home," and "They are in a better place now," are the typical responses. You may have said these same words to someone during their time of loss.

The fact is, when we try to console a bereaved one at a time of a personal loss, the proper response may actually be silence. Compassion and sympathy often need no words. It is in personally having the knowledge that God *IS*, and His word is *True*, that will bring us to terms with a loss in a time like this.

Consider the relationship of faith and salvation as pieces of armor. First, compare two individuals both suffering a similar loss of a loved one. One may be a person of great faith, well founded in their understanding of their life and reward in heaven after their time on Earth. The other, we will say, has very little understanding of Life-after-Life (or Life-after-Death). There is a marked difference in how these two individuals may react to, and recover from, their loss. Second, consider what essentially happens which leads to healing from a loss such as this; as our faith and understanding of God's will may be shaken, we often find ourselves questioning "Why…" this-and-that. It will eventually be our ritualistic belief, traditions, or underlying solace in a Divine Plan that helps us find peace with the loss of a loved one. Spiritually, this may be taken to represent our helmet, or salvation, protecting us and offering us coverage when we have let our shield down. It may be the simplest statement that strikes this cord within an individual, and some aspect of their salvation may be just the thing to kick in when the chips are down, and bring them to a point of emotional healing.[**] This may be taken as an additional

---

[**] It could just as easily be a statement of truth, which brings an individual back, or a simple joy derived from an act of charity for another, which they

benefit of our spiritual armor. The following simple scripture quote succinctly relates two characteristics of a Warrior and the elements of the shield and breastplate.

1 Cor. 16:13-14 *Be vigilant, stay firm in the faith, be brave and strong. Let everything you do be done in love.*

It is by our *Faith* in God and His promises that we can enjoy the protection of the shield, and therefore, salvation. ***For I see no reason to be ashamed of the gospel; it is God's power for the salvation of everyone who has faith…*** **Rom. 1:16.** Faith is required if one is to acquire salvation. Faith will guide one to understand and **_Believe_** in their salvation. In regards to armor, if you have any shield *at all*-any faith-, it will serve to offer protection for your head, your thinking, and your mind. Spiritually, faith is required to obtain any measure of salvation, for it is by *Faith Alone* that we can claim our belief in the existence of God, and believe in the truth of His Word. If one does not have faith in God's existence, or His promises, there will be no shield of protection against doubt, fear, and lies-the principle weapons of the enemy. So you see, faith and salvation are inextricably linked, just as each ring of our chain mail armor.

Love and Faith have been used to describe the elements making up our spiritual breastplate, and they are the principle weapons to be used to vanquish doubt and fear. Faith in this context joins with an element of our breastplate to "double up our protection." We fear less when we are loved filled. This is simply because, ***In love there is no room for fear, but perfect love drives out fear, because fear implies punishment and whoever is afraid has not come to perfection in love.*** **1 Jn. 4:18**. We have been designed by God to be fearless: [7]***For God hath not given us the spirit of fear; but of power, and of love, and of a sound mind.*** **2 Tm. 1:7.** Bear this in mind, and the enemy will have an impossible job of planting "a spy within."

When we claim our victory over our fears and doubts with love and faith, we suddenly find that we are capable of taking criticism, failures, setbacks and obstacles we would otherwise have considered

---

may perform.

as insurmountable, in stride. We become free to act, being no longer immobilized, and we can then implement strategy, or fulfill our orders. Everyone becomes a beneficiary of the freedom of action found in one fearless Warrior.

When we do not have the "back-up" or overlapping protection from all of our armor, there are holes in our spiritual armor. This presents a tempting and vulnerable target to the enemy. The attacks of the enemy and effects of life may then make an immediate impact upon us, resulting in some form of emotional, spiritual, or even physical trauma. What may result from a personal loss, or set back, is a deep depression and long period of recovery. Practicing all the elements of our armor is essential to minimizing our risk, and shortening any recovery. In times of distress and woe, it is holding firm to our relationship with God, and bearing in mind His promises that will bring order to disorder, hope to the hopeless. ***Surely Yahweh's mercies are not over, his deeds of faithful love not exhausted; every morning they are renewed; great is his faithfulness! 'Yahweh is all I have,' I say to myself, 'and so I shall put my hope in him.' Yahweh is good to those who trust him, to all who search for him.*** **Lam. 3:22-25.**

There is additional symbolism in describing faith as a shield. Traditionally, a fallen warrior was carried home on his shield. Using this as an analogy, he is borne by his faith and once interred, his effigy would typically be displayed with his shield covering him as "with his faith for all eternity." You either returned home from battle carrying your shield, or carried-on your shield. Faith will serve to protect you while you live, and carry you through death when you die.

In use, the shield could be held by a center grip that allowed easy control of the shield and the greatest extension of it in use, at arms length. The hand was typically protected on the outside by a raised convex iron cap or "boss." The boss, as well as the edge of the shield, was capable of being used offensively by smashing it into the ribs, shoulder or head of the enemy, and by its shape, cause trauma, if not broken bones. Truly, faith can be used as a weapon against evil. An opponent can be smashed to the ground or pushed aside with a shield. This is how we are to think of our faith. It is not just a defensive shield, held poised in the hand. It is to be thought of as a very powerful weapon capable of ***SMASHING*** the enemy! Never thought of a shield being used as a weapon before, have you? Consider these words: *...so that in their light you may fight like a good soldier with faith and a good conscience for your weapons.* **1 Tm. 1:18-19.**[‡] Alternatively, think over these words: ***Do not annihilate them, or my people may forget; shake them in your power, bring them low, Lord, our shield.*** **Ps. 59:11.** While faith is fully capable of utterly annihilating the enemy, in some ways this is to good for them, and bringing them low not only serves as a reminder to us, but to them as well, of the power of God. In fact, it is found in the book of **Proverbs** that by sparing the violent (the enemy) his crimes are aggravated: ***The violent lays himself open to a penalty; spare him, and you aggravate his crime.*** **Prov. 19:19.** Jesus spoke of the power of faith and directed us thus: *...If ye have faith as a grain of mustard seed, ye shall say unto this mountain, Remove hence to yonder place; and it shall remove; and nothing shall be impossible unto you.* **Matt. 17:20.** Maybe one more scripture will make the utter power of faith clear: ***Nor are his commandments burdensome, because every child of God overcomes the world. And this is the victory that has overcome the world—our faith. Who can overcome the world but the one who believes that Jesus is the Son of God?*** **1 Jn. 5:4-5.** Overcoming adversity is the standard result of the faithful Warrior. No nation can stand before one, no kingdom claim victory over a faithful and persevering Warrior. With faith such as this, you have to wonder if another weapon is needed at all.

That final statement, *"and nothing shall be impossible unto you,"* says it all. Yet, how few of us truly act as though we understood, or believed the above statement to be true. Jesus did not tell us it required a lot of faith to accomplish the impossible, He told us quite literally if we had *ANY* faith, we could move mountains and do the impossible. I doubt many of us would profess having no faith at all, so then why are so many of us acting as though we had none? It is as

---

[‡] Faith and conscience are related several times in the scriptures and with good reason: **1 Tm. 1:19** *...Some people have put conscience aside and wrecked their faith in consequence.* It is important for a Warrior to act in good conscience, for conscience is an extension of one's will, and if we act without conscience, we have left our faith behind.

simple as picking up a shield and holding it before us. We simply have to believe. ***Jesus answered, 'In truth I tell you, if you have faith and do not doubt at all, not only will you do what I have done to the fig tree, but even if you say to this mountain, 'Be pulled up and thrown into the sea,' it will be done. And if you have faith, everything you ask for in prayer, you will receive.'* Matt. 21:21-22.** Being able to say what one believes, as a creed is essential for acting on this faith. Knowing what we may want, how we hope a situation will develop, or simply willing-things-to-be will not cut it, we have to *ACT* as though it were already a fact, no questions asked. Why else do you suppose "acting on faith" and "acts of faith" are so often referred to in the scriptures? This additionally points to the importance and dependence on our "willingness and doing," the spiritual armor with which we shod our feet.

Quite simply, as Jesus said, ***According to your faith, let it be done to you.* Matt. 9:29**. With these words of direction, two blind men were healed. What do you have faith in, what do you truly believe, what can you lay hold of and own with your faith?

Most shields were fitted with straps to allow them to be worn around the neck freely or to allow the weight to be carried on the shoulders. The shield could also be slung over the back to free both hands for heavier detail work. When worn in this fashion, the shield served to offer additional protection from attacks from behind. This allows the Warrior to concentrate efforts more forcibly with the power of both hands in grappling with the enemy. With a shield slung in this manner, it is out of the way and easily borne. Faith should become as comfortable to wear, and carry with us daily, as this. As the smallest amount of faith has the ability to do the impossible, it cannot be very cumbersome. This should give you pause to consider those "people of faith" you know, who are always troubled, or wrestling with matters of belief. This is a telltale sign that something is out of order, or not in proper readiness. This type of situation defies an attribute of the Warrior, which is to be ready on a moments notice for the call, ***"To Arms!"***

The scutum and heater were generally curved across the face of the shield to allow the body to be more or less encompassed by it. The very design of the shield made it easy to deflect hurled stones, javelins and other missiles, as well as turn away pikes, spears and the hacking onslaught of the enemy foot soldiers. The curved, slick surface of the shield contributed greatly to its defensive abilities. In a sense, one could step into his shield (step into his faith), and be covered by it as by a protective wall. *May Yahweh be a stronghold for the oppressed, a stronghold in times of trouble! Those who revere your name can rely on you, you never desert those who seek you, Yahweh.* **Ps. 9:9-10**.

The shield is a piece of armament capable of protecting or covering a Warrior from head to foot. When the Shield-of-Faith of others is shared, an impenetrable mobile Bastion is created. The Romans exemplified this by interlocking their shields to produce a formidable formation called a "Testudo." This was effectively the first "tank" of warfare. *You will pursue your enemies and they will fall before your sword; five of you pursuing a hundred of them, one hundred pursuing ten thousand; and your enemies will fall before your sword.* **Lev. 26:7-8**. With their shields covered with soaked leather, the formation was able to withstand Greek fire, and searing oil. The key to the testudo's success was to not let personal or individual fear destroy the formation. It took *Faith* on the part of every one of the warriors in the formation to keep it together and whole. Just imagine, if you can: 300 to 600 sweating, blood spattered warriors crowded together chin to back, shoulder to shoulder, breathing each others exhalation, tromping across a war torn battlefield covered with the remains of the fallen slain…having flaming pitch poured down over you, and yet you march on…undaunted, unswerving, up to the wall of the defenders, there to bring up a battering ram within your formation…and then **stand there** beating a slow methodical cadence of ultimate doom upon the fortress of the enemy, all the while hoping that none of your comrades crowded around you were more terrified than you. **Yahweh has dispossessed great and powerful nations before you, and no one so far has been able to resist you. One man of you was able to rout a thousand of them, since Yahweh your God was Himself fighting for you, as He had promised you. Jos. 23:9-10.** Although you could only keep your own fear in check with your FAITH in the units performance, it would be the displayed and *Expressed Faith* displayed by all of the companions standing firm about you, that would help bolster you, and keep the formation sound. For you see, without the unified faith of each warrior in the formation, the testudo would founder. If the faith and confidence of the testudo failed, the testudo would waver and become ineffective. The entire formation would become dangerously vulnerable to the onslaught of the enemy, fall apart and endure terrible losses. It was a unified spirit, an expressed and WORKING FAITH that would keep the formation together and ultimately win the day.

Phil. 1:27-29 *But you must always behave in a way that is worthy of the gospel of Christ, so that whether I come to you and see for myself or whether I only hear all about you from a distance, I shall find that you are standing firm and united in spirit, battling, as a team with a single aim, for the faith of the gospel, undismayed by any of your opponents. This will be a clear sign, for them that they are to be lost, and for you that you are to be saved.*

If the *faith* of the soldiers making up a testudo failed, the losses suffered by the unit could be shocking. This may be punishment enough for a unit in combat, but for the survivors of a Roman unit that failed in this manner, the losses at the hand of the enemy were only the beginning. While the loss of a units combat effectiveness is seen today as punishment enough for the survivors, ignominious defeat was not tolerated by the Romans. With the conclusion of the days fighting, the remnants of a faltered unit could be subjected to the disciplinary punishment of "Decimation." This punishment consisted of having the remnants of the unit lined up as if on parade, and stripped of armor. Any merits of distinction would be stripped from their standard, conspicuously dishonoring the entire unit (a tough enough punishment for some having fifteen to twenty years of service). This having been done, rift of armor and honor, the remnant would be counted off by tens. Once counted off, one man out of every ten of the survivors would be **PUT TO DEATH** by the hands of their comrades. A strong lesson indeed to teach the importance of **FAITH**, for it truly is a shield, which covers all.

Now that we have a better idea of how faith may be represented as a shield, let us see how it is defined in the scriptures and look at an example of how it may be expressed. In the book of **Hebrews**, we find a very clear definition of faith. The King James Bible reads: *[1]Now faith is the substance of things hoped for, the evidence of things not seen* **Heb. 11:1.** The New Jerusalem Bible puts it in a slightly different way: *Only faith can guarantee the blessings that we hope for, or prove the existence of realities that are unseen.* Our Lord Christ put the crucial question very simply Himself. As recorded in the gospel of **John**, Jesus put it very simply: *'I am the resurrection, anyone who believes in me, even though that person dies, will live, and whoever lives and believes in me will never die. Do you believe this?'* **Jn. 11:25-26.** It is your answer to His question which will determine whether or not you bear His "coat-of-arms," or heraldic display. After all, if you were to enlist in any army, you can expect to stand before an officer at some time, and take some form of oath of allegiance. God's army is no different. *The sheep that belong to me listen to my voice; I know them and they follow me. I give them eternal life; they will never be lost and no one will ever steal them from my hand. The Father, for what he has given me, is greater than anyone, and no one can steal anything from the Father's hand.* **Jn. 10:27-29.** Reread the definition of faith as found in **Heb. 11.** Our *Faith* is what essentially manifests those things that are unseen, yet hoped for. It is by faith that miracles may be performed, the impossible made possible. It is in having faith and daily living with it, that a Warrior takes on the nature of "the indomitable foe" when facing the enemy. To those around him, a faithful Warrior's life is filled with moments of unbelievable coincidence and chance. It is not chance and coincidence that is being witnessed, it is the very manifestation of things hoped for by faith.

Misplaced faith, or faith in false gods, does nothing to offer protection. *No one who believes in him will be judged; but whoever does not believe is judged already, because that man does not believe in the Name of God's only Son.* **Jn 3:18**. It is when we believe and have faith in the One True God, our Commander-in-Chief, and have faith in His promises that we step up and take charge with our faith secured to our spirits. *For this is how God loved the world: he gave his only Son, so that everyone who believes in him may not perish, but may have eternal life.* **Jn 3:16**.

There is a fine example of how faith may be displayed in the book of Romans, it shows how strength may be drawn from faith, and hope found when a situation seems hopeless: *Though there seemed no hope, he hoped and believed…in fulfillment of the promise: Just so will your descendants be. Even the thought that his body was as good as dead—he was about a hundred years old—and that Sarah's womb was dead too did not shake his faith. Counting on the promise of God, he did not doubt or disbelieve, but drew strength from faith and gave glory to God, fully convinced that whatever God promised he has the power to perform. This is the faith that was reckoned to him as uprightness. And the word 'reckoned' in scripture applies not only to him; it is there for our sake too—our faith, too will be 'reckoned' because we believe in him who raised from the dead our Lord Jesus who was handed over to death for our sins and raised to life for our justification.* **Rom. 4:18-25**.

I hope the Warrior within you has rallied to this chapter's words of faith. How a shield functions and how our faith relates to this type of protection should be clear. It has been stated that a shield of faith is infinitely more powerful and protective than a shield made of metal. Exactly where this power and protection come from and how it is to be grasped and used is the subject of the next section.

It is our faith in God's Word and promises that allows us to go to the armory and strap on this shield. Once we have committed our will to believe in God's Word, *God Himself* offers to become our shield! This is one of the reasons so many Warriors cannot fathom faith and *How* to use it. It is a wondrous mystery that is clearly laid out for us to grasp. It is in simply accepting the *Truth* of God's Word and putting it to work before us as our shield, as a Warrior would present a shield, which enables us to claim and use the shield of faith. *[1]Preserve me, O God: for in thee do I put my trust.* **Ps. 16:1.** This is not rhetoric. This *IS* how it works. You see, just as a physical shield must be hefted, held on to in order that it may be used, so it is with our *Faith*. Bearing in mind that our belts and straps spiritually represent truth, God's truth literally makes up the straps with which we grasp and use our shield, our faith. It is the *Truth* of God's Word, His promises that we must hold on to. We do this in order that we may raise our Shield of Faith and use it in the face of adversity, to stand stoically and move forward. In adhering to God's principles and commandments and claiming the Truth of His promises, we honor God and call upon Him to fulfill His promises. This is *Acting upon our Faith*. This is how we *Raise our Shield*, and garner its protection. The following scriptures very simply present this fact and call all Warriors to claim this assurance and protection.

Ps. 119:86-88 *All your commandments show constancy. Help me when they pursue me dishonestly. They have almost annihilated me on earth, but I have not deserted your precepts. True to your faithful love, give me life, and I shall keep the instructions you have laid down.*

First, we must honor God and His precepts, standing firm in His promises. God is a faithful Master, who will honor His promises. You will not be surprised to see the word-promise-occur so many times in this chapter when you recognize that it is our belief and trust in God's Word which is our initial act of faith, and compels God to make good on His promises and assurances for us.

Deut. 7:7-24 (excerpted) *Yahweh set His heart on you and chose you…because He loved you and meant to keep the oath which He* *swore to your ancestors…This is why God brought you out with His mighty hand and redeemed you from the place of slave-labour…You can see that Yahweh your God is the true God, the faithful God who,…is true to His covenant and His faithful love for a thousand generations as regards those who love Him and keep His commandments…He destroys anyone who hates Him…Listen to these ordinances, be true to them and observe them, and in return Yahweh your God will be true to the covenant and love which He promised on oath to your ancestors. He will love you and bless you…You may say in your heart, "These nations outnumber me; how shall I be able to dispossess them?" Do not be afraid of them: remember how Yahweh your God treated Pharaoh and all Egypt…do not be afraid of them, for Yahweh your God is among you, a great and terrible God… God will clear away these nations disastrous for you. But Yahweh your God will put them at your mercy, and disaster after disaster will overtake them until they are finally destroyed…no one will be able to resist you—until you have destroyed them all.*

If this simply were not true, then there would never be a reason to follow His Word. When His promises are held close to the heart and followed in faith and love, God **WILL** respond. He has to, He has promised to. If God's army of Warriors followed this simple rule, and God did not honor His promise, we would simply all be destroyed. And yet, **WE STAND!** With **God** as our shield before us, incredible incidents of synchronicity commonly occur, and often we are left awed by what has occurred. In a hopeless situation that faithful Warriors have turned over to the Creator, wondrous things will be witnessed: ***Trust wholeheartedly in Yahweh, put no faith in your own perception; acknowledge Him in every course you take, and He will see that your paths are smooth.*** **Prov. 3:5-6.** Seldom will these occurrences make sense to the unbeliever, but to those Warriors who have followed their orders, the hand of the Almighty will be clear enough.

You may have some idea of just how protective a steel shield is. We began this chapter with a look at ancient shields and how they were constructed, so it is only fitting that we do the same for our spiritual shield. *He reserves His advice for the honest, a shield to those whose ways are sound...* **Prov. 2:7.**

Unlike material shields, our spiritual shield of faith is constructed of something ethereal at best, yet, it is far stronger than steel. To relate the invincibility of our shield of faith, it may help to understand why it is stronger than steel. The simple answer is that it is unalloyed. ***Every word of God is unalloyed, a shield to those who take refuge in him.*** **Prov. 30:5.** We are additionally instructed that our shield of faith is indestructible. ***You give me your invincible shield (your right hand upholds me.*** **Ps. 18:35.** The key to understanding what this really means, and why it makes a Warrior's Shield of Faith so powerful, is simple. God, ***Himself***, offers to serve as our shield once we claim ***His*** protection through faith. God speaks plainly, thus our faith shield is unalloyed, pure, and invincible, and it is our faith, which calls upon God to manifest His promises about us.

So how do we as Warriors believe that our Creator will actually serve as our shield? He says He will, so hold Him to it! ...***On the contrary, you must be loyal to Yahweh your God as you have been till now. Yahweh has dispossessed great and powerful nations before you, and no one so far has been able to resist you. One man of you was able to rout a thousand of them, since Yahweh your God was Himself fighting for you, as He had promised you.*** **Jos. 23:8-10.** ***Accuse my accusers, Yahweh, attack my attackers, Grasp your buckler and shield up, and help me. Brandish spear and pike to confront my pursuers, give me the assurance, 'I am your Savior.'*** **Ps. 35:1-4.** And most clearly we see in the following Psalm: ***We are waiting for Yahweh; He is our help and our shield, for in Him our heart rejoices, in His holy name we trust.*** **Ps. 33:20.** God waits for the moment we are faithful to Him, and honor Him by our displaying our willingness to rest in His promises of salvation, and protection. Then we are able to receive the blessings He desires to bestow upon us, and the protection He has promised to deliver.

It cannot be put any more explicitly than we find in Psalms. Any Warrior of God must find security in these words: ...***my God in whom I trust! He rescues you from the snare of the fowler set on destruction;...you find shelter under His wings. His constancy is shield and protection. You need not fear the terrors of night. The arrow that flies in the daytime, the plague that stalks in the*** *darkness, the scourge that wreaks havoc at high noon. Though a thousand fall at your side, ten thousand at your right hand, you yourself will remain unscathed. You have only to keep your eyes open to see how the wicked are repaid, you who say, 'Yahweh my refuge!' and make Elyon your fortress. No disaster can overtake you, no plague come near your tent; He has given His angels orders about you to guard you wherever you go. They will carry you in their arms in case you trip over a stone. You will walk upon wild beast and adder, you will trample young lions and snakes. 'Since he clings to Me I rescue him, I raise him high, since he acknowledges My name. He calls to Me and I answer him: in distress I am at his side, I rescue him and bring him honor. I shall satisfy him with long life, and grant him to see my salvation.'* **Ps. 91:1-16**.

When we have trained as warriors, we learn that our weapons include: prayer, fasting, communal prayer, singing praise and giving thanks. Prayer grasps the promises of God and erects them like a wall between us and the powers of darkness. Prayer can bring God's angels rushing to our assistance. Use a good reference Bible and read this verse, ^{13}***But the prince of the kingdom of Persia withstood me one and twenty days: but, lo, Michael, one of the Chief Princes, came to help me; and I remained there with the kings of Persia.*** **Dan. 10:13**. ^{14}***Are they not all ministering spirits, sent forth to minister for them who shall be heirs of salvation?*** **Heb 1:14**.

Now that the Psalm 91 has been introduced, I would like to relate a very powerful historical story. During World War I, the 91st Infantry Division was formed, and shipped overseas to serve in Europe during the peak of the war. One Brigade in particular, the 91st Infantry Brigade, distinguished itself during many of the bloodiest battles. They were part of the American Expeditionary forces. Its commander was a devout Christian man, and had delivered to each of his men a small card on which he had printed Psalm 91. As agreed, the men met each morning and recited Psalm 91 together. Among other engagements fought in by their Brigade were three of the bloodiest battles of the entire war: Chateau Thierry, Belle Wood, and the Argonne. It is not uncommon to find other units engaged in these battles having suffered better than fifty percent casualties, and several similarly engaged units are on record having suffered up to **ninety percent casualties!** In stark contrast to these records, the 91st

Infantry Brigade **did not suffer ONE combat related casualty!**[§] **Few other examples of true "Warriors of Faith" are as compelling as this notable fact.**

A true Warrior invokes God's protection by honoring God with faith in His Word. When this is claimed, the protection of our spiritual Shield of Faith will then prevail and cover the faithful from attacks above, unseen, and all about. An additional element of the Shield of Faith is the strength that comes with it. *Bow down, then, before the power of God now, so that He may raise you up in due time; unload all your burden on to Him, since He is concerned about you. Keep sober and alert, because your enemy the devil is on the prowl like a roaring lion, looking for someone to devour. Stand up to him, strong in faith and in the knowledge that it is the same kind of suffering that the community of your brothers throughout the world is undergoing. You will have to suffer only for a little while; the God of all grace who called you to eternal glory in Christ will restore you, He will confirm, strengthen, and support you. His power lasts forever and ever. AMEN.* **1 Ptr. 5:6-11.**

It is simple as this. Place your trust in God and His Word, and He will protect and preserve you. *[31]As for God, his way is perfect; the word of the LORD is tried: he is a buckler to all them that trust in him.* **2 Sam. 22:31.** *[5]Every word of God is pure: he is a shield unto them that put their trust in him.* **Prov. 30:5.**

The assurance that we are covered from attacks above and will derive strength can also be found in: *Yahweh my Lord, my saving strength, You shield my head when battle comes.* **Ps. 140:7.** This points out again that it is the strength of our Almighty God, the Father, who empowers us with the strength to fight to the victorious end. The shield of faith is automatically deployed to shield our head from attacks from above.

The following scriptures relate the characteristics of faith and how it serves to protect us from other directions of attack. The typical attack, which is directed at our heart, is often the frontal assault. In this direction our shield is well presented: *'Do not let your hearts be*

[§] This information can be found on the 91st Infantry Division website as recorded by Col. Jack Mohr.

troubled. You trust in God, trust also in me.' **Jn. 14:1.** These words of power were spoken by our Savior, and serve to remind us that when our hearts are filled with His love, those hostile, pointed, needling words aimed at us, are first absorbed, or quenched, by His love. This serves to bestow compassion and understanding on us. Doing so helps to keep us balanced, and efficiently respond with love to those who have offended us. Jesus also taught His disciples *[44]But I say unto you, love your enemies, bless them that curse you, do good to them that hate you, and pray for them which despitefully use you, and persecute you...* **Matt. 5:44**. Additionally, when it comes to those frontal attacks, bear in mind God's promise: *Yahweh is my strength and my shield, in him my heart trusts.* **Ps. 28:7.** Entrusting your heart to God's protection is a sure winner. So you see, a frontal attack will avail the enemy nothing.

The enemy we fight is a cunning and cowardly one. While the enemy may often attack us head on, frontally, they will typically reserve this tactic for a Warrior they feel may be caught napping, unawares, or ill-prepared in faith. The more common form of attack chosen by our cowardly foe is the blind-side attack, the ambush. One of the wonderful things about our shield is that it will protect us from unseen attacks, not just the blows of the enemy we see aimed at us: *For look, the wicked are drawing their bows, fitting their arrows to the string to shoot honest men from the shadows...Yahweh examines the upright and the wicked, the lover of violence he detests. He will rain down red-hot coals, fire and sulphur on the wicked a scorching wind will be their lot.* **Ps.11:2, 5.** Even though the enemy may escape our eyes, the eyes of God always see them.

God also defends us from attacks to our flanks, or our sides: *But you, Yahweh, the shield at my side, my glory, you hold my head high.* **Ps. 3:3.** This effectively means that God is our protection from all directions of attack. Think about it. From above, the front, sides, and the unseen—we are virtually surrounded in God's protection. Can this be shown in the scriptures as well? You bet! *It is you who bless the upright, Yahweh, you surround them with favor as with a shield.* **Ps. 5:12.** There you have it, complete coverage (and better coverage than any metal shield *this* Warrior has ever fought behind).

Let us see how the scriptures instruct us as to the strength and power of faith when applied by a Warrior. The first scripture from

Hebrews shows an example of many of the principles of faith and its might. Claiming the promises God has made, and acting on faith, empowers the Warrior with courage, perseverance, strength, and invincibility: *What more shall I say? There is not time for me to give an account of Gideon, Barak, Samson, Jephthae, or of David, Samuel and the prophets. These were men who through faith conquered kingdoms, did what was upright and earned the promises. They could keep a lion's mouth shut, put out blazing fires and emerge unscathed from battle. They were weak people who were given strength to be brave in war and drive back foreign invaders.* **Heb. 11:32-34.**

When we unquestioningly take our orders and carry them out, we are supported by God's hand and kept from the snares of the enemy (this is a benefit which was related when the spiritual armor of our feet, willingness and doing, was discussed). In order to act on our will, our faith is often called upon. It is then that we can walk over pitfalls on the arm of the Lord, and complete our mission of peace: *I shall rescue you from the people and from the nations to whom I send you to open their eyes, so that they may turn from darkness to light, from the dominion of Satan to God, and receive, through faith in me, forgiveness of their sins and a share in the inheritance of the sanctified.* **Acts 26:17-18.**

All victory and credit is bestowed upon our Lord, who defeated Death and claimed our salvation in fulfillment of God's new covenant. *Thank God, then, for giving us the victory through Jesus Christ our Lord. So, my dear brothers, keep firm and immovable, always abounding in energy for the Lord's work, being sure that in the Lord none of your labors is wasted.* **1 Cor. 15:57-58.**

Just as the elements of salvation and willingness-and-doing are seen in our expression of faith, the elements of our belt of protection can also be found related to faith. The fact that we must display our faith in God's Word shows trust, and acting on our faith shows our belief in God's promises as true.

Ps. 119:33-34 *"Keep my steps firm in your promise; that no evil may triumph over me. Rescue me from human oppression, and I will observe your precepts."*

Many characteristics help us to develop and act on our faith and beliefs. You may have recognized several of them in the above scriptures. Exercising these characteristics makes walking in faith easier, and enables us to accept the seemingly miraculous nature of some of the events that may occur around us when we get it right. Specifically, some of the characteristics which serve to strengthen and support our expression of Faith, and the development of our spiritual "Shield of Faith" are the following: fearlessness, perseverance, willing and doing, humility, devotion to a greater cause, nobility, and strength.

When a Warrior takes "the leap of faith," and sees the completion of his duty before he understands *how* it may yet happen, he has purged any spies within the camp of the mind by his expression, through action, of his faith. Once doubt and fear are checked in our mind, then we are free to accept an opportunity, share, and do what the Spirit leads us to do. This is essential as a Warrior must be free and able to engage, take part, take a stand, or move as opportunity presents itself.[ii] When a Warrior acts in a manner directed solely by his faith and belief in the scriptures, and what he feels led to do by the Holy Spirit, the mind of the Warrior is immune to doubts and fears. As these are the principle weapons of the enemy, and they have been neutralized, the enemy must resort to rash methods or blatant actions. These types of attacks are generally easy to recognize and neutralize by the conscientious, and deliberate acts of a Warrior supported by prayer and fasting. There are times when prayer and fasting are required, as the battle we wage is of a spiritual nature, and it is often required that we add the prayers of others, or personal sacrifice, to mount a successful attack against an entrenched, or powerful foe. Our Lord Jesus taught this lesson to His disciples. **^{29}*And He said unto them, 'This kind can come forth by nothing, but by prayer and fasting.'* Mk. 9:29.**

As difficult, a concept as this perception of using faith may seem, simply by virtue of its simplicity, we are encouraged to act fearlessly

---

[ii] Fear and Doubt typically set in after we have been softened up by Worry. These weapons of the enemy are directed at immobilizing God's Warriors, and Love and acts of Faith destroy these "enemies within."

when it comes to matters of faith. These are the most exciting moments in our life of faith, and when a Warrior begins to "live the ordinary life in the unordinary way," it comes easier and easier to rely upon one's faith. Liken the experience to skydiving. You had better believe the first few times a skydiver "takes the leap," he thinks a lot about that chute opening. But very quickly, with regular success, this no longer pervades the mind, and the leap from the plane is exuberantly looked forward to. In the eventuality of a main-chute failure (liken this to our spiritual enemy pulling a fast one on us), a successful deployment of the reserve chute after many drills in this sort of emergency, results in a successful, although somewhat abbreviated, jump. No matter what happens, God is with us, and we are to give no thought to failure. ***Do not lose your fearlessness now, then, since the reward is so great. You will need perseverance if you are to do God's will and gain what he has promised.*** **Heb. 10:35-36.** A contingency plan will always present itself to the faithful Warrior, for God is in control of the battle, and we are merely to claim the victories for Him! ***A human heart makes the plans, Yahweh gives the answer.*** **Prov. 16:1.**

An important admonishment is found in the above scripture. Perseverance is required if we are to do God's will and accomplish our task. Nobody ever said our faith would be a cakewalk. Quite to the contrary, Jesus warned those wanting to follow Him that their lives would be filled with temptation, trials, and tribulations. His disciples recognized this fact. Now this fact is welcomed as it serves to develop…guess what, Character! ***[3]And not only so, but we glory in tribulations also: knowing that tribulation worketh patience; [4]And patience, experience; and experience, hope: [5]And hope maketh not ashamed; because the love of God is shed abroad in our hearts by the Holy Ghost which is given unto us.*** **Rom. 5:3-5.** Continuing in the face of adversity is a hallmark of the very qualities required of the faithful: perseverance, fearlessness, and strength or fortitude. After all, anyone can simply give up when the chips are down and the outcome looks grim, but that is just the moment a true Warrior is made for. ***So then, now that we have been justified by faith, we are at peace with God through our Lord Jesus Christ; it is through him, by faith, that we have been admitted into God's favor in which we are living, and look forward exultantly to God's glory.***

Not only that; let us exult, too, in our hardships, understanding that hardship develops perseverance, and perseverance develops a tested character, something that gives us hope, and a hope which will not let us down, because the love of God has been poured into our hearts by the Holy Spirit which has been given to us. **Rom. 5:1-5.**

Ultimately, when we most fear to take action, it is then we *MUST ACT!* This is the purest expression of courage. Simply believing something is going to happen does not exclude us from imparting some of our will and exercising our faith to show that we expect an outcome. Faith alone will not cut the mustard. We are expected to "put our actions where our faith is," much like we are asked to "put our money where our mouth is" when it comes to mundane situations. Some time we have to unscrew the jar and dip some mustard out with a knife. It certainly is not going to come out of the jar by itself, now is it? *[17]Even so faith, if it hath not works, is dead, being alone.* **Jm. 2:17.** Even though we may fear in our heart, or question with our mind, we must still be willing to act on this faith of ours and act. This exemplifies our willingness to do, and the doing, both which may become acts of courage and perseverance in light of our faith.

A good example of how this works can be found in **Numbers 21**, and **Deuteronomy 2**. The people of Israel needed to pass through the land of King Sihon, king of the Amorites in the land of Heshbon. When Sihon rejected the peaceful requests of the Israelites and mounted war against them, God's directive to His people was simple and clear *[31]...begin to possess, that thou mayest inherit his land.* **Deut. 2:31**. It was an act of faith that led the Israelites to move against Sihon. This was required of them by God, for they were disposed to peacefully pass through the land, rather than fight. God turned all the land of Sihon over to the Israelites for their obedience. When we are obedient to God's word, expect the unexpected.

Another subtle effect bears pointing out on this note. There is a vast difference between reacting to a situation, and responding to it. Reacting leads to quick, ill-conceived actions, or snap decisions. In contrast, responses come from trained actions, the experience of training and discipline. The proper response to any number of situations through training, removes the demand for thought, or reflection, as the trained response has been instilled with forethought and discipline. This allows an immediate response to a situation without the need for contemplation. At a time when action is called for, there is no time for thinking. Had the Israelites simply *reacted* to King Sihon's actions, they may have just run away.

Another way to consider the difference between reacting and responding, may be to consider the actions required during combat, say a sword fight. When the enemy makes his move, a properly trained Warrior need not consider how to defend himself, he just does it. The proper response has become a trained action. Only through this type of training can we eliminate the natural reflex to flinch. In much the same way, a successful batter will swing only on good pitches, rather than swing on any pitch that seems good, and strike out. Action from a trained and relaxed mind is lucid, fluid, for it comes from a deeper wellspring than those of reactions. Reactions come from emotional states, or natural reflexes, both of which can be used against you by a wily and trained enemy.

As much as our faith is all ours, it is empowered by the selfless act of sacrifice made by our Savior. For this reason, a humble spirit must be carried within the heart of a Warrior, for it must always be remembered that the sacrifice of God's only Son was required to redeem us. ***If we accept the testimony of human witnesses, God's testimony is greater, for this is God's testimony which He gave about His Son. Whoever believes in the Son of God has the testimony within him...This is the Testimony: God has given us eternal life, and this life is in His Son. Whoever has the Son has life, and whoever has not the Son of God has not life. 1 Jn. 5:9-12.*** It would be contemptuously prideful to believe we could ever walk into our Creator's presence without recognizing and accepting this fact. A sacrifice had to be made to redeem us; that is, the sacrifice of God's son. When we accept that we are without justification barring the sacrifice of God's most Holy Son, we represent humility in our heart. None of us can bear up our own pride and have it count for anything.

This understanding fuels one's devotion to a greater cause, and enables a Warrior to offer up his own life to fulfill his mission, as he understands that it is not his limited understanding and desires being fulfilled. This is the example we have been given and we have been instructed that *[13]Greater love hath no man than this, that a man lay down his life for his friends. [14]Ye are my friends, if ye do whatsoever I command you.* **Jn. 15:13-14.** This is a very noble act indeed, one exemplified by our Lord, and this selfless act serves as a good definition of nobility. We are asked to do whatever is required, and His example was to lay one's life down for another if need be. A Warrior must be prepared to follow this example. In ancient times, if a commoner were to handle the shield of a nobleman without permission, he might suffer the loss of a hand. This stands in stark contrast to the desire our Lord has for all of us to accept His ennobling selfless act of redemption, embrace His helmet of salvation, don His mantle of saving blood, freely displaying His Coat-of-Arms as our Shield of Faith, and become co-heirs to his Kingdom.

When a Warrior is aware of this code of behavior which serves as his model, it helps to bear in mind that courage and strength will be provided by faithful action. ***Be vigilant, stay firm in the faith, be brave and strong. Let everything you do be done in love.*** **1 Cor. 16:13-14.** With the strength supplied by God, nothing is impossible, it merely takes courage and strength of will to see our actions to completion.

Col. 1:21-23 *You were once estranged and of hostile intent through your evil behavior; now he has reconciled you, by his death and in that mortal body, to bring you before himself holy, faultless and irreproachable—as long as you persevere and stand firm on the solid base of the faith, never letting yourselves drift away from the hope promised by the gospel, which you have heard...* the impossible will be accomplished.

The Shield of Faith is truly a mighty piece of armor in the arsenal of the Warrior and to take a phrase from a popular credit card, "Don't leave home without it!" While a literal shield is typically the last piece of armor to be picked up and settled into for combat, our walk of faith *begins* with applying faith's principles. Everything else follows in kind, but faith begins us on the road. We never know when our time has run out, so it is imperative that we avail ourselves of faith's protection at the earliest convenience.

Mk. 1:15 *The time is fulfilled, and the kingdom of God is close at hand. Repent, and believe the gospel.*

Philip Paul Sacco

Our last piece of armament will be handled in the next chapter:

"The Sword of the Spirit"

Chapter 11

The Sword of Spirit

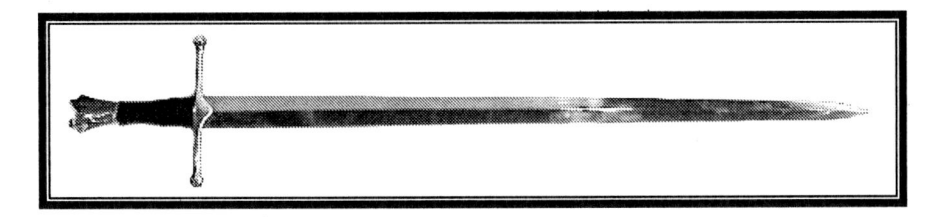

Eph. 6:17 *Receive the sword of the Spirit, which is the Word of God...*

Rev. 19:11-16 *And now I saw heaven open, and a white horse appear; its rider was called Trustworthy and true; in uprightness he judges and makes war. His eyes were flames of fire, and he was crowned with many coronets; the name written on him was known only to himself, his cloak was soaked in blood. He is known by the name The Word of God. Behind him dressed in linen of dazzling white, rode the armies of heaven on white horses. From his mouth came a sharp sword with which to strike the unbelievers; he is the one who will rule them with an iron scepter, and tread out the wine of almighty God's fierce retribution. On his cloak and on his thigh a name was written, KING OF KINGS AND LORD OF LORDS.*

This is our last piece of spiritual armor, "The Sword of the Spirit, which is the Word of God." When you undertake the history of the sword, one acquires the history of mankind. Mankind created many innovations; several led to the deadliest of all of man's creations, the sword. These innovations have shaped our society today, just as markedly as the sword shaped the maps of the world. By having a better understanding of how a sword was fashioned and used, we may gain certain insights into how we may call upon and rely upon our spiritual sword. Having a better understanding of the characteristics of a sword, we may better understand how these characteristics in us apply to our spiritual weapon. While it was mentioned in the preceding chapter how a properly instructed Warrior can use their faith as a weapon, it is our ***Sword*** that is constructed specifically as a weapon. Being it is our sole offensive arm, having a sound understanding of how to use it is essential for a Warrior who looks to engage the enemy and serve well in the ranks of the Lord.

During the Stone Age, we find our earliest examples of swords fashioned out of stone by a process not unlike the knapping of chirk, obsidian, or flint by the American Indians and other ancient cultures for arrowheads, skinning knives, and spear points. While stone-age man left many examples of the stone sword, it took the development and understanding of metallurgy to begin the development of the type of sword commonly known to us today. With constant upgrades in the design and materials used for body protection, there was a continuous need for improvements in the weapons of the day throughout history. A delicate balance existed between the protective ability of the armor of the day and the efficiency of the typical weapons of that time. For a short period the weapons would prove the current body armor ineffective, then some innovation would be developed which would see body protection defeat the ability of conventional weapons to do any damage to the well accoutered soldier of the day. This ever escalating development of arms and armor has continued through today. While body armor is no longer used to the degree it was worn until a few hundred years ago, the arms race is clearly apparent today in the development of artillery, anti-tank weaponry and the constant development of defensive armor for tank. As the armor plating of tanks become more resistant, the artillery rounds fired at them will need to become more penetrating and destructive. This in turn forces the need for new defensive enhancements and so on.

At the top of the list of weapons development, sit our weapons of mass destruction. When weapons are no longer used by one assailant against another, but rather an entire people may be obliterated with the simple push of a button, the concept of defense takes on a new definition. Some envision this insanity to escalate until a real *"doomsday device"* is created capable of destroying our entire world.[*] The question of striking a mortal blow against your assailant on the individual level is no longer the concern, but rather striking a mortal blow against an entire nation or people becomes the issue. When the use of weapons of this magnitude becomes considered, the sentiment, "If *we* go, ***Everyone*** goes!" pervades. That sentiment appears to make sense to an ever increasing and alarming number of people. It should strike the reader that there is something seriously wrong with this mindset. It makes more sense to concentrate on making our presence a blessing and asset to those around us, and on a larger scale, the world. Then, rather than planning to destroy us, thoughts would be towards preserving us. Nevertheless, as awesome and destructive as a dooms-day device may sound, it is nothing to compare with the power of our spiritual sword, The Sword of the Spirit, which is the Word of God! For a hint as to the awesome power of God's Word, we find in Jeremiah that God's Word can be heard in the remotest corner of the earth, verily to its core! ***The noise resounds to the remotest parts of the earth. For Yahweh is indicting the nations, arraigning all humanity for judgment; the wicked he assigns to the sword, Yahweh declares.* Jer. 25:31.** Now the weapons of man are capable of making a nice hole in the ground, but God's Word can make the entire Earth tremble.

Even more profound than the destructive power of the Word of God is the awesome power of His Word to bring about creation itself. It should be remembered that God, by His spoken Word, brought all

---

[*] While it does not seem to make much sense to use a weapon, which will kill oneself if used, such is the insanity of mankind to make sure that "a reprisal strike" may be made if one is annihilated by a first strike. The fear of the ultimate doom of the world by an already eliminated opponent is supposed to be threat enough to prevent the first strike from being attempted. This is supposed to make us feel better somehow, in knowing that those who killed us would in turn be eliminated. It does not seem to matter that the rest of the world's innocents would additionally be destroyed. This makes no sense to the author! **Heb. 10:30-31** *We are all aware who it was that said: 'Vengeance is mine; I will pay them back.' And again: 'The Lord will vindicate His people.' It is a dreadful thing to fall into the hands of the living God.*

of creation into being: ^{3}*And God said, Let there be light: and there was light...*^{6}*And God said, Let there be a firmament in the midst of the waters, and let it divide the waters from the waters...*^{9}*And God said, Let the waters under the heaven be gathered together unto one place, and let the dry land appear: and it was so...*^{11}*And God said, Let the earth bring forth grass, the herb yielding seed, and the fruit tree yielding fruit after his kind, whose seed is in itself, upon the earth: and it was so...*^{14}*And God said, Let there be lights in the firmament of the heaven to divide the day from the night; and let them be for signs, and for seasons, and for days, and years: ...*^{20}*And God said, Let the waters bring forth abundantly the moving creature that hath life, and fowl that may fly above the earth in the open firmament of heaven...*^{24}*And God said, Let the earth bring forth the living creature after his kind, cattle, and creeping thing, and beast of the earth after his kind: and it was so...*^{26}*And God said, Let us make man in our image, after our likeness...* Gen. 1:3, 6, 9, 11, 14, 20, 24, 26.

Once mankind developed the skills and understanding of smelting and metallurgy, everything in society began to change at an increasing rate. One of the earliest metals used to pour molds or hammer into swords was copper; consequently, replacing the need for chopping and cutting weapons of the day. This new found material offered the advantage of resilience and an edge that easily allowed the material to be continuously sharpened if it became dulled. As man grew accustomed to this new material, various means of handling it proved to increase the characteristics of the metal, such as heat-treating it. This was a process by which the metal was heated, and then cooled slowly. This process eventually led to tempering of metal that proved advantageous hundreds of years later when yet another, more durable, metal was discovered which could fully take advantage of the tempering process. While copper swords were found to be a great improvement over stone ones, it was simply a matter of time before a new metal was discovered which would render the copper sword as obsolete as its predecessor.

This new metal was an alloy of different metals, a true accomplishment of metallurgy. Man entered a new epoch with the advent of this new metal, and we refer to this period by its name. Mankind entered the Bronze Age. This new metal held an edge longer, did not tarnish as readily, nor was it as heavy as copper. It was stronger than copper, and would not deform when stressed beyond a certain point. These characteristics made it possible for a weapon made of bronze to cut a copper sword in half and chop through copper plating, the material of the day for body armor. It seemed as though a miracle had been invented. The cultural shift of power and influence for vast regions of the world revolved around which culture developed this new improved metal for use on the battlefield first. What could be better than this new found material— why another, more durable metal, of course.

As mankind's technology and ability to work metals improved, so did the characteristics of the metals he produced. This continuing process proved to have such an impact on society that the next epoch of societal evolution bears, yet again, the name of man's next most profound discovery. With the discovery of iron, mankind entered what we call today the Iron Age. During this epoch, with man's creative genius and skills in working this new metal, the process of tempering iron was discovered and with it all sorts of inventions began to make their way into society. Tempering allowed iron to take on resilience unseen in metals, providing the metal with "spring." By sheer good fortune and luck, the process of tempering iron incorporated carbon into the metal. This led to improving the characteristics of iron by converting it into steel.[†] Steel is even more durable, stronger, and more resilient than iron and proved to be an excellent material for use in the construction of body armor. An added benefit was the ability to increases steel's resistance to rusting with annealing and case hardening. Steel became the standard for generations to construct armor with, as it would take a finer grade of

---

[†] The Japanese were among the very first people to master the process of making tempered steel, and this some 2,000 years before its common use in Western Europe. The Japanese Samurai sword has a unique distinction as some of the finest steel ever produced. The exact process is only known by a few craftsmen today, and the tradition is passed by the old world tradition of apprenticeship. The few remaining masters of the art are dying off, and their knowledge of this ancient art stands being lost for all time due to the lack of "proper students to learn the mysteries."

steel blade, one that was tempered to perfection, to compromise steel armor.

The process of tempering was said to add "life" to a steel sword, such was its characteristic to spring, or rebound, when a solid object was struck, as if the weapon had a life of its own. A well-tempered spring steel sword also had the ability to be bent grossly out of true and yet spring back to true from its own "memory." The development of spring steel made possible, of all things, *springs*, which were useful in all kinds of new machines and contrivances, such as the clock. Knives and implements of seemingly indefinite longevity were produced. Iron, and subsequently steel, proved to be incredibly more durable than even bronze had seemed when compared to copper. Whereas bronze was a rigid metal which could snap if stressed too heavily, not unlike the earlier stone swords, a steel sword was capable of withstanding tremendous deformation and resist breakage. Some of the finest tempered blades can be bent into a complete circle, not break, and still return to true.

Smaller and more intricate tools could now be made with this new metal and craftsmanship, in virtually all disciplines, accelerated as more and increasingly powerful and intricate tools were fashioned. Hundreds of years passed in Europe before what had been discovered in Asia some two thousand years earlier was stumbled upon. This was the perfection of the tempering process to the point that reliable results could be regularly reproduced in a finished piece.

There are many historical accounts that describe the destructive capability of the sword. However, by virtue of the fact that we no longer see swords in society, it is easy to lose sight of just how deadly a weapon the sword is. To date, no other weapon has been responsible for the loss of more human life than the sword! History is full of recordings that tell of the brutal and savage power and authority levied by the sword. One of the most striking accounts can be found in the book of **Judges 12**. Jephthah had served as judge of Israel between 1143 and 1137 B.C., and after the defeat of the Ammonites, he was confronted by the men of Ephraim for excluding them from the battle. Jephthah led the men of Gilead to war against the Ephraimites for raising arms against him, and some forty-two thousand Ephraimites were put to the sword.

One of the most well known swords of all history is the Roman short sword. The short thrusting sword of the Roman Legions has the honor of being the single most destructive weapon ever fashioned by man. The Roman "Gladius," as it is called, is on record as having slain upwards of quarter million Gauls in one battle alone. In the year 51 B.C., Julius Caesar with an army of some 50,000 Romans, surrounded a Gallic force almost twice his army's size in the fortified city of Alesia. To accomplish this feat, Caesar surrounded the fortress with a double set of ramparts, a doughnut, as it has come to be called. The inner perimeter involved some eleven miles of ramparts, and the outer perimeter some 14 miles of fortifications. Facing outwards from both perimeters were a combined 50 miles of trenches and beyond that another hundred yards of field obstructions and pitfalls. These measures were found necessary by Caesar as he had word of an additional 250,000 Gallic tribesman coming to the assistance of their besieged kinsmen. This seemingly hopeless situation for the Romans brought them to fight against a combined enemy force in excess of six times greater than their own number. In a flawless display of Roman military perfection, with his blockaded and surrounded Legions hard-pressed from both sides, in a position both surrounding a force and themselves being surrounded, Julius Caesar exacted a triumphant victory using primarily the Roman weapon of choice—the Roman Gladius—a weapon of terrible destructive force in the hands of a trained professional soldier. Only a few scattered remnants of the Gallic forces escaped the Romans.

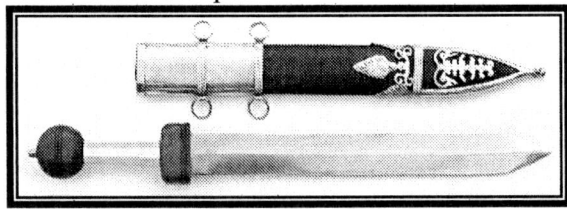

The Roman Gladius was well known to the Apostles, as they would have been seen everyday on the streets as the Roman patrols made their rounds. It may come as a surprise to you that one of Jesus' closest friends carried a sword. In fact, we are told Simon Peter carried a sword: ***Simon Peter, who had a sword… Jn. 18:10.*** For that matter, many of those with Jesus during His arrest had swords and offered to use them to defend Jesus: ***His followers, seeing what was about to happen, said, 'Lord, shall we use our swords?' Lk. 22:48.***

The short sword, being double edged, is a weapon capable of cutting in both directions as well as being capable of delivering a terrible thrusting wound. The distinct advantage of a two-edged blade such as this is simple. Having used it to ward off a blow from one side of the body the reverse edge always presents an immediate attack to respond with: ...***in the word of truth and in the power of God; by using the weapons of uprightness for attack and defense...* 2 Cor. 6:7.** This makes the short sword not only a weapon suited for attack and defense, but one that is exceptionally swift in its delivery. ***¹²For the word of God is quick, and powerful...* Heb. 4:12.**

As for the awesome cleaving power of a sword, I would like to retell the story of Richard the Lionhearted in one of his battles against the forces of Saladin in the Holy Land. Richard, single handedly, charged headlong into a company of the enemy and killed some thirty men in single combat with just his sword. The last man Richard is recorded as having killed was an enormous monster of a man, and a champion of the Saracen army. Standing in his stirrups with his sword raised high, Richard allowed the enemy champion to charge with lowered spear aimed at his armpit. At the last moment, just as the Saracen multitude expected to see the last of the Frankish King, Richard slipped the point of the spear and neatly clove the man in two, from shoulder to hip, through Saracen armor, leather, and padding. This alone is a heroic example of the cutting ability of the sword, not to mention the fact that with this one blow, Richard also severed the head of his opponent's horse from its body through the thickest part of its neck.

Spiritually, it is fitting that the Word of God is symbolically related to us as a sword. A quality of a sword is that it has the ability to cut through all meat clean to the bone. This is another way of saying the Word is incisive enough to cut away all the fat and chaff of a situation, position or matter to reveal the underlying structure, the bones, or true heart of the matter. Just as a sword, *the Word* has the ability to lay bare the essentials, the vitals. As mentioned earlier, a well-tempered sword is often described as having a life of its own. This also is a quality referred to in describing the Word of God. ***The Word of God is something alive and active; it cuts more incisively than any two-edged sword; it can seek out the place where soul is divided from spirit, or joints from marrow; it can pass judgment on*** *secret emotions and thoughts.* **Heb. 4:12-13.** Now to me, I am sure for you also, something that can pass judgment on our secret emotions and thoughts is incisive.

Just as a sword is used offensively and defensively, we must be wary of the manner in which we use the Word of God as it can be used against us if we are not careful. The Word of God, itself described as a "terrible two-edged sword," is often used by our adversary against us. In the book of **Matthew** we are told of an instance when Jesus himself was tempted by the devil using words of the old testament as a test: *'If you are the Son of God,' he said, 'throw yourself down; for scripture says: He has given his angels orders about you, and they will carry you in their arms in case you trip over a stone.'* **Matt. 4:6.** There are several instances in which the devil shows himself to be quite versed in the words of the scriptures and readily uses them to force his point. False prophets are another example of how the enemy may use God's Word against us (Ref. **Ps. 91:11-12**).

There is another way to say the Word cuts both ways. A two-edged sword, if used carelessly and without control, can lead to personal harm. There is a very fixed manner in which a sword such as this can be safely handled. To carelessly grasp the blade can lead to personal injury. The Word of God should not be used in a manner that causes harm in a callous way, unkind, or unthinking manner either.‡ If used in this fashion, we may have our words used against us in turn. The Word of God is a glorious thing to be used in a constructive way and not for our personal agenda. Remember, a Warrior is given to a greater cause, taking orders from a higher authority. He does not fight for his personal gain, but for the good of a greater cause. *Though the wicked draw his sword and bend his bow to slaughter the honest and bring down the poor and the needy, his sword will pierce his own heart, and his bow will be shattered.*

---

‡ A good example of careless or uncontrolled use of God's Word would be to use the scriptures to judge others and their flaws while refusing to note our own flaws, This is just one simple and typical example of how the Word of God may be used in a fashion not intended for its use (**Matt. 7:1-5, Luke 6:41-42**). The result is self-judgment, or personal condemnation.

What little the upright possesses outweighs all the wealth of the wicked; for the weapons of the wicked shall be shattered, while Yahweh supports the upright. **Ps. 37:14-17.**

The Christian Warrior is described as being armed with the Word of God as a Sword. Aside from our spiritual armor, there are several other forms of weaponry we as Christian Warriors are to become proficient with. Jesus tells us, *In truth I tell you once again, if two of you on earth agree to ask anything at all, it will be granted to you by my Father in heaven. For where two or three meet in my name, I am there among them.* **Matt. 18:19-20.** He taught us that *Prayer* is a very powerful tool to be used and that prayer joined together in unity is more powerful. Jesus specifically admonished His disciples that there are times when the prayers of only one of us will not suffice. In fact, He also tells us that fasting adds power to prayer. This means that a Christian Warrior has the following arsenal at his disposal:

1. The Word of God.
2. Personal Prayer.
3. Communal Prayer.
4. Fasting.
5. Fasting and Prayer.

All of these Spiritual Weapons are to be used in Faith and acted upon in the knowledge of the promises made by the King.

The weapons of the enemy include fear, lies, and all manner of deception. To oppose attacks specifically of these types, we are fortified with the Belt of Truth, the Breastplate of Righteousness, and the Shield of Faith, as has been the subject of the proceeding chapters. When we perfect our spiritual armor, the attacks of the enemy can find no breach in our defense. When the Christian Warrior understands this, there can hardly be enough opposition to stop *but one* steadfast and loyal Warrior following the direction of the Almighty. The enemy in this war has no weapon of power, or armor for protection. This coupled with the understanding of God's might and power of protection through our spiritual armor allows us to take the best shot of the enemy and yet…**To STAND! Eph. 6:10-13.**

As a further assurance that we may always be able to avail ourselves of prayer, we are instructed to hope and wait with perseverance and confidence for those things we do not see, but hope for. Additionally, the Holy Spirit will aid us and help us pray when we cannot find the words ourselves. *But having this hope for what we cannot yet see, we are able to wait for it with persevering confidence. And as well as this, the Spirit too comes to help us in our weakness, for, when we do not know how to pray properly, then the Spirit personally makes our petitions for us in groans that cannot be put into words...* **Rom. 8:25-26.** Even at our lowest moment of despair and frustration, we can find solace in knowing that the Holy Spirit is with us and we merely have to turn our concerns and frustrations over to Him. He knows our heart and will carry our deepest concerns to the throne of the Father.

There are times when we must be quiet and listen for the Word of God. To do so brings security, quiet and aversion of calamity...*but whoever listens to me may live secure, will have quiet, fearing no mischance.* **Prov. 1:33.** This exercise of the Word has a certain reliance upon our Helmet of Salvation and Shield of Faith. Just as the other pieces of our spiritual armor have been shown to be interrelated to derive complimentary and total protection, so it is with our Sword as well. While the Sword, the Word, is mighty enough to offer us complete protection by itself, the enemy will seldom afford us the luxury of attacking us simply. It is prudent to prepare oneself as completely as possible. I would never say that the Word is not swift enough to stop an arrow of the enemy in mid-flight, but let's get real for a moment. While a Warrior often finds himself outnumbered and surrounded, we are entreated to protect ourselves with all the promises of the Lord, not just a few. This is prudent. I would never relish the thought of taking to the field of combat with just my boots on, nor would I look to carry only my sword. To truly enjoy confronting the enemy, fearlessly, and with zeal, a Warrior must prepare himself. To confront the enemy otherwise is foolish.

Besides its use as a weapon of war, the sword has traditionally been used as the symbol of authority, or sign of kingly might. Historically, all knighting ceremonies entailed the use of a sword in the bestowing of the title of nobility. It was with the sword that justice was meted out, and for this reason, it was the symbol of authority used in the conveyance of the lord's wishes.

The sword has a long tradition as being recognized as the emblem of justice. In Medieval Europe, a "trial by combat" was typically settled with the defendant of a crime, or his/her designated champion, coming to blows with an advocate of the throne, or court. When a sentence of death was to be carried out upon one of nobility, the sword, not an axe, was used in the execution. The cut of the sword has always been revered for its swiftness, as the length of the blade allowed the full severing of a limb, or neck, while the axe with its shorter cutting edge, while able to chop more severely, often left the job incomplete. The axe was reserved for those of a lower station in society. Justice dispensed by the swift, deliberate, and clean blow delivered by the executioner's sword was in comparison much quicker than the often required second blow of the axe, as the axe was a wieldy weapon and often missed its mark; not a pleasant prospect.[§]

To be clear in understanding God's Word, our Sword may be taken to include all of the promises to be found in the scriptures, as well as the prophecies, assurances, and Covenant Laws. These are given to us for our understanding of the character of God, and He desires us to grow in our familiarity with His recorded Word. Once we accept and understand the full nature of God's Word, we can then use the Sword of the Spirit as intended by the scriptures. God's Word is a truly majestic and beautiful gift, an awesome and deadly weapon in the hands of a trained Warrior.

Now that we have a broader understanding of swords in general, let us look at some scriptures and compare some of the characteristics of swords to the Sword of the Spirit-the Word of God.

One verse in particular which, if read liberally with a slant on the wording, can be taken to refer to the Word as a Sword literally worn on one's hip. *This I know, that God is on my side. In God whose word I praise, in Yahweh whose word I praise, in God I put my trust and have no fear; what can mortal man do to me?* **Ps. 56:10-11.** If

---

[§] So secured was the authority of the wielded sword, if a person not entitled to bear a sword were to pick up his lords sword, High Justice could demand the striking off of the offenders hand, or the taking of his life.

we were to envision literally carrying God's Word on our side as our protection, what *would* you fear? This is in fact exactly the way we should think about the Word of God. It is God's empowerment and protection for us, His assurance.

The two scriptures below build on the principle of the power inherent in the word of a king, and how powerful this is when understood. Jesus shows the power of His Word in casting the unclean spirit out of the man in the synagogue. It is from the power imbued in our Lord's promises and assurances that we may speak with His authority in His name, by virtue of His Word.

Ecc. 8:4 *[4]Where the word of a king is, there is power...*

Lk. 4:32 *[32]And they were astonished at his doctrine: for His Word was with power...*

The pronouncement of a king's word carries plenty of weight in its own right, but the power carried in the Word we are to hold, commands evil spirits to obey, and if our faith is great enough, to move mountains. In the Gospel of John, we read of an instance in which Jesus' spoken word has the power to knock the entire mob, those come to arrest Him, backwards and off their feet: ***[6]As soon then as he had said unto them, 'I am he,' they went backward, and fell to the ground.* Jn. 18:6.** Continuing a little further from the previous scripture in Luke 4, we find that spectators were astonished when they witnessed the evil spirits leave the possessed man when commanded by Jesus. The people who witnessed this event declared the power and authority they had borne witness to: ***What a word is this! For with authority and power he commandeth the unclean spirits, and they come out.* Lk. 4:36.**

We wield this voice of authority when we speak in the name of our Lord and use His voice of authority and commanding Words of the Spirit, as this is our sword. This is much the same as a nobleman dispensing justice in the name of the king, with the sword he had been bestowed by the king. Remember, authority is wielded in a sword and justice is dispensed by it. The following scriptures are specific in relating the element of justice and vengeance to the Word of God, and specifically relate the Word to being as a sword:

1 Kng. 3:24-25 *²⁴And the king said, 'Bring me a sword.' And they brought a sword before the king. ²⁵And the king said, 'Divide the living child in two, and give half to the one, and half to the other.'*

Rom. 13:4 *...it is not for nothing that the symbol of authority is the sword: it is there to serve God, too, as His avenger...*

Ps. 149:5-7 *The faithful exult in glory, shout for joy as they worship Him, praising God to the height with their voices, a two-edged sword in their hands, to wreak vengeance on the nations, punishment on the peoples...*

God in His infinite patience and love is always clear in His judgments, and spells out the ramifications of ignoring His warnings. It is in our nature to seek God only in times of distress and need. Seldom do we give honor and praise to His goodness in times when we are blessed. Surely, God revels when we turn to Him in need but even more does he cherish our thankfulness for His blessings when we enjoy peace and harmony.

Prov. 1:23-33 *Pay attention to my warning. To you I will pour out my heart and tell you what I have to say. Since I have called and you have refused me, since I have beckoned and no one has taken notice, since you have ignored all my advice and rejected all my warnings, I, for my part, shall laugh at your distress, I shall jeer when terror befalls you, like a storm, when your distress arrives, like a whirlwind, when ordeal and anguish bear down on you. Then they shall call me, but I shall not answer, they will look eagerly for me and will not find me. They have hated knowledge, they have not chosen the fear of Yahweh, they have taken no notice of my advice, they have spurned all my warnings; so they will have to eat the fruits of their own ways of life, and choke themselves with their own scheming. For the errors of the simple lead to their death, the complacency of fools works their own ruin; but whoever listens to me may live secure, will have quiet, fearing no mischance.*

Rom. 8:1-16 (excerpted) *Thus condemnation will never come to those who are in Christ Jesus, because the Law of the Spirit which gives life in Christ Jesus has set you free from the law of sin and death...What the Law could not do because of the weakness of human nature, God did,...This is so that the Law's requirements might be fully satisfied in us as we direct our lives not by our natural inclinations but by the Spirit...And human nature has nothing to look forward to but death, while the spirit looks forward to life and peace, because the outlook of disordered human nature is opposed to God, since it does not submit to God's Law, and indeed it cannot...You, however, live not by your natural inclinations, but by the spirit, since the Spirit of God has made a home in you...*

...we have no obligation to human nature to be dominated by it. If you do live in that way, you are doomed to die; but if by the Spirit you put to death the habits originating in the body, you will have life.

All who are guided by the Spirit of God are sons of God; for what you received was not the spirit of slavery to bring you back into fear; you received the spirit of adoption, enabling us to cry out, "Abba, Father!" The Spirit himself joins with our spirit to bear witness that we are children of God.

Give glory to God and sing Praise to His name! *[12]To the end that my glory may sing praise to thee, and not be silent. O LORD my God, I will give thanks unto thee for ever.* **Ps. 30:12.** Through His protection and blessings, we may tread the traps of the wicked and fear no harm. The devastation of the sword and protection of God's Word are easily recognized in the following verses.

Deut. 13:15 *[15]Thou shalt surely smite the inhabitants of that city with the edge of the sword, destroying it utterly, and all that is therein, and the cattle thereof, with the edge of the sword.* This scripture bears testimony to the truly destructive capability of the sword as the men of Belial were killed to a man and their city laid waste by the sword.

Ps. 57:5-6 *Be exalted above the heavens, God! Your glory over all the earth! They laid a snare in my path—I was bowed with* *care—they dug a pit ahead of me, but fell in it themselves.* Surely the enemy thought they were doing good, yet they transgressed against God's Word, and their plans backfired on them…This is how God will deal with those enemies of His and those in His care.

Jdg. 4:15-16 *[15]And the LORD discomfited Sisera, and all his chariots, and all his host, with the edge of the sword before Barak; so that Sisera lighted down off his chariot, and fled away on his feet. [16]But Barak pursued after the chariots, and after the host, unto Harosheth of the Gentiles: and all the host of Sisera fell upon the edge of the sword; and there was not a man left.*

The awesome destructive ability and application of the sword can be found documented readily in the scripture. For more instances in which the sword was specifically used to bring the utter destruction of cities and peoples, read the following chapters: **1 Sam. 15, 22**, **Deut. 13, 20**, **Jos. 6, 8,10,11**, **2 Sam. 15**, or **2 Sam. 22:34-37**. It may not be an atomic bomb, but when God directs one to act, any tool He places in the hand of His Warriors will be sufficient to destroy countries.

As the sword has been described as a two-edged weapon of offensive and defensive capabilities, it would be fitting to sample a few scriptures that contain these elements. We have seen from the above and previous discussion how devastating a weapon the sword is, but specifically, how may we hold to the Word of God for offense and defensive protection?

Ps. 145:18-20 *He fulfills the desires of all who fear him, he hears their cry and he saves them. Yahweh guards all who love him, but all the wicked he destroys.*

Ps. 57:2-3 *I call to God the Most High, to God who has done everything for me; may he send from heaven and save me, and check those who harry me; may God send his faithful love and his constancy.*

The following scriptures show how the Word may actually be used to spar with the enemy. In a wonderful display of the deft incisiveness of the Word, Jesus shows us that the enemy often never knows how severely they have been wounded. There is never a stroke made upon our Savior, which He fails to return to expose and lay open a completely unprotected or defenseless position of the foe. Read the following exchange slowly and relish the biting and deep penetration the Truth of the Word can administer.

> **Jn. 8:31-58** *To the Jews who believed in him Jesus said: 'If you make my word your home you will indeed be my disciples; you will come to know the truth, and the truth will set you free.'*
> *They answered, 'We are descended from Abraham and we have never been the slaves of anyone; what do you mean, 'You will be set free?' Jesus replied: 'In all truth I tell you, everyone who commits sin is a slave. Now a slave has no permanent standing in the household, but a son belongs to it forever. So if the Son sets you free, you will indeed be free. I know that you are descended from Abraham; but you want to kill me because my word finds no place in you. What I speak of is what I have seen at my Father's side, and you too put into action the lessons you have learned from your father.'*
> *They repeated, 'Our father is Abraham.' Jesus said to them: 'If you are Abraham's children, do as Abraham did. As it is, you want to kill me, a man who has told you the truth as I have learned it from God; that is not what Abraham did. You are doing your father's work.'*
> *They replied, 'We were not born illegitimate, the only father we have is God.' Jesus answered: 'If God were your father, you would love me, since I have my origin in God and have come from him; I did not come of my own accord, but he sent me. Why do you not understand what I say? Because you cannot bear to listen to my words. You are from your father, the devil, and you prefer to do what your father wants. He was a murderer from the start; he was never founded in the truth; there is no truth in him at all. When he lies he is speaking true to his nature, because he is a liar, and the father of lies. But it is because I speak the truth that you do not believe me. Can any of you convict me of sin? If I speak the truth, why do you not believe me? Whoever comes from God listens to the words of God; the reason why you do not listen is that you are not from God.'*

> *The Jews replied, 'Are we not right in saying that you are a Samaritan and possessed by a devil?' Jesus answered: 'I am not possessed; but I honor my Father, and you deny me honor. I do not seek my own glory; there is someone who does seek it and is the judge of it. In all truth I tell you, whoever keeps my word will never see death.'*
>
> *The Jews said, 'Now we know that you are possessed. Abraham is dead, and the prophets are dead, and yet you say, 'Whoever keeps my word will never know the taste of death.' Are you greater than our father Abraham, who is dead? The prophets are dead too. Who are you claiming to be?' Jesus answered: 'If I were to seek my own glory my glory would be worth nothing; in fact, my glory is conferred by the Father, by the one of whom you say, 'He is our God,' although you do not know him.*
>
> *But I know him, and if I were to say, 'I do not know him,' I should be a liar, as you yourselves are. But I do know him, and I keep his word. Your father Abraham rejoiced to think that he would see my Day; he saw it and was glad.'*
>
> *The Jews then said, 'You are not fifty yet, and you have seen Abraham!' Jesus replied: 'In all truth I tell you, before Abraham ever was, I am.'*

Jesus makes several powerful points in this dialogue in reference to the Word of God. What Messages do you hear? Do you see how the Jews were misusing Gods Word in an attempt to deny and refute Jesus? What will be their fate for doing so?

God entreats us to know Him, and not deny, or refuse, His Word. There are countless examples of people of faith turning from God and His teachings, and the result is typically the same. After a time of chastisement and separation, the early Jews would offer sacrifices for their sins in the hopes of regaining God's love. God never held His love from anyone; it is the weak nature of mankind, which has directed us to turn away from God so often in the past. Can you honestly say that God has ever left you? It is our denial of God that separates us from His unconditional love. God's desire to protect us and lead us can be found in the following verses. It will help to follow these scriptures in your Bible as there is much more information to be found in the entire chapters from which they are gleaned. These specific quotes are the significant part and are easily remembered. Bear in mind the nature of relationship that is mentioned in these scriptures as well, as God desires us to remain close to Him and learn of Him. Think of "holding to His precepts" as another way of saying wielding the Sword of His Word.

Ps. 56:3-4 *When I am afraid, I put my trust in you, in God, whose word I praise, in God I put my trust and have no fear, what can mortal man do to me?*

Hos. 6:5 *This is why I have hacked them to pieces by means of the prophets, why I have killed them with words from my mouth, why my sentence will blaze forth like the dawn—for faithful love is what pleases me, not sacrifice; knowledge of God, not burnt offerings.*

Deut. 33:29 *Who Is like you, O victorious people? Yahweh is the shield that protects you and the sword that leads you to triumph. Your enemies will try to corrupt you, but you yourself will trample on their backs.*

Ps. 56:5-6 *All day long they carp at my words, their only thought is to harm me, they gather together, lie in wait and spy on my movements, as though determined to take my life. Because of this crime reject them, in your anger, God, strike down the nations.*

Ps. 37:39-40 *The upright have Yahweh for their Savior, their refuge in times of trouble; Yahweh helps them and rescues them, he will rescue them from the wicked, and save them because they take refuge in him.*

Mk. 13:11 *And when your are taken to be handed over, do not worry beforehand about what to say; no, say whatever is given to you when the time comes, because it is not you who will be speaking; it is the Holy Spirit. Brother will betray brother to death, and a father his child; children will come forward against their parents and have them put to death. You will be universally hated* *on account of My name; but anyone who stands firm to the end will be saved.*

Ps. 119:33-34 *Keep my steps firm in your promise; that no evil may triumph over me. Rescue me from human oppression, and I will observe your precepts.*

Ps. 119:169-170 *May my cry approach your presence, Yahweh; by your word give me understanding. May my prayer come into your presence, rescue me as you have promised.*

These scriptures entail many of the benefits of wielding the Sword of the Spirit. Look at them again and see how many different attributes of protection, power, victory, and character are expressed in them.

This leads us to the last topic with which we shall close this chapter: the characteristics that support, enhance, and develop our Sword of the Spirit. As has been shown with each prior piece of our armor, many of the attributes of a Warrior's character will assist in the development of our use of the Sword of the Spirit. As many of these character attributes have been noted in the various scriptures used throughout this chapter, pause and consider what personal characteristics you believe will be beneficial in this regard. It may come as no surprise to find included among them: devotion/honor, nobility, mercy, discernment/wisdom, justice, strength, courage/fearlessness, and willingness-and-doing.

The Sword of the Spirit is the very Word of God, which we are to learn to wield, you might have a valid argument to say that every characteristic may be found in support of and supported by the Word. However, if we consider the Word having the characteristics of a sword, the above listed attributes fit nicely with the symbolism of a sword.

In that a sword has traditionally been used for virtually all of recorded history in the ceremonies of investiture of kings and the dubbing ceremonies of knighthood, there is a certain reverence in regards to swords and their place in these very solemn and often ecclesiastical ceremonies. When a king is invested, he is reminded of his oath to God and his devotion to the principles of justice and the good of mankind under his care and rule. Honor is always paid in this type of solemnity to the higher authority by which one takes his place. This is no different for a candidate being elevated to knighthood. The newly dubbed knight is made to take solemn pledges of fealty upon the sword of his lord. It is by this very sword, which the candidate is raised to his new social status and position.

A candidate for either an investiture, or a dubbing, typically spent the entire previous night in prayer or standing a vigil. A tremendous amount of reverence and solemnity would be evident during the ceremony due to the devotional overtones and prominence of the church during either ceremony. This combined with the recognition and honor paid to a higher authority in either case make for a distinctively sober ritual. Both of these rituals bear, by their nature, an obvious transfer of a noble station. Thus, when one bears a sword, the heart of nobility is expected to be displayed. To draw one's sword was a grave decision, whether it be to combat the enemy or dispense justice. In either case, when one knows the duty of the sword is obligatory, the sword is quick to deploy: *[24]And the king said, Bring me a sword. And they brought a sword before the king. [25]And the king said, Divide the living child in two, and give half to the one, and half to the other.* 1 Kng. 3:24-25.

When the sword is drawn to decide issues of justice, a wise decision requires that discernment be applied so that justice is dealt and mercy not withheld. Justice without mercy yields a cold and dispassionate decision. Historically, it was he that bore a sword that levied justice, as the bearer was honor-bound to the cause of a higher authority and duly granted the right to dispense its justice.

As the sword is swift, its mercy is likewise swift; both in the execution of a death sentence or the sparing of an innocent. On the battlefields of medieval Italy, if a kinsman were mortally wounded and all prospects pointed to a long and protracted death in pain, it was felt the merciful thing to do was to speedily absolve the loved one and end their suffering. This was facilitated with a specially designed dagger, a Misericorde.[#] Likewise, if innocents were in danger from a

---

[#] Misericorde means "Mercy for the Body."

foe, the quick response of the sword enabled the defenseless a new day.

As the constant daylong use of a sword would demand strength, it should come as no surprise that being strong enables one to quickly use the sword when called for. Being strong in spirit enables one to quickly turn to our Lord for all of the attributes required on a moments notice. Likewise, daily exercise in the Word enables a Warrior to rely on its strength when needed. The Word carries all the food we need to nourish every aspect of our being. When one considers how the Word may be involved in any one aspect of our being, or character, it becomes evident that hardly an aspect of our being remains untouched for the benefit of another. When this realization permeates one's spirit to the very depth of the marrow in the bones, then all personal fear, reluctance, or hesitance can be faced with courage and a ferocious demeanor. *⁷For God hath not given us the spirit of fear; but of power, and of love, and of a sound mind. 2 Tm. 1:7.*

When we have exemplified the full nature and character of the Warrior in ourselves, we then become totally ensconced in the protection or our Armor of God. Being true to the Word in word and deed, we are so royally accoutered that the stars and angels themselves do witness the goodness of the Lord, the divine Creator. Never stopping in the pursuit of the enemy, never fearing the hidden danger, always bearing love, forgiveness, forbearance, mercy, and goodness in our heart as our divine example instructs. Who could help but revere our Lord, our King, who so nobly prepares His Warriors!

All the armor is now made ready. Be not limited by your understanding, but hold secure to the assurances and promises of the King, the Almighty Creator of all. As a Warrior in the Army of God, avail yourself of all these blessings as the hand of man has never forged armor such as this, but by the hand of God Himself, each piece is crafted for your individual, personal edification and protection. Strap each piece about yourself and be ready at a moment's notice for the approach of the enemy as well as the approach of our King (**Jdg. 16:20, 2 Ptr. 3:10**). Be not found sleeping, unprepared and unwitting as the five virgins were (**Matt. 25:1-13**), suffer not the punishment of the sleeping or unwary guard (**Ezk. 33:1-9**). Rather, be strong in the

Lord always (**Eph. 6:10**), and goodness and mercy shall by yours all the days of your life (**Ps. 23:6**).

Chapter 12

The Twelfth Hour

Once the decision is made to train for the fight and become a fully empowered Warrior in the Army of God, many will ask, "How do I avail myself of this information now that I accept the reality of Spiritual Warfare and the need for the Armor of God?" This final chapter will answer this question and encourage any reader wishing to become truly empowered by God's Word and promises, and become so blessed.

Now that you have a better understanding of the Armor of the Christian Warrior and God's promises concerning the Armor itself, I ask you now to look within your heart and answer the following questions.

Have you felt a void in your life? Have you been searching for something to give meaning to your life? Could it be something is missing from your life, a commitment never made, or fulfilled? Are you willing to take on the task of inner revelation and development?

Do you recognize the need to awaken the Warrior within and join the ranks of the fully empowered Christian Warriors?

Are you ready to look within to that hurt area of your character which you want to finally take claim of, find the brokenness within that needs the healing touch of another Warrior, and take control of your life by turning it over to God?

Be aware that the battle is at hand and the rally cry has gone out. What is your response? Will you answer the call to arms for your own sake…for all our sakes, FOR GOD'S SAKE?!

The challenge is now before you. Are you willing to take a stand under the authority of the King? Are you willing to really put your faith in God and learn what He would have you do? These two questions will find you in one of two most likely spiritual dispositions: 1) You have never accepted Christ as your personal redeemer and feel the call of the Holy Spirit in your life to bring you to God. 2) You are a believer in Christ, but have never experienced the empowerment of the Holy Spirit or trained to face the reality of Spiritual Warfare.

God's army is recruiting. Are you ready to enlist? If so, then what can be done is to offer yourself an initiation. It can be held within the Temple of your body with the Holy Ghost as your Mentor. The symbolic death is that of your old way of behavior, the old "self" which you put away for the sake of developing a new Self! Become a fully armored Warrior in the Army of God!

Salvation and Redemption

The call is first placed before those yet uncommitted to saving grace of God by the sacrifice of His son Jesus. Are you ready to accept Jesus' redemption of you, or would you rather remain blissfully ignorant of true spiritual matters and face the consequences? The only way to secure the Armor of God is through accepting God's Word. If you feel the calling of the Spirit in your life, and desire to come back to God, I encourage you in your decision and offer the following prayer for your guidance. Your life will be forever changed.

If you are ready to accept Jesus as your personal Saviour, or desire to renew your faith, go to a place of quiet, or call upon someone you know to be a Christian, and pray with them the following prayer. There is nothing magical about this prayer. It need not be followed word for word. It is offered here only as a guide if you are new to faith and are ready to profess your faith before God. What is important is that you pray this prayer aloud, with your mouth profess your faith because...*the word of faith, the faith which we preach, that if you declare with your mouth that Jesus is Lord, and if you believe with your heart that God raised him from the dead, then you will be saved. It is by believing with the heart that you are justified, and by making the declaration with your lips that you are saved.* **Rom. 10:8-10**.

Pray the following:

Philip Paul Sacco

Most Holy and ever-caring God, You created all things to Your glory, and answer all contrite and faithful prayer. Accept the cries of this repentant sinner, and bless me with the saving grace of your Son, Jesus Christ. I acknowledge that I am a sinner, forever separated from your love by my sins. I know there is no way back to your loving presence, but by accepting the sacrifice of Jesus for all my sins, past, present and future.

Most Holy and Eternal Father, Jesus died on the cross in full payment for my sins, and by His resurrection from death, I claim my redemption by His saving blood, and sacrifice.

Most Gracious and loving God, you are faithful to your Word, and I thank you for hearing my prayers of repentance and faithful acceptance of Your promises. I ask that you guide my life from this moment on, giving me the strength and courage to forever change my sinful ways, and become more Christ-like in all ways. Jesus defeated death, and accepting His sacrifice for my sins entitles me to full fellowship as an heir to the heavenly kingdom, and I welcome full brotherhood with all faithful believers.

As a scriptural sign of your conversion, I entreat you to read the Word concerning Water Baptism, and seek it out for yourself. Rising from the waters of Baptism, you arise a new creature in the eyes of God. Being baptized will also put you in contact and loving fellowship with other believers who will help you grow as a child of God. Fellowship and community are essential to those new to the Word, and infants in Christ need the support and nourishment which may be readily found among a fellowship of Christians. Some suggested scriptures to read concerning water Baptism follow. It is recommended that you turn to your Bible and read more than just the following scriptures for a better understanding.

Matt. 21:25 *[25]The baptism of John, whence was it? from heaven, or of men.*

Mk. 1:4-5 *[4]John did baptize in the wilderness, and preach the baptism of repentance for the remission of sins. [5]And there went* *out unto him all the land of Judaea, and they of Jerusalem, and were all baptized of him in the river of Jordan, confessing their sins.*

Acts 19:4-5 *⁴Then said Paul, John verily baptized with the baptism of repentance, saying unto the people, that they should believe on him which should come after him, that is, on Christ Jesus. ⁵When they heard this, they were baptized in the name of the Lord Jesus.*

Fire and Empowerment

In the fall of 1962, a great resurgence of interest in the power of the Holy Spirit was begun when Pope John XXIII's called for a "New Pentecost." By the mid 70s, this movement was acknowledged widely within the Catholic Church, and came to be known as the Charismatic or Pentecostal movement. Whole books have been written about the basis for the "Baptism of the Spirit," and I encourage those questioning this as a legitimate teaching of the Bible to search out one of these books and prayerfully study it, or God's Word, concerning this empowerment.

If you are a Christian whose life has been, well, shall we say "mundane," without the presence of God being felt, it may be that you have not understood what living a life of faith is all about. Perhaps you have not recognized the reality of the Powers and Principalities at work around you because you have been asleep in your faith or exercise of God's authority. What I have found to be the case is that many Christians deny any empowerment beyond the act of confession and redemption of their sins, as above. The fact is that before Jesus physically ascended into heaven, He had promised to send the Holy Spirit of God to his disciples to be with them and empower them until His return. This new baptism has been referred to as: "The infilling of the Spirit," the "Baptism of Fire," or the "Baptism of the Holy Spirit." Whatever you may call it, this is the means by which believers become empowered by the full blessing of the Holy Spirit.

From my personal experience, I can tell you that there are two distinct camps when it comes to those who believe in the "Baptism of the Spirit." Some believe that the infilling of the Spirit occurs at the time of repentance and salvation. It is commonly pointed out that as repentant believers in Christ, we have the Spirit of God in us. *⁶And because ye are sons, God hath sent forth the Spirit of his Son into your hearts, crying, Abba, Father.* **Gal. 4:6**. This is better referred to as the gift of the Spirit, or the promise of the Spirit, and occurs when one accepts the redeeming quality of Jesus' redemption of sins into their heart. This gift is what is responsible for changing our heart and soul upon conversion. Others point to the specific incident in which Jesus came to baptize His followers with the Spirit of God *'⁵For John truly baptized with water; but ye shall be baptized with the Holy Ghost not many days hence.'* **Acts 1:5**. This "Baptism of Fire and the Spirit" was inaugurated on the Day of Pentecost, when the Apostles were meeting in the upper chamber. As this was a separate occurrence from their individual conversion experiences, some believe this Baptism is distinct and separate from the gift of the Spirit which occurs at the time of salvation. Either way, believing first in Jesus is crucial to accepting His baptism of the Spirit. It is the separate empowerment promised as distinct from salvation that is entailed in the "Baptism of the Spirit." It is not the purpose of this book to decide this issue for you. What is important is that you *experience* the infilling, and become empowered; however, you believe it doctrinally. Personally, I experienced the Baptism of the Spirit as a separate experience, brought on by a lying on of hands. I know of many people who simply petitioned God in prayer for guidance and empowerment, and God answered their prayers. As God is faithful to His promises, God will bless you as well.

Turn in your Bible and read the following scriptures. They involve several aspects of the Baptism of the Spirit. The first scripture is one of the many references in the Old Testament to the future pouring out of God's Spirit upon all men. There are many Old Testament references to God's outpouring of His Spirit in a later age, and this should serve as confirmation that what occurred to the Apostles in the upper room during Pentecost was the fulfillment of prophecy.

Isa. 44:3 *³For I will pour water upon him that is thirsty, and floods upon the dry ground: I will pour my spirit upon thy seed, and my blessing upon thine offspring.*

John the Baptist later identified Jesus as the Baptizer with the Spirit:

Mk. 1:8 *[8]I indeed have baptized you with water: but He shall baptize you with the Holy Ghost.*

Jn. 1:33-34 *[33]And I knew him not: but he that sent me to baptize with water, the same said unto me, Upon whom thou shalt see the Spirit descending, and remaining on him, the same is he which baptizeth with the Holy Ghost. [34]And I saw, and bare record that this is the Son of God.*

We have it from Jesus' mouth that He would send the Holy Spirit to the Apostles:

Jn.14:16-17 *[16]And I will pray the Father, and he shall give you another Comforter, that he may abide with you for ever; [17]Even the Spirit of truth; whom the world cannot receive, because it seeth him not, neither knoweth him: but ye know him; for he dwelleth with you, and shall be in you.*

Jn. 16:7 *[7]Nevertheless I tell you the truth; It is expedient for you that I go away: for if I go not away, the Comforter will not come unto you; but if I depart, I will send him unto you.*

Moreover, we have it from Peter that the Baptism of the Spirit is to be experienced just as water baptism and salvation:

Acts 2:38-39 *[38]Then Peter said unto them, Repent, and be baptized every one of you in the name of Jesus Christ for the remission of sins, and ye shall receive the gift of the Holy Ghost. [39]For the promise is unto you, and to your children, and to all that are afar off, even as many as the Lord our God shall call.* It should be noted that Peter refers to the gift of the Holy Ghost in this instance, and you may find a slight variation in the translation you use. This gives cause to division as to whether the Baptism of the Spirit is a separate experience.

Acknowledge that Our Bodies are the Temple of the Holy Spirit:

1 Cor. 6:19 *¹⁹What? know ye not that your body is the temple of the Holy Ghost which is in you, which ye have of God, and ye are not your own?*

Many Christians fail to explore, enrich, and fully experience the walk of faith that can be so greatly enriched by the empowerment of the Spirit. If you desire to accept the full richness of our Christian inheritance, then I entreat you to pray the following prayer, or one like it. If you have any charismatic Christian friends, or you know of a special meeting night when the prayerful meet, I entreat you to join with them and have one or two of them pray with you. In my experience, this is always a powerful and personal experience.

Many prefer to pray alone in the solitude of their home, and for those I offer the following prayer:

Most Holy Spirit, author of the Word of God, place within my heart a growing desire and thirst to know your Word, to have it become alive in my life. Enlighten me, as the Author of the Word, to the true richness of the blessings, gifts, and mysteries enclosed with the Scriptures. Remove anything blocking me from receiving Your full Blessing and infilling. Bless me with understanding as I study and meditate upon your Holy Word, and empower me to walk in life with greater faith. Bless me with your gifts.

Praying a prayer, such as the one above, is a sure fire way to "supercharge" the ho-hum life many Christians otherwise experience. Pray upon the gifts of the Spirit and seek them out.

The Epilogue highlights some of the interesting turns of events that have brought me to writing this book. What I felt was inspired as a simple presentation some ten years ago, I see now has been in development throughout my entire life. A good expression that may sum up my experience is: "That which doesn't kill us, makes us stronger." With countless troubles have come countless blessings. On many occasions, I have received a very personal meaning to the scripture. *Not only that; let us exult, too, in our hardships, understanding that hardship develops perseverance, and perseverance develops a tested character, something that gives us hope, and a hope which will not let us down, because the love of God has been poured into our hearts by the Holy Spirit which has been given to us.* **Rom. 5:3-5.**

The hardship the enemy presses upon you will give you some indication of the threat you, as a Christian Warrior, pose to them. You are worthy of the fight. Bolster your spirit, polish your armor, and declare yourself as taking a stand; the Lord will count you and you will enter into His "roll call." Don't be lukewarm in your indecision. You see there is no room for fence sitting—we are directed to be hot or cold in our faith. *Here is the message of the Amen, the trustworthy, the true witness, the Principle of God's creation: I know about your activities; how you are neither cold nor hot, I wish you were one or the other, but since you are neither hot nor cold, but only lukewarm,* **I will spit you out of my mouth.** *You say to yourself: I am rich, I have made a fortune and have everything I want, never realizing that you are wretchedly and pitiably poor and blind and naked too. I warn you, buy from me the gold that has been tested in the fire to make you truly rich, and white robes to clothe you and hide your shameful nakedness, and ointment to put on your eyes to enable you to see.* **I reprove and train those whom I love**: *so repent in real earnest...Anyone* **who proves victorious** *I will allow to share my throne, just as I have myself overcome and have taken my seat with my Father on His throne. Let anyone who can hear, listen to what the Spirit is saying to the churches.* **Rev. 3:14-19, 21-22.**

Once we become empowered by the Holy Spirit, to the outward world, we become larger than life. This becomes apparent for two primary reasons. First, because we start expressing values not commonly found adhered to in society today; consequently, this alone sets us apart. Secondly, our experiences show themselves to be miraculous at times. This should not come as any surprise, as we are protected by the Armor of God. Remember what the scripture says about God's Warriors, *but the people that do know their God shall be strong, and* **do exploits. Dan. 11:32.** We are transformed when we accept a commission under Jesus. The old ways are put away and the new ways become like a breath of fresh air. Excitement follows an active Warrior. Read any fairy tale and you will see that it is typically the hero who is the only one *doing the exciting stuff.*

In the every day world, a kind word, a helping hand are always there for the asking, but how often is it offered? There are not enough Warriors out there in society offering a helping hand, taking a stand, willing to make a difference, not waiting for the opportunity or having to be asked. They are to busy *doing*. We all know that friendly acts are always appreciated. A simple adage recognized in the world today is, "There's no such thing as a free lunch," or "You don't get something for nothing." If this is true, then the converse must also be true: "You can't give something away without receiving something in return." When this is applied to God's promises, you can expect to receive payment many times over what you have given. There is an incredible reciprocity in a simple smile, a kind word, or a helping hand. These should be the forms of "currency" ready at hand to a Warrior. More important than thinking of rewards should be the pleasure derived in taking a stand and doing what is right for that reason alone. Satisfaction in having done this should be payment enough for a Warrior. Additionally, it should be kept in mind always to **remember to welcome strangers, for by doing this, some people have entertained angels without knowing it. Heb. 13:2.** Remember this next time you see a stranger in need of a helping hand.

Warriors from the past had to condition themselves to carry the weight of their armor daily so that moving in it became second nature and they conserved their energy. There is a lesson in this for us as Christian Warriors as we accustom ourselves with living our lives in the Armor of God. In dealing with the affairs of the world and the many moments of tribulation a Warrior will encounter, two simple rules should be borne in mind: **1)** Faith before Fear, and **2)** Prayer before Pessimism. These two simple rules will aid us in conserving our spiritual and physical energy. If these two simple rules are practiced, many wondrous encounters will be experienced. These two rules will help keep one from panicking, and thus, rather than wasting energy in a personally destructive way, a Warrior will be acting positively.

God Bless you and welcome to the fray. No better comrades can a man have in life than the ones who would join him in a fight!

We need not search far to find the Powers and Principalities against which we struggle. In many various ways, they have taken control of powerful positions in our society and the world. Some of the greatest oppression in our country today comes from the system of bureaucrats who relish exercising their power or "authority" while forgetting whom they are appointed by and work for. Many of our representatives and public officials are more interested in pleasing special interest groups and lining their own pockets, rather than in enacting and enforcing truly liberating legislation or operating under the Godly principles this country was founded upon. It is easy to find out what is being done on the local and regional levels within our political system. This is a good arena to take a stand and make your voice heard.

As an example of how a Christian Warrior may apply the Word in daily affairs, I would like to share with you a story shared with me by a brother Warrior in Christ, Barry Smyth. Barry has had to confront "Evil in High Places" many times. This is one of many stories which I can relate which shows how "the system" often retaliates against the private citizen, and how one Christian Warrior has found a way to combat it.

County Sheriff Gets Rebuffed By Front Line Master
by Barry Smyth

I was having a hard time getting the Sheriff of Logan County, Colorado to acknowledge any of my God given rights while I was incarcerated in the county jail. In a moment of inspiration, I wrote him the following notice:

Dear Sheriff Bollish:

I'm writing this to you because it seems to me that you do not consider my religious convictions to be firmly and sincerely held. From our conversation in your office, it seemed apparent that you may have some of your own. I use the Holy Bible as my authority, I hope you recognize it. Here's some of what I believe and why:

I believe even though I came to believe in Jesus the Messiah in 1981, that I could still sin (Rom. 6). Sin is the transgression of the law (I John 3:4). Keeping the law is wisdom and understanding (Deut. 4:5-6). A wise man fears and departs from evil (Prov.14:16). If I get wisdom I love my own soul: and if I keep understanding I find good (Prov.19:8). If anyone despises his ways and doesn't keep his commands he shall die (Prov.19:10). If I wander out of the way of understanding I will remain in the congregation of the dead (Prov.21:16). Without the Lord's commandments, there is no wisdom (Prov. 21:30). If I keep the Law, I will be considered to be a wise son (Prov. 28:7). If I keep the least of the commandments, and teach other men to do so, I shall be called great in the kingdom of heaven (Matt. 5:19).

I want to be considered great in the kingdom and to do so I must teach others to obey the least of his commandments and do them myself. I must do this whether I'm in or out of your jail. I have a duty to teach you regarding His commandments. If you as much as give me a drink of water, you will not lose your reward (Matt.10:42). If you receive me in His name, you have received Him (Matt. 18:5). However, if you offend me, as a believer in the Messiah, it would be better for you that a millstone were hanged around your neck, and that you were drowned in the depth of the sea (Matt. 18:6). Jesus warned, "Woe unto the world because of offenses! For it must need that offenses come; but woe to that man by whom the offense cometh!" (Matt. 18:7). If you mock at my attempts to keep the law by not helping me and causing me to sin, the Bible says you are a fool (Prov.14:9). It is an abomination to kings (and sheriffs) to commit wickedness: for the throne (or office of sheriff) is established by righteousness (Prov.16:12), and thorns and snares are in the way of the froward (Prov.22:5). If you forsake the law you praise the wicked: but if you keep the law you contend with them (Prov. 28:4). If you keep the law you are wise (Prov. 28:7). If you turn away your ear from hearing the law, your prayer will be an abomination (Prov. 8:9). If you cause me to go astray in an evil way, you will fall into your own pit (Prov. 28:10). If you try to contend that you did not know about any of this, and that you are therefore justified in causing me to sin, the Lord, who keeps your soul, doesn't he know it (Prov.

24:11-12)? Don't you think that He will render unto you according to your works (Prov. 24:12)?

I sincerely believe that the following foods are deceitful foods as mentioned in Prov. 23:1-3: milk, iceberg lettuce, refined white flour, refined sugar, and margarine. They, therefore, are not permissible to eat. Lev. 11 and Deut. 14 list edible foods. Deut. 22:1 commands not to wear blend garments, therefore, it follows that my sheets and blankets should be 100% also; Heb. 10:22 covers drinking pure water; Gen. 1:29 covers fruits and vegetables; Isa. 7:22 covers butter and honey. In Proverbs, a scripture mentions that I should not take a man's garment because then he will have nothing to sleep in. I also have a scripture regarding water in plastic but can't find it right now. I do not think it is your job to make an inquiry into the validity of my claims and I only cite scripture to show my beliefs are sincere.

Rest assured that I would not take matters into my own hands. Instead, I leave your future in the Supreme Ruler of the universe's hands. In Gal. 3:14 the scripture says that the blessings of my father Abraham come upon me. The Lord, in blessing Abraham said, "I will bless them that bless thee, and curse him that curseth thee:" (Gen. 12:3). The Lord is longsuffering toward you and He is not willing that you should perish, but that you should come to repentance (I Ptr. 3:9). If you repent I will be first in line to remit your sins pursuant to Jn. 20:23 and I Jn. 5:16. If you got this far, thanks for reading."

Barry Lynn Smyth

Barry's story continues: During my eighty-six day stay in the Logan County Jail I was given my own private cell and was able to have the light on or off at my request. Before going to jail, I was given long distance calling cards with 120 minutes on them. I was allowed to use the Sheriff's phone as opposed to calling collect at exorbitant rates payable by friends and family. The cook gave me my biblical diet in its entirety. A local baker delivered whole wheat bread to the jail. The local Deep Rock distributor delivered pure water to my cell. I had an extra mattress, extra pillow, and an extra blanket. I was allowed to keep these in spite of the fact that there was a shortage and I offered to give them up. I had all my law books lined up under my bed. During my stay, I read *Blackstone's Commentaries* and the

Colorado Constitution Annotated in their entirety. The jail's head administrator approved my having vitamins in my cell and told me not to let the Sheriff know that he had done it. I had an Oral B toothbrush and natural toothpaste in my cell. Ultimately I was given trustee status even though the jail had no trustee program.

During my stay, I filed a motion for Post-Conviction Review. The Court set a hearing. On the morning of the hearing, about 4:00 a.m., there was a clap of thunder over the jail that was so loud it shook the combination jail/courthouse that was made of brick. It was the loudest clap of thunder I have ever heard in my forty-two years. I was reminded of a couple of scriptures:

...And as Samuel was offering up the burnt offering, the Philistines drew near to battle against Israel: but the LORD thundered with a great thunder on that day upon the Philistines, and discomfited them; and they were smitten before Israel **(1 Sam. 7:10).**

The LORD thundered from heaven, and the most High uttered his voice **(2 Sam. 22:14).**

The LORD also thundered in the heavens, and the Highest gave his voice; hailstones and coals of fire **(Ps.18:13).**

The people therefore, that stood by, and heard it, said that it thundered: others said, An angel spake to him **(Jn. 12:29).**

The hearing lasted five and a half hours. I called seventeen witnesses. The hearing could not have gone better.

I felt like the prosecutor had his tail between his legs. I had done enough study to know that he had a burden in the hearing and he was not meeting it. When the hearing was over, and they had returned me to my private cell, softball sized hailstones fell on the jail/courthouse. They were breaking the light-bars on the sheriff's cars. They hit one deputy, by his own admission, twice (He had violated my rights more than once and was less than a blessing to me.). Other deputies told me that one deputy, that had not been a blessing to me, had her car worked over like someone had taken a ball-peen hammer to it. Another deputy, that had been a blessing to me, had his car parked up under a cover, and it was not damaged at all. The car that I drive was parked by the jail, and you could not tell that it had been in a hailstorm. This all reminded me of another instance in the Bible from

Awaken The WARRIOR

Exodus the 9th chapter:

[18] *Behold, tomorrow about this time I will cause it to rain a very grievous hail, such as hath not been in Egypt since the foundation thereof even until now.* [19] *Send therefore now, and gather thy cattle, and all that thou hast in the field; for upon every man and beast which shall be found in the field, and shall not be brought home, the hail shall come down upon them, and they shall die.* [20] *He that feared the word of the LORD among the servants of Pharaoh made his servants and his cattle flee into the houses:* [21] *And he that regarded not the word of the LORD left his servants and his cattle in the field.* [22] *And the LORD said unto Moses, Stretch forth thine hand toward heaven, that there may be hail in all the land of Egypt, upon man, and upon beast, and upon every herb of the field, throughout the land of Egypt.* [23] *And Moses stretched forth his rod toward heaven: and the LORD sent thunder and hail, and the fire ran along upon the ground; and the LORD rained hail upon the land of Egypt.* [24] *So there was hail, and fire mingled with the hail, very grievous, such as there was none like it in all the land of Egypt since it became a nation.* [25] *And the hail smote throughout all the land of Egypt all that was in the field, both man and beast; and the hail smote every herb of the field, and brake every tree of the field.* [26] *Only in the land of Goshen, where he children of Israel were, was there no hail.* "In closing…**Rev. 22:10-15**…" *This, too, he said to me, 'Do not keep the prophecies in this book a secret, because the Time is close. Meanwhile let the sinner continue sinning, and the unclean continue to be unclean; let the upright continue in his uprightness, and those who are holy continue to be holy. Look, I am coming soon, and my reward is with me, to repay everyone as their deeds deserve. I am the Alpha and the Omega, the First and the Last, the 'Beginning and the End. Blessed are those who will have washed their robes clean, so that they will have the right to feed on the tree of life and can come through the gates into the city. Others must stay outside: dogs, fortune-tellers, and the sexually immoral, murderers, idolaters and every one of false speech and false life.'*

(End of Letter)

I can relate with Barry and I tell you this. I have seen the injustice of our system firsthand. I am a law abiding and God-fearing man. I know how the forces of evil will marshal against a child of God. It was not until I started to take a stand for my God given rights, rights that are supposed to be recognized and respected in America, that I became intimately aware of how far this country has departed from adhering to the principles of God. I have been arrested more than once for professing my Christian beliefs. In none of these incidents were other people or property involved. On more than one occasion, the "authorities" went beyond their legal authority to harass and make an example of me. I sympathize with Barry and all others "made object lessons of" by our "legal" and corrupt system.

On the other end of the spectrum, I can relate many incidences in which a divine plan is more easily seen. Six months after I began writing this book, I was impressed upon by the Holy Spirit to make preparations to travel to California and present my first "Warrior of God" appearances. Many fantastic answers to prayer made the trip possible. Some of them were so remarkable that I began writing them down. One of them in particular exemplifies the power of prayer and the results of being obedient. I called my friends in California and told them that I was planning a trip out their way just as soon as it could be arranged. This was near the end of April 1999. Within two weeks, preparations had been made and several appearances had been arranged for the second week of June.

One of the first of these was to an assembly of five to ten year old children at a Christian School. When I met with the school's administrators, I found out that when they were initially contacted about the possibility of having me for an assembly, they had already scheduled one, however, the topic had not been arranged. My friend, Ellen, called them back a week or two later, and asked if they had decided on the topic for their assembly. Their director of programs informed Ellen that several of the teachers had been praying about it, and they felt they should do something on the armor of God. Ellen then informed them, "Boy have I got someone for your program!" When I met the program director, I asked her when the teachers had been praying about the topic for their assembly. "The end of April," I

Awaken The WARRIOR

was told. God had obviously been working in the background. Recorded occurrences such as this now half fill a book of their own.

Within a month of my return from California, I chanced into a VIP pass to attend a national fantasy/science fiction convention in Atlanta. The pass allowed me access to a private suite where I made several very good connections with writers, editors, and a publisher. While I am confident that these contacts will prove to be more than incidental in substance, I had one profound experience at the convention.

A large number of the participants at this particular convention dress up in costumes from their favorite movies or fantasy novels. I happened to be attending in one of the outfits I wear for "Warrior of God" presentations as an advertisement. To the casual observer, I appeared as a monk, wearing a brown habit and cowl. Underneath I wore the armor of God. As it turned out, the Warrior was called to duty on the last night of the convention.

A girlfriend of mine, Chrissy, and I had been looking for one of the many dance halls we knew to be rather lively, and I came across an auditorium in which there appeared to be a performance starting. There were several hundred people crowded around a stage upon which three individuals were preparing themselves for a show. The music was quite loud and heavy in nature. I believe some people call this particular form of new music "Gothic." I went to get Chrissy and returned to watch the show. Two of the "performers," a young man a and woman, were restrained to pillars by leather bonds and had needles that looked to be the size of crochet needles pierced through various parts of their body and face. Metal studs of various sizes were also pierced or attached to their bodies. Playful "assistants" used whips on the "performers," What we witnessed was so vile and decadent, Chrissy was forced to leave the room. As I would not let Chrissy leave unescorted, I escorted her out to fresh air and left her in the care of friends. I then returned to see what could be done to end the spectacle.

Working my way close to the front of the stage, I raised my hands in petition and prayer and lowered my head to beseech God that something be done to shut this spectacle down. After some ten minutes, I claimed victory in the name of God, and left the auditorium. I had no sooner left the assemblage, than I noticed two plain clothed security guards speaking on walkie-talkies. As I approached them, I heard they were calling for backup and officers were on the way to take care of some disturbance. I approached them not knowing what other matter they were tending to and asked them if they were aware of what was occurring in their venue. They asked me if I had been in there, and when I said yes, they asked if I was registering a complaint. I most certainly assured them that I was, and they immediately got back on their radios to confirm my objection to their superior. As it turned out, they were trying to figure out what to do about the situation, but as no complaint had been filed, there was no clear protocol.

Within two minutes, several uniformed guards appeared and the assemblage was dispersed. In filing my complaint, I found out that the hotel did not sanction the activity, and that they would make sure that such activity never occurred again on the premises. I sang joyful triumph and victory over the protests of those being removed. None of them saw anything wrong in what they were doing, and they verbally objected to having their entertainment arrested.

The young man had close to two dozen piercings to his body and face, his entire body was covered with streams of blood. It was apparent that he had not enjoyed the performance. The young girl seemed oblivious to what had happened, and it was not until Chrissy talked with her, that she realized how she had been disfigured. She broke down in tears crying and Chrissy stayed with her for some time to console her.

I praise God for the opportunity of bearing witness to this victory, and whatever small part I may have played in shutting it down.

Remember that you are not a puppet in the hands of God. He will not force you to act against your will, nor will he take your free will from you. His desire is that you be a willing suppliant. Put God's will first, and be prepared for the amazing to occur. Once you begin to experience the Holy Spirit taking part in your life in this way, you will better understand this little poem:

> I asked for Strength…
> And God gave me Difficulties to make me strong.
> I asked for Wisdom…
> And God gave me Problems to solve.

> I asked for Prosperity…
> And God gave me Brain and Brawn to work.
> I asked for Courage…
> And God gave me Danger to overcome.
> I asked for Love…
> And God gave me Troubled people to help.
> I asked for Favors…
> And God gave me Opportunities.
> I received nothing I wanted
> I received everything I needed
> (author unknown)

When we listen to the voice of God within us, and are obedient, many times surprising results will immediately come to our attention. The following story was sent to me from an acquaintance named Wendy. It is a true story that she had been sent by a friend of her's:

God has a way of allowing us to be in the right place at the right time. I was walking down a dimly lit street late one evening, when I heard muffled screams coming from behind a clump of bushes. Alarmed, I slowed down to listen and panicked when I realized that what I was hearing were the unmistakable sounds of a struggle: heavy grunting, frantic scuffling and tearing of fabric. Only yards from where I stood, a woman was being attacked.

Should I get involved? I was frightened for my own safety and cursed myself for having suddenly decided to take a new route home that night. What if I became another statistic? Shouldn't I just run to the nearest phone and call the police? Although it seemed an eternity, the deliberations in my head had taken only seconds, but already the cries were growing weaker. I knew I had to act fast. How could I walk away from this? No, I finally resolved, I could not turn my back on the fate of this unknown woman, even if it meant risking my own life.

I am not a brave man, nor am I athletic. I do not know where I found the moral courage and physical strength but once I had finally resolved to help the girl, I became strangely transformed. I ran behind the bushes and pulled the assailant off the woman. Grappling, we fell to the ground where we wrestled for a few minutes until the attacker jumped up and escaped. Panting hard, I scrambled upright and approached the girl, who was crouched behind a tree, sobbing. In the darkness, I could barely see her outline, but I could certainly sense her trembling shock. Not wanting to frighten her further, I at first spoke to her from a distance.

"It's OK," I said soothingly. "The man ran away. You're safe now." There was a long pause and then I heard the words, uttered in wonder, in amazement. "Daddy, is that you?" Then, from behind the tree, stepped my youngest daughter, Katherine.

Do all the good you can, In all the ways you can, In all the places you can, At all the times you can, To all the people you can, As long as you ever can.

You see, we can never be sure whose life we may affect with our concern and care. Prayerfully petitioning God for guidance and discerning His will is a sure fire way to live the ordinary life in an unordinary way. I could have filled this book with stories relevant to every piece of the Armor of God, as well as lessons I have learned about the character development of the Warrior within. What is more profound and certainly more personal is for you to open your life to the instruction of God, and have your own experiences in developing your Warrior character, and polishing and proofing your own Armor of God. I hope you make the decision to join the ranks of the Lord, for surely we are in the 12th Hour.

To this end, I hope God had a message for you in this book, and I pray for your revelation, growth, empowerment, and protection in the Masters hand.

Epilogue

When Christians awaken to the full power, we may reward ourselves; we may fulfill God's plan for our life and we all benefit. When we keep mindful of God in our life, we immediately recognize certain events as confirmation, or evidence of God's will. Events we may have otherwise called coincidence, or serendipity, take on a new meaning when the purposefulness of a divine plan is apparent. I desire the reader have a better understanding of my position in regards to these matters, as well as the type of events to which I am speaking. God's hand has been active in my life, and understanding how I have come to recognize this may help you to come to a greater understanding of incidents that may occur in your life as well. Please indulge me, as I believe these lessons are faced by us all.

If your faith-life seems to be on hold, could it be you are not the empowered Christian you think you are? Jesus taught us to welcome our trials and tribulations, as this develops us in understanding and wisdom. The point is, that it is easy to find out how threatening the enemy considers you, for the enemy only leaves the sleeping and non-threatening warriors alone. Only if the enemy sees you as a threat, will he come against you. You can take it as a compliment the more arduous his attacks upon you. For the enemy, this is an exercise in futility; but do not let-on to the secret! The victory has already been given us. Learn what it means to walk the way of Faith…it is a very interesting walk!

My walk of faith has been an ongoing state of preparation to present the message of this book. It is only in hindsight that many of the unusual and seemingly disjoint episodes of my life have come into proper focus and the hand and design of Creator God seen. To complicate His divine plan (if any of us can truly complicate anything for Him), I have often unwittingly strayed from the path He had set me upon. Some of us never "get it right," some of us are "late bloomers," and some of us are *"just plain stubborn."* What is important is that any one of us **"WAKES UP"** and gets with the program.

Philip Paul Sacco

I have learned not to question God's timing. Not only is He the keeper of time itself, but He has a sense of humor as well. It is infinitely more fun to get out of my own way and let God bless me as He sees fit rather than direct Him in His ways. Though telling God how to act in our lives is typical of human nature, it is as fruitless as telling an orange tree to bear apples. While apples are sweet, they bear the seed of poison. God knows our hearts better than we do, and as a just and loving God, He knows best. It is when we interfere that we generally have complications occur.

Surely, the enemy knew what God had planned for me. Death approached my crib when I was an infant, and had I not been born with a quiet spirit, when I whimpered, my mother may have otherwise "let the baby be." As it was, she was not accustomed to hearing my cries. It took her a few seconds to realize what it was she was hearing. She was so surprised to finally hear me cry out, she hurried to check on me. As my cries were so unusual, she carried me in her arms from the room. As she carried me through the doorway, the entire ceiling collapsed filling my crib with plaster and wood. This was the enemy's first attempt to "plaster me" at an early age.

I was yet three or four years old when the next incident occurred. I was nearly separated from my intended support structure, my loving family. My family was on vacation in Florida. My six year old sister Lenore, Mom, and I, were sitting by the pool just beyond the French doors to our room. Mom wanted to make us some sandwiches. She left me with my sister, instructing her to watch me for a few minutes while Mom made lunch. Within scant minutes, Mom returned to find my sister alone, sucking on a lollipop. "Where's the Baby…?!" my mother put to her…" Oh,-…that nice lady wanted to take a picture of him…" was the response. A frantic scene followed as my mother rushed down the corridor throwing open any open door, no doubt near hysteria. Quickly, she came upon a room with several couples standing around a bed illuminated by studio lights, with me sitting on the bed, sucking on a lollipop of my own. In a moment, I was retrieved by my mother who didn't give anyone a chance to explain anything. In the blink of an eye, I was gone. Just as quickly, by my mothers quick thinking and speedy actions, I was thankfully recovered. No doubt, within minutes, my entire future would have been quite different in the hands of strangers.

Awaken The WARRIOR

As I grew up, it became evident I had some special skills. As early as the fourth grade, I began to be groomed for public speaking. It was years before I discovered public speaking is ranked as one of the three greatest fears among people. It was also during the fourth grade I had my first on-stage experience, a passion that I actively engaged in until the late 80s.

Over my adolescence, I had a strong inclination towards things chivalric in nature. I displayed an inborn knowledge of martial combat. So pronounced was my understanding of things well beyond my experience, or study, I was asked to speak before my fourth grade class on—of all things—the Roman gladiatorial games and the persecution of the Christians in the arena. My teacher was so impressed with my delivery and knowledge of arms and armor, as well as the Roman games, she had me speak to all the other fourth grade classes as well.

When I was just a few years older, the feeling that I had somehow missed my time, that the days of knighthood had escaped me, weighed so heavily upon my young mind, I cried myself to sleep many nights. I can still remember my mother's concern when she held me and desperately tried to understand what bothered me so. I would put it to her simply, "*I want to be a knight...*" I just want to be a knight..." *I'm supposed to be a knight...*" She tried to help me understand that was a time long gone by. I could not understand why this was so, or what she meant. I am sure my mother was both confused and concerned for me, but no more confused and concerned than I was myself. I tried to find other ways to get back to that ancient time, always wanting to learn how to sword fight as I had watched in so many movies. As sword fighting isn't exactly commonplace today, I turned to archery, drawing castles and armor, building models of knights in armor, and dreaming of days (and knights), gone. Watching Richard Harrison in *Camelot* and reading every tale of King Arthur's Court only made things worse. These were too strong a reminder of what I wanted for my life. It would be years before I began to "come into my own" again.

Even at this early age, my father saw in me an aptitude for the military way of life. He approached me with the idea of going to a military school. Had my mother not intervened, I would more than likely been a Lieutenant at the time of the Vietnam War. The Lord only knows what may have become of me. Personally, I am sure I was spared many horrible experiences; perhaps the most tragic of all. As it was, dear Mom would have no more consideration of me going to a military academy, and that was that. Dear Mom took a primary role in a major course adjustment which effected my life, yet again.

Death followed me, however, and sought many opportunities to prevent me from raising the Sword of the Spirit; military man or not. His next attempt to take me was while I slept, in a car accident. We were on vacation at the time of the accident. The turn of events necessitated our waiting for our car to be repaired before we continued our journey cross-country. The good Lord provided us with a gracious family that took this family of six strangers in to their home. While awaiting car repairs, I was treated to "celestial fireworks" while watching Fourth-of-July festivities at a local park. Hailstones the size of oranges struck the field from which my older brother, sister, and I watched the fireworks. As we ran for cover, I slipped, falling to the ground. My brother ran back and snatched me from the ground by my arm just before three of the "hammers from the heavens" embedded themselves where I, mere moments before, had lain. We ducked for cover in a concession stand. No sooner had the door slammed upon my heels behind me than a rapid hammering jarred and dented the aluminum door. These hailstones crushed car roofs and smashed windshields. I could easily have been killed. Death would have to wait again.

Evil is an insidious thing. Its attacks are fluid and dynamic. When the subject of an attack is to well guarded, attacks against supporting elements can be expected. In considering the tremendous preventive shield my mother had to date shown in my life, it is quite possible that the goal in the above mentioned wreck was in fact the elimination or disablement of my mother. The injuries she sustained in the accident continue to effect her to this date.

Being born into a Catholic family, I was raised Catholic. At the proper age, I was confirmed in the church. I took quite seriously the solemn vow of becoming a soldier in the army of God. To me, this was something real. I expected orders at any time. Unfortunately, at that young age, I did not understand the teachings of the church, nor the reality and nature of Spiritual Warfare. I was young and uninvolved in true spiritual study. For a time, my life of faith lay dormant.

Other attempts were made on me, though more diabolical in nature. To kill my body is one thing, but to kill my spirit is another. **^{28}*And fear not them which kill the body, but are not able to kill the soul: but rather fear him which is able to destroy both soul and body in hell.* Matt. 10:28.** As I grew older, I searched for power and meaning in my life. With the promise of control and power, I was lured into witchcraft and tarot, casting a spell, which nearly cost my father's life. Fortunately for me, God took this time to get my attention in a very real and personal way. In my sophomore year of High School, I repented and accepted the redemption of Jesus for my then worthless hide. God blessed me with close prayer friends over the next year, especially Hank Edmondson, who provoked me to study and receive the Baptisms of Water and Fire. My life changed immediately and radically. When I found the power of the Book of Ephesians and the spiritual gifts discussed in Corinthians, I beseeched God to show me His majesty and allow me to engage in spiritual warfare, if it still existed. This was just before the release of the movie *The Exorcist*. Everyone was sure such things were not real. Only a small number of spiritually aware individuals attempted to bar the release of the movie. They understood the danger of releasing this information upon the unaware masses. I found out within one week of my prayer that they were correct. I was about to learn just how real this war is.

My best friend in those days, Danny Merrill, called upon me to assist a friend of ours who had been cursed by his grandfather, a confirmed warlock. Steve maintained contact with this malevolent spirit with a Ouija board. Steve had a blood lust and had taken to attacking humans, as small animals no longer filled the bill. Realizing the gravity of what he had done, Steve cried out to Danny for help. God directed Danny and me in praying over Steve, and in the saving of his spirit. After some three hours of uninterrupted spiritual confrontation clasped in prayer over Steve, the spirit of oppression and blood lust was soundly defeated by the power of the Holy Spirit and in the name of our Lord Jesus. Steve was delivered from the malevolent grasp of his grandfather. During the process, I witnessed a wooden cross actually blister flesh! This entire encounter took place in his front yard.

The Lord saw to it that we had not one interruption or the prying eyes of neighbors to contend with. When Steve was delivered from the oppressive spirit, it was evident in his demeanor, countenance, and in that, the light of his eyes was restored. Steve was led in a prayer of salvation and he immediately felt the dark oppression of his past replaced by the love and acceptance of our Savior. Praise God. I lost contact with Steve as he attended another school and graduated that year.

Almost ten years later, Steve looked me up and filled me in on how his life changed following that monumental night. He married his girlfriend of the time, completed seminary training, became a minister, and had a son. Steve admitted that had Danny and I not answered the call, he most likely would have been driven mad, ended up in jail, or been killed. To God belongs the victory!

Having now squarely declared myself for God, and having "thrown down the gauntlet," Death approached me with renewed vengeance. I was assailed by brute force; this time, a racially motivated attack. Following a gym class, I was brained with a detached locker door. This resulted in my having some eight to twelve stitches and a mild concussion from the blow to the rear of my head. A prayer friend, Wally, was immediately at my side. He led me away from a bloody confrontation and to the nurse's aid station to be taken to the hospital. At that time, I made no connection between the incident and my spiritual stance. I continued merrily on my way in my life seeking out ways to embrace chivalry and honor in my "normal," every day life. Throughout high school, I crusaded against witchcraft, tarot, and Ouija boards, burning any boards and tarot decks I could lay my hands on.

It was the summer of my high school graduation when I had one of the most harrowing experiences of my life, one that would be repeated several years later. I had gone to Savannah Beach with my girl friend Debra, her girlfriend Diane, and Diane's boyfriend Larry. We all enjoyed watching dolphins playing in the surf. When the tide changed, Larry and I mounted air mattresses and swam out to the primary breakers about half mile out in the hopes of entertaining ourselves with the dolphins. It was at this time, when I started horsing around with Larry, trying to dunk him, then he tells me he *can't swim*! This was bad enough, but just after laughingly telling me this, Larry points towards what he believes is a dolphin between us and the beach. Larry starts paddling towards it. I was horrified, for I knew the triangular dorsal fin coursing along the beach was characteristic of a shark, not a dolphin! I quickly stopped Larry's splashing, then calmed him down to brace for a harrowing experience. The shark turned in our direction, and began to circle us. This monster of the deep swam closer each time it circled. It finally began what I knew to be a feeding approach…directly towards me! I prayed as I don't think I *ever* prayed before as I watched, transfixed, this monster approach the end of my air mattress. The shark was close to the surface, the shape of its snout and back clearly visible. As the shark raced under the length of my float, I could see its back was wider than my raft. I had the feeling it could swallow me whole…almost. It seemed like it took forever for this nemesis of the deep to pass under me. It must have been some 12-16 feet long.

We waited a few minutes, and not seeing the shark again, I took a grave and calculated risk. I had my Scuba fins on, "turbo fins," capable of propelling one at incredible speed in the water. I got in the water and had Larry get on top of my mattress as well as his. I told him to keep a sharp eye out for the shark. Keeping my body as low in the water as possible, I began pushing Larry towards shore using a very powerful stroke known as the "dolphin kick." I hoped the near and recent presence of dolphins would aid in camouflaging the turbulence I created with this powerful stroke. Larry joked about the wind he felt in his hair as we sped towards shore. I certainly felt the protection of angels as I noted we left a wake through the waves behind us. When we made it to shore, the girls asked us where we got the motor. Fortunately, they had missed the episode with the shark, as I am sure they would have been terrified for us.

Ever since I was a kid, I had feared water. It was not until I was almost twelve that I learned to swim. I never felt comfortable with the ocean, and this experience did nothing to endear me further towards the deep blue sea. Several years later, I gave up any interest in the ocean after having yet another similar experience. Such is my life.

The following year, I had the good fortune to meet three time Cuban fencing champion Eliana Salizar, and her husband Rudy. I began training in—you guessed it—*Fencing* (a modern day version of sword fighting). The ante was raised, as this Warrior-in-training was still on track to meet his destiny as a recruiting officer for God's army. If the spiritual combat had not been serious enough yet, it soon would take a more severe turn as the minions of darkness formed a new strategy.

I had developed a thirst for the power of God's Word, and studied the spiritual gifts listed most literally in **1 Corinthians** and **Acts**. I became active with a very charismatic and Spirit filled worship group. I bore witness to singing in tongues, several miraculous healings, prayer in tongues, interpretation, and prophecy. My interest in eschatology began at this time. I became convinced that our days would see many signs described in the Bible, which we have been cautioned to watch for. Shortly after this, our prayer group was ousted from our meeting hall. The directors of the Catholic school and my church at that time did not ascribe to the "full gospel" teachings we were manifesting. It was a number of years before a sympathetic and understanding priest took charge of our church and the group began reforming. I, however, never found another group as profound and spirit filled, and my life had taken me elsewhere. I no longer met with them. My access to a strong supply depot had been eliminated.

Darkness crept close to me during my first year of college. On one memorable morning, I encountered what I can only refer to as an advance guard of evil. I was roused from sleep to a feeling of oppression and dread. I tried to go back to sleep. When I found the oppression physically perceptible, I turned to my Bible and ensconced myself in the Word.

The entire house was still, very still, unnaturally still—even for it being three in the morning. I prayed in earnest for protection and strength as I could feel the breath of evil nearby. No matter how many lights I turned on in my room, the darkness never seemed to leave the corners of the room. I felt an unnatural chill in the air. Matters came to a head when I turned and looked out my partially opened door to see a black, shadowy figure standing in contrast against the darkness of the house beyond. Gleaming red eyes peered at me from without and an audible hiss met my ears as it quickly darted from my sight.

Ⅰ The spirit of fear welled up within me and I turned to the Lord in prayer. Part of me thought I was surely still asleep, a hard slap and pinch assuring me otherwise. I felt an instinct to check on my sisters, Lenore and Carole, in the adjacent room. I was afraid of waking my sisters and crept into their room quietly. I leaned over them to find my younger sister sleeping fitfully in her bed while my older sister, Lenore, lay perfectly still, seemingly asleep. She seemed to be holding her breath. I prayed the good Lord to watch over them as they slept and moved towards the door.

Before I had left the room, I heard Lenore's hushed voice tentatively call out my name, quaking and full of fear. She asked me if I had been in the room earlier. She had seen a dark figure lean over the bed of our younger sister. It had just leaned over her bed before my entrance. Lenore said she felt its presence as it pressed down on her bed just as I had entered the room. She thought she was dreaming, but as I prayerfully entered the room the figure of darkness had hissed audibly and rushed from the room through the wall between their beds. Numb with fear and lack of understanding for what was happening, she lay perfectly still watching as I then prayed over them and moved to leave the room. I knew I was not dreaming. More than that—so did my sister. I knew what I had to do. The Holy Spirit led me to go to the bathroom, fill a glass with water and bless it in preparation for cleansing the house.

Now that I knew I was not seeing things, and sensing the tangible cast of evil, I proceeded to move through the entire house, blessing it with Holy Water in the name of God the Father, the Son, and the Holy Spirit. Unfortunately, I awoke my parents. Initially alarmed, I prayed the Lord bless them with restful and secure sleep and proceeded throughout the remainder of the house while my sister stayed and explained to them what had happened and that I was not mad, that I had not "lost it." They were soon asleep again, secure in the blessed protection of our Lord, assuredly circled about by His angels of goodness and light. It took some time to bless the entire house. When I was done, I spent some time in the scriptures praising God for the victory. I climbed back in bed sometime near six in the morning.

The following morning I removed the old hold-out vestiges of the lies I had bought into prior to turning to the Lord: writings of Allister Crowley, *The Satanic Bible*, books of witchcraft, tarot cards, and a Ouija board. Burning them was truly a blessing, as the Ouija board uttered the most profound groans and screams when having been blessed and burned. To date I have managed to destroy some seven to eight Ouija boards and several tarot decks. They are tools of entrapment used by the enemy. I found out the hard way the traps of the enemy are regularly tended.

After the incident with the minion of darkness, my elder sister and mother took an avid interest in what I had been saying about the power and Baptism of the Holy Spirit. My mother came to me some time later and shared with me her personal acceptance and empowerment of the great Comforter in her life. While my sister Lenore never mentioned anything as specific as having received the "Baptism of the Spirit and Fire," she no longer doubted my tales and has been blessed since this episode with several angelic visitations. Her kids and husband have also seen these messengers from God in their home when they prayed for protection and blessings. Both of my sisters and my mother continue a strong and very involved life in the spirit and are active with their respective churches. My father, while a spiritual man, is quiet and conservative in his devotions and tends to keep his professions of faith to himself.

By this time, I had been competing for about two years as a regional novice in the fencing circuit and was gaining notoriety. Time was ripe for the enemy to attack again. The pre-emptive strike came in the Savannah River one summer afternoon. In the same spot I had saved a dear friend of the family from drowning, evil smote me in the foot in an attempt to slow me down and, no doubt, see me drown. I had heard of people stepping bare footed on broken glass in the river, so I made a habit of wearing thick-soled sneakers. While crossing an area of rapid and intense water flow in the rapids, I stepped upon what, at first, felt to be a smooth rock with my right foot. As I bore my weight down upon my foot, I felt the rock give under foot and heard conveyed through my body the sound of imploding glass. A stab of pain shot upwards through my leg and reflex action drew my leg up, forcing me to be carried away in the stiff current. As I swirled down river, I attempted to gain handholds to pull myself from the current. Kicking with my apparently injured foot felt most peculiar.

Once I had managed to pull myself to some rocks out of the deep, rushing current, I drew my leg up out of the water and noticed moss clinging to the bottom of the sneaker. Considering where I was, the bottom of my sneaker should have been clean. I took a closer look, as something was not right. It was not until I grasped the toes of my foot and pulled it higher for a better look that I noticed the razor fine slice across the middle of the sole and up the instep of the sneaker, almost as far as the laces. When I pulled on my foot to examine it, it folded eerily and easily upwards. The moss had been forced up into the bottom of the sneaker, and I assumed, my foot. I could put no weight on the foot and struggled to leave the river. Struggling against the current without the use of both legs was tiresome.

Once on shore, I removed the severed sneaker to closely inspect my foot. The sole of the sneaker had been very neatly sliced completely through as if I had trod on the edge of a sword. I found my foot had also been sliced as neatly, to the bone, up through the instep—two tendons deep within had been cut. Being versed in first aid, and thanks to the bone chilling water, blood loss was minimal.

Leaving the river entailed an arduous climb up a hundred foot bluff and then a one mile hike to a friend's car before we could make the quick ride to an emergency center (my friends enjoyed having a good excuse to get a speeding ticket). It took a while, but my foot was tended to that evening and with its repair I had concluded yet another interesting escapade. It would be some time before I was fencing again.

The best was yet to come. It was Easter Sunday, 1975. Dad stayed at home and the rest of the family all collected ourselves to enjoy the clear, blustery day and fly kites. Off to the local college campus we went. We settled the ladies on a blanket. My brother Rick and I laid out the kite and line and gave it a yank. The kite quickly found the brisk air, and was sailing effortlessly in a moment. Having the kite up and out about seventy feet, the heavy-duty kite string suddenly snipped as if cut by scissors just before my fingertips. The kite played in the air at just the right height to keep the fleeting string scant inches from my grasp as the kite raced me over hundred yards to settle in the top of a tree. Neither my brother nor I could understand how that kite stayed in the air for that distance. It was rather eerie as the kite had a picture of Herman Munster on it that gave us cause for a good laugh. We were having too much fun to lose that kite so abruptly. Besides, I wanted it back as I had been flying that kite since I was eight. It seemed obvious to both of us that by climbing a four foot wall and using my brother as a ladder to scale a nearby causeway, easy access could be gained to a roof from which the kite could be reached. Simple plans so often simply go awry...

To make a long story short, in scaling the roof I fell, landing on my head and spending a brief period on the other side of life. I could write a book about this incident alone and the many lessons I learned from it. Suffice it to say, I became the veteran of a "Life-after-Life" experience and once again cheated Death. Just before my return, I was told "It wasn't my time" as "I hadn't done *'it'* yet..." I was not the same for quite some time after this little episode. My bell had been decidedly rung. The experience changed my life in many ways. While I gave my brother the scare of his life, experienced a breath of Paradise, broke my wrist, suffered from a major concussion and bruise to my brain, and experienced amnesia for the better part of a day—all in an instant—this little episode took me over ten years to settle out over because of the spiritual experience it brought me. In one afternoon some ten years later, I brought all my issues and questions to a priest at Christ the King Catholic Church. I was able to lie to rest all of my questions and spiritual conflicts concerning my "After Life" experience. I was finally at peace with what I had gone through, having reconciled what I *thought* I had been taught by the church with what I had experienced.

Always persistent and not to be outdone, Death came knocking again within three short months of my fall from that roof. I had broken my left wrist in the fall. I had the cast removed three days before a trip to Myrtle Beach with my friends Perry and Bobby. Death stalked again—another car accident—this time a severe one. All of us, some nine friends having convened at the beach, had all been heavily involved with a Christian fellowship club. We all found it peculiar that everyone seemed to have the same foreboding about the Opal GT two of the girls had come to the beach in. Its owner was Bobby's girlfriend. Bobby, Perry, and I discussed the situation and we came to a decision. The three of us had taken Bobby's car, an SJ, to the beach. It was much larger than the little Opal GT, so we offered the girls the larger car to ride home in just as a precaution. If they were to have a wreck, they would be far better protected in the SJ. What we had not discussed widely with the girls was our feelings that, if in fact the Opal were to have a wreck, we would rather be in it than see them endure the accident. The Opal did, in fact, have that wreck, a fairly high speed one. We went under the rear end of a Mustang, nearly decapitating me, costing me my "boyish good looks," nearly lacerating off my nose, the tip of my tongue, two-thirds of my upper lips, and causing severe lacerations to several muscles of my face. I was nearly blinded in my right eye. It was almost an hour before a rescue 'copter made it to the scene. We were airlifted to a hospital and in route I stopped breathing (these facts I found out years later when I discovered a copy of a letter of thanks my father had sent to the rescue unit). I discovered that the flight crew had revived me and kept me breathing until I was under hospital care. Hey…this was only three months after I was assured it wasn't my time to go as I hadn't done *"it"* yet, so as I certainly hadn't had time to do *"it"* yet; It must not have been my time yet again. Death was a little too anxious perhaps…[28]***And I give unto them eternal life; and they shall never perish, neither shall any man pluck them out of my hand. John 10:28.*** I was being obedient and God had a mission for me yet…I just had to do *"it."* Now if I could just figure out what *'it'* was.

In my junior year of college, I decided my life apparently was not exciting enough so, I took up skydiving. I decided that skydiving was not for me after I watched three malfunctions in one day (while no one was killed or dangerously injured, it was a wake up call for me). Need I say the previous year had created many "issues" to settle in my life. I was searching for more direction, more answers in my life at this time. I became very involved with my church, St. Mary's On The Hill, training for and becoming an ordained Extraordinary Minister of Communion. I also began reading the Gospel selections at mass as a Lector. It was only a year or so since the fall and the accident. I was still very foggy minded. It would be some ten years before I started putting my mind back together again. I was searching for answers to the questions the "After-Life" experience had raised in my mind. Spiritually I had become very unsettled.

At this time, being a little uncertain about the direction my life was to take I decided maybe I should have some vocational and psych tests done. I was a pre-med student and had many friends in the military, another primary interest as a possible career choice (I was only interested in becoming a flier, but my poor eyesight snuffed that possibility). Additionally, I had talked to a local priest about possibly working in the church, given the experiences I had. I felt torn in three directions. It was suggested by my sister that I go to a college counselor for some tests. While the good doctor did ask me if I thought I had a "death wish," I assured her she just didn't understand the experiences I had. Testing told me that a career in, well, do I need to say, the military, theology, or medicine all were equally and highly rated. A lot of help there, right? No clear decision was reached.

I graduated from college needing to take an extra year to complete my studies. Recession and corporate cut backs in research-and-development and quality control made it very difficult for me to find a job with my degree in science. I took a job in a major local gun shop. With the owner's assurances, I had hopes of becoming a gunsmith. After almost two years of working for them it became evident, I had no future in this direction. I was quite distressed one night and confided in my brother that I felt as though God was repeatedly heating me in coals and hammering me into some weapon of His design. If I was to become a "Sword for God" I just wanted to know what I was to do. My dear brother Rick told me to be patient. If God had some special service for me to do, *"it* would become clear"...*It* eventually did.

My brother Rick was a practicing dentist at the time. After some discussion, he and I decided it would be great if I completed a degree in Dental Technology and worked with him as his in-house lab tech. I applied for the program at the Medical College of Georgia. On the Fourth-of-July weekend of 1980, I was informed that my application had been accepted. This news came to me as I sat dumbstruck on the floor outside of the Intensive Care Unit (ICU) my brother was admitted to that weekend. He had fallen prey to a car accident, literally having his brains knocked out. God must have been watching after him. There was an ambulance in route to another accident in his immediate vicinity. They were rerouted to his accident site instead. There was an entire scrub team already being gathered at the emergency ward to receive the other accident victim who had likewise received severe head injuries (while his injuries were not as severe as my brother's, Toby was not as fortunate as my brother, never recovering from his wounds and becoming physically disabled. He was in a room next to my brother's in the ICU.).

While Rick arrived at the hospital alive was nothing short of miraculous, hopes for his surviving through the night were grim. I had been watching Rick's monitors from the hallway outside the ICU when they flat lined, setting off alarms. My brother was on his way to his personal visitation with our Lord in Paradise, becoming a veteran of an "After-Life" experience of his own. I had collapsed to the floor and was on the verge of tears when the news of my acceptance to the dental program was delivered to me by Dr. Vericella, a personal friend of the family. He was also the admissions officer at the Dental School. Needless to say, the news was a little anticlimactic. What good was pursuing the dream of working with my brother after just witnessing his apparent death.

Rick eventually regained consciousness, making a miraculous recovery, the likes of which none of the doctors involved with his treatment had ever before witnessed or even read of concerning injuries of his type. He became known as the "Miracle Patient" by the doctors and staff of the hospital. His recovery was certainly one for the books as none of the doctors gave him any chance of ever recovering to live a normal life again, let alone without serious debilitations. While my brother was hospitalized and speechless, I was the only one he was able to convey information to. We had a special connection. I was the first person he spoke to upon regaining his speech. Nothing short of the touch of the Master's hand could have saved him.

During the initial two years of his recovery, I completed and received my Dental Technology Degree, receiving State honors and graduating with the second all time highest grade point average in the history of the school. I had given it my all in the hopes that my brother and I would still work together. It was not meant to be. Shortly after my graduation from the program, he sold his office and retired from dentistry. Nevertheless, that summer as my brother was living alone in Atlanta I moved there to be with him and started my career in the dental industry.

My move to Atlanta positioned me for the next phase of my preparation. Soon after moving to Atlanta, I discovered and became involved with an internationally established medieval interest group. I began training in what I had always wanted to learn-armored combat, medieval martial arts. I was squired to a knight within a year. Over the ensuing years, I researched and developed an accurate thirteenth century fighting style. I became versed in combat with the single sword, sword and dagger, sword and shield, double sword, Bastard and Great-Sword, glaive (pole-ax), spear, spear and sword, and spear-and-shield fighting techniques. I purchased and learned how to make armor and learned the proper way to wear and fight in it. My many years of training, practice, and competition in Fencing went a long way towards enhancing my abilities and skills in armored combat. My fighting style became known within four kingdoms and I gained a reputation as an opponent to be respected, taking relish in fighting several opponents at once. Little did I know that my martial arts training was to have far more implications upon my life than my personal enjoyment of martial combat, competition, and staying fit. The basis for my understanding of the warrior had been laid.

During this time, I was active with a young-singles group where I attended church. I was asked to speak to them several times at retreats and weekend gatherings about my "after-life" experience and my experience with the power of the Holy Spirit. I made many entreats to my friends to study the Word and become spiritually alert, joining in the fray. I explained to them that there were few of us in the front lines. One friend later came forward and accepted the empowerment and blessings of the Holy Spirit. Her name was Jennifer. Jennifer became a solid warrior for God's army. We had many interesting stories to share with each other. I was with her when her car's engine blew up in the middle of nowhere in southern Alabama. That was another unforgettable weekend. It was also around this time that I approached one of the priests of my church whom I knew quite well. I asked him for guidance, as I felt our Lord intended for me to be more involved with spiritual warfare. His message to me was "to not commit the sin of spiritual pride" and the church was the place to deal with such matters. Not exactly the kind of help or guidance I was looking for, and he certainly "cooled my heals."

God was nearly done setting the stage for me; Death was still in pursuit. The summer of 1990 saw me open my dental lab. I became involved with a civic society, the Jaycee's. After the first year of founding our chapter of the Jaycees, the organization held a statewide convention at Jekyll Island. My new friends and I all attended. As we would be spending five days at the beach, I had taken with me a recently acquired portable pontoon sailboat to enjoy with my good friend Derrick. On our second day at the beach, Derrick and I took the small sailboat out and had quite an adventure. We were caught in a rip tide, having to sail down the beach and eventually having to reef the sail and swim the small craft in. At dinner that night, we were told by many of our friends that where we had been was the middle of the hammer-head breeding grounds and it was mating season. We counted our blessings and had many a good laugh about it while we had our feet on dry ground.

The following day, I took the boat out by myself. I was careful to stay close to shore, my experience of the day before fresh in my mind. I sailed uneventfully for about an hour, and then made one bad mistake. I turned away from the beach, just once, to come-about and wound up in contrary winds going—you guessed it—right back out to where I had been the day before with Derrick. I steadily attempted to sail the boat back to shore. The wind and current continued to drift me further out and down the beach regardless of how I maneuvered the tiny misfit craft. I could easily see my friend Derrick following my progress along the shore at first. When he was becoming unidentifiable by the distance, I knew I would have to do something quick. I put on my life vest, reefed the sail, and tied the small rig to my belt. I had become a strong and accomplished swimmer after years of Scouting and swimming in the family's pool. I thought more about what was in the water than the distance I would have to swim. My fears were amplified when something brushed my legs and attached itself to my right foot. I can only assume it was a young hammerhead looking for a meal. Fortunately, I was wearing a pair of heavy leather sandals (they were in fact a pair of caligae that I had made) that completely covered my feet. The entire sole of the sandal was nearly torn off my foot. I prayed that "Mamma" was not around to give junior a lesson in proper dining and steadfastly kept swimming for shore. I thanked God for being with me that day as it was a beautiful day for a swim. I hoped that it would not be my last. I swam for over an hour and a half to reach the beach against the current, towing the troublesome sailboat behind me, praying the entire way. When I finally reached and collapsed upon the shore, I was met by my friend Derrick, a cold beer in his hand. Shore patrol arrived shortly after I left the water. They were glad the dangerous waters off the beach had not offered up another drowning or shark attack for them to deal with. Again, I was told how lucky I was. I did not go back into the water again on that trip. While I have been to the beach since, I have no fondness for the ocean. I keep the sandals as a keepsake.

By this time, I had about eight years of training and combat experience in armor. It was time for the birth of "The Warrior." A friend of mine, Cathy, ran a series of weight loss clinics. She approached weight loss as a spiritual matter. She had a brainstorm one day and approached me to discuss the pertinent aspects of being, or becoming, a warrior, and how this may be applied to help her subscribers with their weight loss. We discussed it for some time. She hit upon an idea: I would be introduced during the third or fourth meeting of each group. I would do a presentation on what being a warrior was all about. She would call her clinics "Weight Warriors." My appearances were always well received and very powerful.

It was at one of these meetings that I made a friend who would prove to be instrumental in the future of my presentations. Ellen Marks, the wife of a Baptist minister, had really liked what I had to say during one of these sessions. She apparently received a spiritual message. She approached me afterwards and asked if I would come and speak to their church youth group. Prior to my appearance with them, I met her husband Al, and we enjoyed the growth of a wonderful friendship. It turned out that Ellen was in the process of writing a book of her own. It was a medieval period work centering on the education of a young lad by a Christian knight who teaches the lad about values, morals, and Christian ethics. Ellen found me to be a fountain of information and inspiration for her book.

As it was, our continued friendship in Atlanta was not to be. Within a year of our meeting, Al and family were moved to California. The hand of God was certainly at play. While they had been moved about as far away as possible, once they had become settled they asked me to come out to their new church and do a presentation on the armor of God. Ellen and Al were very supportive of the message. They expressed their feeling that I should consider making it a ministry. As I had just tied up all of my resources and energy in starting up my lab business, the timing did not seem right. It would be another six or seven years before this message was heavily impressed upon my spirit again. The seed for "Awaken the Warrior" had been planted many years before, but now it was being watered and about to sprout new life and grow into its own.

I had several more harrowing experiences, including being bitten by a black widow during the ensuing years. Probably the two most death defying incidents involved yet again an automobile. The first occurred while taking a road trip for Valentines Day with my girlfriend in 1995. We were in an all-wheel-drive sports car traveling in the center lane of a four-lane highway doing a little better than 75mph when the car's entire drive train locked up. The forces of the transmission were sufficient to break a rear axle, an inch and a half thick steel bar. The car went into an uncontrolled four-wheel skid in the middle of highway traffic, all four wheels having been completely seized. We crossed two lanes of traffic and came to a rest on the inside shoulder of the road three feet from the concrete highway barrier. Other than the frayed nerves and the total destruction of the transmission, we were fine. Nothing short of God's angelic protection could have spared us.

The second and even more amazing incident occurred the weekend of Thanksgiving 1997. This was just one short year before I would start writing *Awaken the Warrior.* I was taking one of my godsons, Alberto, home to visit my family in Augusta. We were traveling on the same strip of road my brother had his accident on so many years before. This was a very well known road to me as I had driven it countless times over some twenty-five years. We were moving at the posted speed of 45 mph as we approached a long curve in the road. Suddenly, all traction on the wheels was lost. We had come upon a stretch of black ice. The car felt as though it was sailing on a cushion of air. I mentioned to Alberto that the car was out of control, as it was not responding to the wheel. We expected to go straight off the road at the curve and into the culvert or hit one of the many high-powered electrical poles along the shoulder. As we entered the curve, the car began to spin, making two complete turns. Magically, we stayed on the pavement while spinning and traveled the entire distance of the curve, over a half-mile stretch of road. As the car came out of the curve, it actually reversed its spin and came-about 180 degrees. This put us traveling backwards as we came out of the curve. The entire episode seemed to take forever, occurring in slow motion.

We both felt as though we were on a carnival ride. I was looking over my shoulder trying to regain control of the car that had been spinning wildly out of control when the car abruptly straightened. The only problem was we were headed down the road backwards now. Pole after pole flashed past the car. I eased the car off the roadway and onto the shoulder. We were still doing a full 45 mph, the car not having slowed down at all, as we hit the shoulder. Dirt and mud went flying everywhere as I braked the car. It was a bumpy ride, but we ended up in a ditch three feet deep in mud and a scant three inches short of hitting a concrete pillar. I have traveled that road many times since, and know the distance we spun out of control to be a little over ½ of a mile from just before the curve to our final stopping point. The entire time, the car stayed in its lane and never left the road for the entire stretch of the curve. We both felt as though the car had been "played with" in the hand of a giant, invisible child, much as a toy car is played with on the floor of a playroom. I sensed the hand of my Guardian Angel, yet again.

Throughout the 90s, I busied myself with the demands of my laboratory, things staying as frustrating as they always had been in the industry. I prayed that if God wanted me to make better use of other talents and skills He had blessed me with, the proper doors be opened for me as I was knocking on many of them. It was late September of 1998 when my orders came to me loud and clear. I was driving home from a delivery run and the Holy Spirit touched my heart. Actually, that puts it far too tamely. He grabbed it and shook it REALLY HARD! I was impressed upon to go home, put on my full armor, and just start walking down the street spreading the news of God's message. Now I had been called upon to do many rather unusual things in the past, but this took the cake. The message was so pronounced, however, that I simply could not ignore it. Full of emotions, I immediately went to my church and asked to speak with a priest. There were several new priests at the church at the time. Father Ron was the only one in particular I would have felt comfortable talking to. I had no idea which priest would be available but God most certainly blessed me as it turned out to be Father Ron.

I explained to Father Ron the gravity of the message I felt. He could tell that I was certainly having to contend with tremendous emotional strain as I recanted to him my need for direction. He simply suggested that I go home and when I felt calmed down sufficiently, that I write down the message or information I felt directed to relate. I was compelled to do just that. I was home in a flash. After calming down enough to put pen in hand, I began writing. I wrote more than twenty pages in one sitting and had a complete outline of the book that would take me two and a half years to complete.

Looking at one's life, many instances may be found which strangely work towards a common good. With God, all things work to accomplish His design. I relate this information so that the reader better understand the reality of Spiritual Warfare and recognize how God may be operating in their own life. Reflect upon your life and consider how situations may have directed you to a certain point in your life.

Philip Paul Sacco

This is not the end, but rather the Beginning…

I have fought the good fight to the end; I have run the race to the finish; I have kept the faith; all there is to come for me now is the Crown of Uprightness which the Lord, the upright Judge, will give to me on that Day; and not only to me but to all those who have longed for His appearing.

2 Tm. 4:6-8

Bibliography and Suggested Reading

Caesar, Julius. *The Battle for Gaul*. David R. Godine, Publisher. 1980.

Evans, Sebastian. *The High History of the Holy Grail*. E. P. Dutton & Co., New York, 1913.

Fliegel, Stephen N. *Arms and Armor*. Published by the Cleveland Museum of Art, and distributed by Harry N. Abrams, Inc., Publishers, New York, 1998.

Frager, Robert, Ph.D. *Who Am I*. G.P. Putnam's Sons, New York, 1994.

Moore, Robert, and Douglas Gillette. *King, Warrior, Magician, Lover: Rediscovering the Archetypes of the Mature Masculine*. Harper, San Francisco, 1991.

Nitobe, Inazo. *Bushido: The Warriors Code*. Ohara Publications, Incorporated, Burbank, California, 1982.

Parker, H.M.D. *The Roman Legions*. Dorset Press, New York, 1992.

Pearson, Carol S. *Awakening the Heroes Within: Twelve Archetypes to Help Us Find Ourselves and Transform Our World*. Harper, San Francisco, 1991.

Simkins, and Embeleton. *The Roman Army from Caesar to Trajan*. Osprey Publishing, London, U.K., 1984.

Steinmann, Anne, and David Fox. *The Male Dilemma*. Jason Aronson, Inc., New York, 1974.

Stott, John R.W., *Baptism & Fullness*. Inter Varsity Press, Downers Grove, Illinois, 1975.

Philip Paul Sacco

The Holy Bible. King James version.

The New Jerusalem Bible. Doubleday & Company, Inc. Garden City, New York.

Tobin, Eamon. *Open to the Holy Spirit.* Liguori Publications, Liguori, Missouri, 1986.

Tzu, Sun. *The Art of War.* Shambhala, Boston, 1988.

Then call me forward and I shall answer, or rather, I shall speak and you will answer.

Job 13:22

About the Author

Having over twenty-five years experience in the art of medieval arms, Philip Paul Sacco is uniquely qualified to speak on the merits of armor, and it's various characteristics. Being delivered from the bondage of occultism, the true power of God's Word has been manifested in his life.

With the history of the warrior as a life long fascination, his studies have included the contemporary understanding of the warrior archetype within us all. His studies have revealed an alarming dilemma—the character assassination of the warrior. With the demise of the warrior, he finds our society and our very souls without guard, and in imminent jeopardy.

Drawing on over ten years of presentations, his expression of the subject matter is incisive and clear for all to understand and incorporate.

Printed in the United States
746800003B